Beyond
the
Shadow
of
Camptown

NATION OF NEWCOMERS

Immigrant History as American History

Matthew Frye Jacobson and Werner Sollors
GENERAL EDITORS

Beyond the Shadow of Camptown: Korean Military Brides in America
Ji-Yeon Yuh

Mary Louise Roberts
Fall 2013

JI-YEON YUH

Beyond
the
Shadow
of
Camptown

Triumphalism:
Can do no wrong
Never stupid, lazy or
non-industrious
Never passive even
in passivity
???

Korean Military Brides
in America

NEW YORK UNIVERSITY PRESS
New York and London

NEW YORK UNIVERSITY PRESS
New York and London
www.nyupress.org

First published in paperback in 2004

Library of Congress Cataloging-in Publication Data
Yuh, Ji-Yeon.
Beyond the shadow of Camptown : Korean military brides in America /
Ji-Yeon Yuh.
p. cm. — (Nation of newcomers)
Includes bibliographical references and index.
ISBN 0-8147-9698-2 (cloth : alk. paper)
ISBN 0-8147-9699-0 (pbk. : alk. paper)
1. Korean American women—Social conditions—20th century. 2. Korean
American women—Biography. 3. Korean Americans—Cultural assimilation.
4. War brides—United States—History—20th century. 5. War brides—
United States—Biography. 6. Military spouses—United States—History—
20th century. 7. Military spouses—United States—Biography. 8. Women
immigrants—United States—Social conditions—20th century. 9. Women
immigrants—United States—Biography. 10. Korean War, 1950–1953—Women.
I. Title. II. Series.
E184.K6 Y85 2002
305.48'8957073—dc21   2002002674

Manufactured in the United States of America

c 10 9 8 7 6 5 4 3 2 1
p 10 9 8 7 6 5 4

To the Korean women whose trust and friendship made this study possible,
in the hope that their talking and my listening will not have been for naught.

Ten hours, twenty hours, no matter how long you sit and listen, it's no use. You have to have experienced it to understand it. You have to have lived through it together. The young women working in clubs and bars, only if you have worked with them can you understand their hearts, only if you have experienced it. So, have you ever sold your body? Only if you have sold your body, can you understand that person's heart. Have you ever gotten rid of a baby inside you? Only if you have had an abortion, can you understand that person's heart. Everything, you have to go through it yourself. That's how you learn about life, by living.

—Mrs. Sommer, Tuesday, January 24, 1995

We are all Koreans, the same people, all of us. The women who married foreigners, we are all the same Koreans. Don't look down on us.

—Mrs. Brennan, Monday, November 11, 1996

CONTENTS

ACKNOWLEDGMENTS

A book is never written by just one person alone, for the writing is but one step in the making of a book. This book would not have been possible without the many women who welcomed me into their homes and their lives throughout the course of my research. It is to them that the book is dedicated. They have both my gratitude and my deepest respect. Many members of the Philadelphia Korean community, especially Moonbum Lee, provided contacts that aided my research. They have my grateful appreciation. Members of My Sister's Place, Sae-oom-tuh, and the Rainbow Center were generous with their time and assistance. In particular, I'd like to thank Geumhyun Yeo, Kim Myungboon, and Kim Hyunsun.

Numerous scholars have provided intellectual support and advice. Lee Kwang Gyu of Seoul National University, now retired, gave me the idea for this study during a conversation in his office and generously commented on the unfolding project. My graduate advisor at the University of Pennsylvania, Walter Licht, has been a staunch supporter. Even in those long months when absolutely nothing was written but simply sat stewing in my brain, he insisted that this would be a terrific study. Gary Y. Okihiro and Kyeyoung Park have been both patient and generous with their support and critical readings. Cameron G. Hurst provided thoughtful, moving comments. Daniel Moshenberg has been an outstanding mentor and comrade. Franklin Odo and Jean Wu, who were my introduction to Asian American Studies, provided generous advice throughout my years in graduate school. Colleagues at Northwestern University, particularly Laura Hein, Sarah Maza, Michael Sherry, Tessie Liu, Adam Green, Nancy Maclean, and Ed Muir have graced me with their generosity. Elaine Kim has been a wonderful source of support and a trusted colleague. My editor at New York University Press, Eric Zinner, inspired confidence from the start and has proven to be a superb editor.

My brother, Sokgu Yuh, has been the best research assistant a sister could ask for, patiently tracking down people and books when I was unable to do so. I am also indebted to the University of Pennsylvania, the

Mellon Foundation, and the Y. H. Park Fellowship for Korean Studies for generously supporting my work.

But a person does not survive with scholarly support alone. I want to thank the members of Oobae, especially Jaebo Kim, Jin Hyung Lee, and Namsu Park, and good friend Sookju Song for their comradeship. Working and playing with them was a joy and a balm to my weary spirit. My mother put up with my very bad temper, my father kept his in check for my sake, and they both gave me their unconditional love, most especially during the bleakest years. My brother is simply the best brother, unsurpassed in all of siblingdom. My husband expressed his deep love in action, taking charge of our household and our newborn son so that I could write this study as a dissertation. He then took charge of our newborn daughter and our son (by then a rambunctious toddler) so that I could revise it into this book. He was also a patient sounding board and coach, nudging me to keep refining my ideas with his gentle but persistent nightly questions: What did you write today? How does that advance your thesis? What's significant about it? Without him, this book would have remained unwritten. Our son and daughter have taught me the wondrous mathematics of life, that one plus one makes more than two. Most importantly, they give us joy, for with their births we became a family.

EXPLANATORY NOTES

Korean names are given family name first in the Korean style for those who are in Korea, and family name last in the Western style for those in the United States.

All interviews for this study were conducted in Korean by the author. Translations into English were done by the author. All names of military brides are pseudonyms, and some identifying traits have been changed as necessary to protect confidentiality. In quoting from the interviews, the following conventions are used:

- { } enclose notes on nonverbal behavior, such as laughter, cries, sighs, gestures;
- [ ] enclose background explanations added by the author;
- ( ) enclose questions asked by the author;
- *italic typeface* is used for words of the speaker that do not require translation, including English and occasional Japanese words where the meaning is made clear;
- regular typeface is used for words of the speaker that have been translated into English.

CHRONOLOGY OF SELECTED EVENTS
IN MODERN KOREAN HISTORY

1866 The *General Sherman*, an armed U.S. merchant marine schooner, tried to open Korea to the United States, but the ship was burned by the residents of Pyongyang.

1871 The United States took revenge for the burning of the *General Sherman* by dispatching the military and conducting what the *New York Herald* called the "Little War with Heathen." About six hundred and fifty Koreans died in the battle.

1875 Korea and Japan signed the Kanghwa Treaty, which gave Japan access to Korean ports, reduced tariffs and gave extraterritorial rights.

1882 Korea and the United States signed their first treaty. In short order, Korea was forced to sign similar treaties with Britain and Germany, giving benefits such as port concessions, extraterritorial rights to the citizens of those countries, and reduced tariffs on their goods.

1892 The Tonghak Peasant Rebellions began. In 1894, the reigning Korean monarch sought help from China in putting down the rebellion, and Japan viewed this as cause for war.

1894 The Sino-Japanese war was fought on the Korean peninsula, over the issue of which country had greater influence on Korea. Japan wins. The Tonghak Rebellions were put down.

1895 The Japanese killed Queen Min, enraging Koreans.

1904 The Russo-Japanese war was fought on the Korean peninsula, again over Korea. Japan won, shocking Western nations who had thought that an Asian country could not defeat a Western power.

1905 Japan declared that it would henceforth manage Korea's international affairs. This was the first official step toward colonization.

1910 Japan annexed Korea.

1919 Koreans staged a nationwide, peaceful demonstration against Japanese imperialism and for Korean independence, which was brutally smashed by the Japanese military. Known as the March 1 movement, this demonstration spread to Koreans overseas. Koreans in the United States, led by Philip Jaisohn (Suh Jaepil), organized a Korean Independence Parade in Philadelphia in April 1919.

In the coming decades, the Korean independence movement was active both domestically and overseas, especially in China, Manchuria, and the United States.

1945 Yo Un-hyung, a respected Korean independence leader, was advised by a Japanese official that Japan would soon be defeated and that Yo should prepare his people for self-rule. Yo began to form People's Committees in each neighborhood district throughout the country.

In early August, the United States dropped atomic bombs on Hiroshima and Nagasaki. Among the dead and wounded were thousands of ethnic Koreans.

On August 15, Korea was liberated as Japan declared unconditional surrender, and simultaneously was divided at the 38th Parallel, with Soviet troops occupying the north and U.S. troops occupying the south.

The United States declared a military government in the south in the same manner that it declared a military government in Japan, and began to disband the People's Committees, accusing its members of being procommunist.

1945–53 Until the north-south border was sealed in 1953, a significant migration of people north and south took place. The movement north largely consisted of workers, landless peasants, tenant farmers, proindependence activists, and communist sympathizers, while many wealthy landlords, large farmers, merchants, intellectuals, and collaborators with the Japanese colonial government moved south.

By the end of 1945, South Korea's first camptown appeared in Bupyong, near the western port city of Incheon.

1946 In U.S.-occupied southern Korea, labor strikes, demonstrations against the American military government, and any activities deemed "procommunist" were put down with the active assistance of the U.S. military.

1948 Southern Korea held unilateral presidential elections while under U.S. military rule, electing Syngman Rhee as its first president and declaring itself the Republic of Korea.

Shortly thereafter, northern Korea declared itself the People's Democratic Republic of Korea, with Kim Il Sung as its president.

1950 The Korean War broke out. Under the leadership of the United States, the United Nations sent troops to Korea. The U.S. government, which never declared war, called it a "police action."

The first Korean women to marry Americans began to arrive in the United States.

1951 China entered the Korean War, fighting with North Korea. Among the Chinese troops were ethnic Koreans from China.

1953 The Korean War ended with an armistice agreement signed by North Korea, China, the Soviet Union, and the United States. South Korea could not sign because officially it had not partaken in the war. South Korea had signed over all military authority to the United States. The armistice declared a Demilitarized Zone (DMZ) that roughly followed the 38th Parallel. The war destroyed the Korean peninsula and left it utterly devastated.

Although the war was over, the supreme commander of the Korean military remained a U.S. general.

1960 A student revolution toppled the Syngman Rhee regime and a new government was established.

1961 Park Chung Hee, an army general, led a military coup and began nearly two decades of military dictatorship. A student movement devoted to democratization began to solidify.

1965 South Korea and Japan signed a normalization treaty, as student activists in South Korea protested what they term "a sellout."

1966 South Korea and the United States signed a Status of Forces Agreement (SOFA) that gave wide latitude to the U.S. military, including the free use of any and all South Korean land necessary for military activities.

Early 1970s The U.S. reduced the number of troops in South Korea and, with the Korean government, launched a camptown cleanup campaign. The South Korean government sent officials to the camptowns to tell the women that they were patriots for earning foreign exchange and serving as civilian ambassadors.

1979 Park Chung Hee's hand-picked commander of the Korean Central Intelligence Agency assassinated him, claiming that he was mishandling labor unrest in Masan that had spread to mass rioting.

1980 Chun Doo Hwan, another army general, led a military coup with the assistance of Roh Tae Woo. In May, the military brutally suppressed prodemocracy demonstrators in Kwangju, killing thousands of citizens in what came to be known as the Kwangju Massacre. Student activists later began to blame the United States, arguing that Chun could not have ordered such troop movements without the consent of the United States.

1981 Chun was the first head of state received by newly inaugurated U.S. President Ronald Reagan.

1987 Middle-class Koreans joined students in prodemocracy demonstrations after Chun named Roh his successor. Roh agreed to democratize Korea in a July statement. Roh and two long-time prodemocracy politicians, Kim Young Sam and Kim Dae Jung, ran for president. Roh won.

1988 Seoul hosted the Summer Olympics.

1992 Kim Young Sam and Roh formed a new political party and Kim was elected president of Korea a few months later.

Yoon Geum-yi, a bar hostess in a camptown near Seoul, was murdered by an American soldier in what South Korean police described as the most horrendous crime they had ever encountered. Her murder sparked a movement against the unequal Status of Forces Agreement and called for its revision. It also added momentum to the student movement calling for the expulsion of U.S. troops from South Korea.

1995 Kim Il Sung died after leading North Korea for half a century, leaving his son, Kim Jung Il, as his successor.

1997 The IMF crisis hit South Korea as the value of its currency, the South Korean won, plummeted to half its precrisis level.

Kim Dae Jung won the South Korean presidential election, along with an economy in crisis.

In the camptowns, women joked that their work had become valuable again for the earning of foreign exchange.

2000 Kim Dae Jung and Kim Jong Il met in a historic summit in Pyongyang, the North Korean capital. They released a joint declaration that called for steps toward a reunification without interference from external powers.

INTRODUCTION

A young Asian woman in Western clothing steps off a boat and is greeted with flowers by middle-aged Americans. She is a Korean war bride meeting her in-laws for the first time, announces the narrator, who then intones a platitude about embarking on a new American life.[1]

Images similar to this grainy scene from a Korean War-era government newsreel could also be found in popular American magazines such as *Life* and *Time* during the 1940s and 1950s. For the most part, these numerous depictions of war brides featured smiling young women waving from ships as they arrived in the United States to join their American soldier husbands. At the dawning of the so-called American Century, these women, who had left behind all that was familiar for an American man, were seen by the American public as proof positive of America's superiority. The very term "war brides" emphasizes the women's dependence on men and their link to war, conferring an identity on them as human war booty. There were even "war bride ships" that took entire groups of young women from Europe to America to join their husbands.

But despite the burgeoning sense of American superiority that came with victory in World War II, there was some doubt among the general public as to the wisdom of American men marrying foreign women, and couples were made to jump through quite a few bureaucratic hoops before gaining the necessary permission to marry. It was, however, generally assumed and expected that the women were eager to become Americans, both out of wifely love and admiration for the American way of life.[2]

When the brides in question were Asian, these expectations were simultaneously tempered by a keener suspicion and bolstered by a stronger confidence. The generally held view at the time was that women from such alien cultures would not make suitable wives for American men and would likely have great difficulty really becoming American. Their choice of America, however, validated America's confidence in itself as the greatest country on earth. In the early years, legal barriers to Asian immigration greatly restricted the number of Asian war brides permitted to enter America. A series of laws culminating in the 1924

Immigration Act prohibited all Asians from immigrating and the War Brides Act of 1945 made no provision that allowed for an exception in the case of Asian women who married American soldiers. It was not until the immigration laws were revised in 1952 that the prohibition against Asian immigration was lifted. Until then, Asian war brides—primarily those from Japan, but also a few from Korea—were allowed to immigrate only through special acts of Congress that established temporary windows of opportunity through which American soldiers could bring home their Asian wives.[3]

Despite suspicions as to their ability to do so, Asian war brides were fully expected to Americanize as quickly as possible. After all, they were now married to American men. That their new lives as Americans were structured by racial, cultural, and gender ideologies privileging white male authority and mainstream American culture is made explicit in the 1957 movie, *Japanese War Bride*. The heroine's troubles are linked to her friendship with Japanese American neighbors. She achieves happiness only by rejecting Japanese Americans and ensconcing herself within a nuclear family household headed by her white American husband. This kind of cinematic portrayal of the expectations that Asian war brides had to meet was based on real-life experiences. A survey of Korean war brides in the 1970s, for example, revealed that their primary conflict was with in-laws who demanded that they renounce Korean culture, even restricting their contact with fellow Koreans.

For war brides, then, becoming American meant discarding one's culture and forsaking relationships with ethnic kin in order to cleave to the culture of a husband and serve as housewife and mother within an all-American family. In other words, war brides were expected to fulfill a role defined by others. In the case of Asian war brides this was further complicated by the particular suspicions, stereotypes, and racism that Americans directed at Asians.

Between 1950 and 1989 nearly a hundred thousand Korean war brides immigrated to the United States. It is their lives that are the focus of this book. Until recently, few Koreans or Americans really knew who these women were. They existed as stereotypes at the fringes of consciousness. For Koreans, they were women of questionable character who had married American soldiers because such marriage was their only escape from poverty. For Americans, they were foreigners whom red-blooded American men had inexplicably married, and the "mama-sans" who operated illicit black-market businesses out of the military-operated PX general stores or worked in massage parlors. For second-generation Korean Americans, they were the women sitting alone, without husbands, during church service and fellowship, the ones they'd ignore because everyone else did. Their presence has barely been acknowledged and their histories have been marginalized. But their presence is significant and Korean women continue to marry American soldiers every year.[4]

Korean women met and married American soldiers in the historical context of U.S. military domination over South Korea that preceded the 1950–53 Korean War and extends into the present. Thus for Korean war brides, as well as for most other Asian war brides, the term "war bride" is misleading. The majority of Korean war brides married their soldier husbands during times of suspended armed conflict, that is, during times of relative peace, not war.[5] Their marriages are a direct result of ongoing U.S. military troop deployments in South Korea since 1945. U.S. military domination is what made these marriages possible and it has also had far-ranging effects on the tenor of Korean-American marriages. For this reason, in the pages that follow, I call these women "military brides."

Korean military brides were born and raised in a country that went from being a Japanese colony to being sundered in two by the superpower rivalry between the United States and the Soviet Union. They come from a nation-state, South Korea, that has served the needs of U.S. national security in the name of anticommunism and defense against North Korea, often at the expense of its own citizens. South Korea has been politically, militarily, and economically subordinated to the United States since before its inception in 1948. Thus its citizens, former and current, have been subject to various forms of American hegemony throughout most of their lives.[6]

Military brides, like most South Koreans, are in constant negotiation with American cultural hegemony, accepting some of its demands and constraints while seeking to reject others. The neoimperialist relationship between South Korea and the United States has shaped the ways in which these women have experienced and encountered America, as well as the ways in which they are positioned within their families and American society as a whole. Korean military brides have been on the front line of Korea-U.S. cultural and social contact for the past half-century.

Their relationship with South Korean hegemony as it influences Koreans both within the nation-state and abroad is equally complex. As women, they have been shaped by Korean gender ideology to view marriage and motherhood as the ultimate feminine goals. But as women who have married non-Koreans and as women who—regardless of their social background—are stained by presumed association with U.S. military camptowns and prostitution simply because they married an American soldier, they are left standing outside the bounds of both respectable Korean womanhood and authentic Koreanness. Thus military brides are constantly defending their respectability as well as their Korean identity.

Beyond the Shadow of Camptown focuses on the negotiations Korean military brides engage in with both American and Korean cultures. Chapter 1 explores the phenomenon of Korean military brides within the context of the U.S.-Korea military relationship, arguing that American cultural dominance is introduced to South Koreans through this relationship. The second chapter discusses the lives of the women in Korea, tracing, over a half-century of Korean history, the changes and continuities that have led to Korean women marrying American soldiers. Beginning the discussion of their lives as immigrants and wives, chapter 3 unearths these women's struggles within the private, intimate spaces of their intercultural families. Chapter 4 highlights food as a form of cultural expression that emphasizes the women's attempts to be both good Korean women and good American wives. Chapter 5 argues that the women have been the critical first link in chain migrations of Koreans throughout the 1970s and 1980s and, as such, have been instrumental in the construction of Korean immigrant communities. Military brides eventually constructed their own communities. Chapter 6 explores how these communities were put together and the ways in which they challenge rigid self-definitions of both Korean and American communities.

The stories presented in these pages are based primarily on oral history interviews and fieldwork conducted over a three-year period. The women and families I interviewed and observed were found through personal contacts throughout the Korean immigrant community. The women I met led me to other women, who led me to three regional associations of military brides and a Korean church composed of military brides and their families. I attended meetings and fund-raising dinners held by the associations and became a member of the church for two years, participating in church life and, at the request of the mothers, teaching the children a weekly class in the Korean language.

Throughout my research, I was acutely aware of my outsider-insider status. I too am a Korean woman but I am not a military bride and I'm usually not of the same generation as the women I interviewed for this book. Like them, I'm an immigrant Korean woman, but unlike them, I came as a child rather than as an adult. I am a racial and ethnic minority in America, as they are, but I'm also fluent in English. That fluency has allowed me many privileges, including an advanced education, higher social status, and greater earning power.

While growing up in immigrant Chicago and attending Korean churches in the 1970s and 1980s, I'd seen my share of military brides and knew they were different. I'd heard adults talk about them in disparaging or pitying tones, and their status as pariahs in "our" communities was clear. And like many other Koreans, I too have a military bride in my own family. My older cousin from Seoul married an American soldier who was the instructor of her English class in the early 1980s, and she has lived with him on various U.S. military bases in the United States and elsewhere since that time. Like most military brides, she married despite the opposition of her extended family, including my parents in the United States. Unlike the majority, however, she has not sponsored any relatives for immigration.

But whether or not military brides and other Koreans have familial ties to each other, our histories and our experiences are inextricably linked. The majority of the women I interviewed and studied were much older than I was, and they treated me like a daughter, niece, or youngest sister. They punctuated their conversations with worried asides about whether I was getting enough to eat, about my face looking pale and wan, or whether I was working too hard. They were generous with exhortations to gain weight, admonitions that I get married, suggestions that I try wearing makeup, and other such maternal advice. Several even offered to find me a suitable husband.[7] For my part, I took an interest in their children, offered my English services to help decipher official letters, and generally tried to be a family friend rather than just a researcher.

Even as they brought me into their lives and treated me with great warmth, the women were as keenly aware as I was, if not more so, of my role as a researcher. Many of them seemed to view me as a stand-in for Koreans at large, so that in explaining their lives to me they felt they were explaining their lives to all Koreans. They expected me to carry their stories to a wider audience and several of them explicitly expressed the hope that I would be able to tell Koreans "the truth" about military brides. Interestingly, no one expressed similar hopes about having their stories told to an American audience, though they were keenly aware of prejudice from Americans. Perhaps they didn't view me as a "real" American and a suitable vehicle for carrying their story to an American audience. Perhaps they were just not as interested in reaching Americans.

For the women I met, granting interviews and participating in conversations meant revealing their personal lives to an outsider. Accustomed to contemptuous treatment from fellow Koreans, most women were unwilling to speak with me. The majority of women declined formal interviews, saying that their lives were of no significance. In many cases, this was simply a polite way of refusing a researcher's advances. Many women feared that I might simply be looking for confirmation of widespread stereotypes about military brides. A 1994 Korean television documentary had been widely viewed and critiqued by the women as another instance of "those intellectuals" portraying Korean military brides in a bad light, which only made them more wary of outsiders looking for sensational stories.

In general, however, they did want the world to know that they were people trying to live decent lives just like everybody else. This was their primary reason for allowing me into their lives, a generous and gracious act that could include the occasional coffee, the weekly encounter at church, invitations to association meetings and events, numerous extended conversations at their homes, and formal interviews.

Although Korean military brides are the focus of this book, their husbands and children are not absent. The lives of the latter are depicted from the perspective of their wives and mothers and they serve as an important and necessary background to the story being told. Many husbands were either ambivalent about or opposed to their wives' participation in my research. Their opposition effectively prevented many women I approached from consenting to formal, taped interviews. But several of the women allowed me to interview them despite their husbands' objections, and many others met me for secret informal conversations when their husbands were at work. The fact that their wives spoke to me in Korean, a language they did not know, seemed to heighten the husband's anxiety about the content of our conversations and interviews. This is not to say that all husbands objected. In my fieldwork I came to know a good number of them, primarily at the military bride church, and our informal conversations have immeasurably enriched this book.

Through visits to their homes or weekly encounters at church, I also came to know many of the women's children, who ranged from toddlers to young adults, with a few in their thirties or even early forties. I refrained from seeking out formal interviews with the children, but my conversations with them, particularly those in their teens and twenties, helped develop my understanding of the life experiences of their mothers and also gave me insights into their own lives and their family dynamics.

Studying the lives and history of Korean military brides has profound ramifications for American history, Asian history, and Asian American history. Broadly speaking, a serious consideration of Asian military brides forces a reconsideration of the whole of U.S.-Asia relations and the social consequences that are a part of these relations. Attention should be paid to the unequal nature of U.S. relations with Asian countries as well as to the gendered and racialized ideologies that are part of this relationship and which have greatly impacted the lives of Asian and Asian American women. Even interpretations of Asian immigration need serious reconsideration. Additionally, the bicultural and biracial families that have been created by the kinds of military bride marriages discussed in the following pages have the ability to provoke new understandings of the concepts of race and multiculturalism.

The history I tell of Korean military brides reveals a history of American involvement in Korea and Korean involvement with America seen from "way, way, way down below," as Robin Kelley might say.[8] The linkages I make—between the imperialist nature of Korea-U.S. relations and husband-wife dynamics, between pressures to Americanize and Orientalist images of Asian women and family relations—demonstrate that even the most personal of relationships are deeply rooted in and shaped by historical and social circumstances. In this history, I trace the

contours of an everyday resistance not against strangers or social supe-
riors in public spaces, but against family intimates in private spaces. It
shows us the hollowness of American multiculturalism even as it shows
us the ways in which military brides contest that particular hegemony.
And it offers us a glimpse of the transformative potential of imagining
and locating community beyond the nation.

CHAPTER 1

Camptown, U.S.A.

The first Korean woman to enter the United States as the bride of a U.S. citizen arrived in 1950. She was the only one that year, and in all likelihood her husband was an American soldier. In the nearly half-century since then, close to a hundred thousand Korean women have followed as brides of U.S. soldiers.[1] These marriages have been made possible by the continued American military presence in South Korea, which provides the immediate context in which Korean women and U.S. soldiers meet and marry. The American presence not only creates the physical context—military bases and nearby camptowns, towns that revolve economically around the bases and which contain red-light districts catering to U.S. soldiers, where the two meet—but it also helps create the social and cultural contexts—militarized prostitution, local civilian employment on military bases, and the lure of America—that make marriage to U.S. soldiers, an appealing option for Korean women.

Relationships between Korean women and American soldiers have been shaped by the unequal relationship between the United States and Korea. These marriages might be based on personal choices made at the individual level but they are also a consequence of a half-century of American military domination over Korea. At least for the women, the choice to marry an American soldier is profoundly shaped by this larger context of Korean subordination. America's military presence in Korea serves as a constant reminder of the glaring contrast between Korean poverty and American wealth, which is too often interpreted as the contrast between Korean backwardness and American modernity. Additionally, the sexual subordination of Korean women on and around U.S. military bases in the region cannot be overlooked when examining the nature and the origins of relationships between Korean women and American soldiers.

The relationship between Korea and the United States is itself gendered, with Korea inscribed as the feminine other in need of protection and the United States playing the role of the masculine superior and guardian. This gendered context of neoimperialism is a major factor in the skewed gender profile of intermarriages between Koreans and Americans, the overwhelming majority of which are between American men and Korean women.[2]

The flip side of protection, of course, is that the masculine guardian also has the power to exploit the feminine other. This aspect of the gendered nature of the U.S.-Korea relationship is perhaps most notoriously reflected in the phenomenon of militarized prostitution, which can be found around every U.S. military base in Asia. South Korea, Okinawa, the Philippines, Thailand, and Vietnam have been or still are locations where Asian women serve the sexual desires of U.S. soldiers in clubs and bars clustered in so-called camptowns (also known as base towns or GI towns) that develop near military bases.[3] In Korea, these camptowns are found next to every major U.S. military installation, small ones near the small bases, larger ones next to the larger bases. Camptown activists estimate that between twenty to twenty-five thousand women are currently engaged in sex work within these communities.[4]

Itaewon, located in the heart of Seoul, South Korea's capital, is one of the better known and larger camptowns. Replete with U.S. fast-food restaurants and stores selling Korean-made goods such as leather jackets and baseball caps, by day Itaewon serves as a shopping district for American tourists and expatriates longing for a taste of home. By night, it becomes the red-light entertainment district for soldiers stationed at nearby Yongsan, home of the Eighth Army and headquarters of the USFK, U.S. Forces Korea. An American reporter describes Itaewon this way:

> A mile or so outside of Yongsan U.S. Army Garrison in central Seoul, past the tourist shops and street vendors selling Bulls, Raiders, et al ap-

parel, past the Burger King and the newly-opened Orange Julius and down a series of narrow roadways packed with American soldiers who are falling in and out of ramshackle clubs—Cadillac Bar, Love Cupid, Texas Club, Boston Club, the King Club, the Palladium, the Grand Ole' Opry—is one of the 180 GI camptowns that exist outside of every significantly sized military base in South Korea. . . .

On any given night in Itaewon, women in prostitution costume hang out club doors soliciting GIs: one part come on, one part contempt. An old Korean woman, hands clasped behind her back, spends the night strolling up and down Hooker Hill, approaching young GIs in their downy sports jackets, asking, "Lady?" as the GI, after questioning "How much? How old?" follows her up the hill and down an alley.[5]

My own 1997 visit to Uijongbu, a much smaller camptown near Seoul, highlighted both the social distance between mainstream Korean society and the camptowns, and the pervasiveness of the U.S. military presence in South Korea. I boarded the subway in central Seoul, along with students, smartly dressed middle-aged women, younger women in office garb, and business-suited men. Only one foreigner, a woman, was visible. During the fifty-minute subway ride, the composition of the passengers changed. The middle-aged women became more shabbily dressed and the young women more heavily made-up, while the business-suited men were nowhere to be seen, having been replaced by men in work clothes. Black and white American GIs, identifiable by their military fatigues, could be seen in nearly every compartment of the train: alone, in groups, or in pairs with young Korean women who were almost invariably dressed in short skirts, with permed hair and heavy makeup. Although perms, heavy makeup, and short skirts are in vogue among young urban women in Korea, the cheap quality of their clothes and the sparkly disco club style of their slightly smudged makeup set these women apart from the chic urbanites who stride through Seoul's fashionable districts.

Uijongbu itself was a bustling small town with what appeared to be a thriving commercial district. English signs made it clear that Americans were among the customers and several American fast-food chains were within walking distance of the station. American soldiers mixed with

Korean pedestrians and U.S. military vehicles were visible among the cars and buses. I boarded a city bus along with several GIs and asked the driver to let me off at *bbaet-bul,* the local name for the Uijongbu red-light district.[6] We headed for the outskirts of the town. Evidence of the U.S. military was everywhere: in addition to military jeeps and trucks, there were signs pointing to Camp Red Cloud and Camp Stanley, the gates of Camp Stanley itself, and the road, which was too wide for such a rural area and was obviously constructed to accommodate military vehicles.

The Uijongbu camptown is actually two neighborhoods, one in front of each U.S. military camp. The *bbaet-bul* bus stop is in the Gosan-dong neighborhood in front of Camp Stanley. It is a shabby, obviously poor area, with narrow streets and back alleys honeycombed with small houses. At first glance, it could be mistaken for any poor neighborhood in any semirural area of South Korea. But the local establishments and clubs, with names like Diamond and Mustang, and the presence of American GIs walking with Korean women, indicate that this area is somehow different. According to camptown activists, Uijongbu has about fifteen clubs in which fifty women work.

Many of the Korean women who marry American soldiers are assumed to have been prostitutes and club hostesses in camptowns such as this. Although no reliable statistics are available regarding the number of camptown women who married American GIs, the existing literature still concludes that the majority of Korean women-American GI marriages involve camptown women.[7] Most of these conclusions are based on ethnographic evidence, casework with Korean military wives living in the United States, speculation based on INS statistics of Korean women who immigrate to the United States as wives of American citizens, and/or statistics kept by the Korean government on emigration and marriages between Korean and American citizens.[8] One Korean wife of an American GI told a researcher that nine out of ten Korean women met their GI husbands at clubs catering exclusively to American soldiers, thus implying that they were prostitutes, and then added that nine out of ten will deny it.[9] Another researcher, however, found that the assumption that most women who marry American soldiers are prostitutes was unsupported by her data, which included a random sampling of applications made in 1978 by soldiers seeking permission from their commanding officers to marry Korean women and a survey of Korean women who had married American men and were seeking emigration visas from the Korean government.[10]

Among the wives that I encountered, it was considered a "known fact" that many of their compatriots had once been camptown women. However, only a few women spoke of camptown backgrounds, and most of the other women had detailed stories about meeting their husbands through friends, on-base jobs, and other encounters.

A satisfactory demographic profile of Korean women who marry American soldiers will probably never be compiled, given the dearth of data. However, it is clear that even though camptowns are one place where Korean women and American soldiers meet and form relationships, it is not the only place. And although it may have been the primary place in the past for the blossoming of such international marriages, it can no longer be assumed that this remains the case. Yet there is no doubting that militarized prostitution figures prominently in the phenomenon of marriages between Korean women and American soldiers. Research in the camptowns and with Korean women who came to the United States as GI wives consistently reveal that many marriages do involve former camptown prostitutes. Research also shows that many come from areas near camptowns and U.S. military bases, regardless of whether or not the women themselves were prostitutes.[11]

But more important, the very existence of militarized prostitution looms like a shadow over both Korean society and the lives of Korean women who marry American soldiers, even if those marriages began in locales other than camptowns. To take only the most blatant example, the sexual virtue of all women who marry American soldiers is immediately suspect, as one Korean woman found upon her engagement to a soldier. The woman, who worked in the same U.S. military base office as her fiancé, recalled the reaction of her coworkers:

As soon as people in my office heard about my engagement with John, they looked down on me. I was made to feel dirty and unworthy. Some soldiers asked me to go out with them, obviously thinking that I was now an easy mark for propositions. I quit my work rather than put up with such nonsense.[12]

Her fiancé, for his part, found that his military colleagues and commanding officers tried to dissuade him from the marriage. Some showed him pictures of sisters and female cousins, offering to introduce him to them. Korean women, it seems, were generally deemed acceptable as sexual companions, but not as wives to take home.

Along with unfavorable reputations, the stereotype of the camptown woman results in social alienation. It helps to keep Korean military wives isolated from both mainstream American society and mainstream Korean society, whether in South Korea itself or in Korean immigrant communities in America, for it makes the women an easy target for contempt. This in effect leaves them isolated within tightly restricted social circles where their primary relationships are either with their immediate families or with other Korean military wives.

It is therefore absolutely necessary to examine militarized prostitution in order to fully understand the historical and social contexts in which marriages between Korean women and American soldiers occur.

America's Comfort Women

For many American soldiers, Korea is synonymous with the proverbial rock 'n' rolling good time, and Korean women—treated as playthings easily bought and easily discarded—are essential to that experience. The women are seen by the soldiers as innately sexual, even depraved, and doing what they do for fun and money. If anyone has forced them into prostitution, in the eyes of the soldier, it is the Korean madams and pimps, not the U.S. military and certainly not the soldiers themselves.[13] The continuing prevalence of this belief is apparent in an April 1999 discussion about militarized prostitution in Korea on an e-mail list whose members, judging from their self-descriptions, are primarily Western males (mostly American) who spent some time in South Korea and maintain an interest in the country. The discussion also demonstrates that soldiers are not the only ones who hold this opinion. Most of the list members who posted on this topic refused to acknowledge that the women in this situation are victimized in any way by the U.S. military or individual soldiers. Instead, the discussants insisted that the majority of the women had made free choices to become prostitutes. One man called camptown women "women who are husband hunting, having fun, or in such [sic] of some sucker with a PX Ration Card." He suggested that "what you really need to do is 'follow the money,'" implying that since money flows from the soldiers to the women and pimps, it is the women and pimps who are benefiting from prostitution. Another man argued that without camptown prostitution, "there would be more rapes, and that the Army is thus keeping down violence against the local community (although that is a terrible thing to say)."[14]

Racism and sexism cannot be discounted as powerful factors in such discourses.[15] These are military manifestations of a deep-rooted American racism against Asians, which in the twentieth century has been expressed in the vilification of Asians as the "yellow peril" or the "yellow horde," as the villainous Fu Manchu, and the sexy but dangerous Dragon Lady. Combined with sexist and racist stereotypes of Asian women as exotic sex objects, this kind of thinking encourages and permits U.S. soldiers to treat Asian women, especially but not only prostitutes, as dispensable sex toys.

As Katherine Moon notes in her groundbreaking study of militarized prostitution in South Korea, the U.S. military condones and even encourages such behavior among its troops. One sailor told her that some commanding officers told their men that Asians like prostitution, calling it a way of life.[16] Articles in the *Pacific Stars and Stripes*, the primary military newspaper for U.S. troops in the Pacific, actively encouraged soldiers to seek out the camptown by reviewing clubs. One 1977 article, for example, touted the *kisaeng* party—a night of drinking and dancing with female entertainment—as the "ultimate experience" and "the Orient you heard about and came to find."[17] A U.S. Army manual from the 1980s turned a blind eye to the troops frequenting prostitutes with a "boys will be boys" attitude, telling the reader that "being a red-blooded American soldier, you will undoubtedly get your chance to experience the various aspects of the village." The manual then provided "tips" for patronizing camptown women, advising the soldiers to check the women's VD cards, stick to the licensed club women, and stay away from the streetwalkers.[18]

A U.S. Army chaplain interviewed in 1991 by Moon explained:

> What the soldiers have read and heard before ever arriving in a foreign
> country influences prostitution a lot. For example, stories about Ko-
> rean women being beautiful, subservient—they're tall tales, glamor-
> ized. . . . U.S. men would fall in lust with Korean women. They were
> property, things, slaves. . . . Racism, sexism—it's all there. The men
> don't see the women as human beings—they're disgusting, things to
> be thrown away. . . . They speak of the women in the diminutive.[19]

These distorted and dangerous ideas on the part of Westerners are embedded in the very fabric of the relationship between U.S. soldiers and
local camptown women. These women are America's comfort women, the
victims of a system of militarized prostitution that is supported and regulated by the U.S. military for the benefit of its soldiers.[20]

Although it is usually Japan that is vilified for the creation of a corps
of comfort women during World War II, virtual slaves serving the sexual
desires of Japanese soldiers, America also has a history of forcing women
and girls into similar situations of sexual subjugation and exploitation.[21]
In Vietnam, an installation of prostitutes servicing four thousand U.S.
soldiers was specifically created by and for the benefit of the U.S. military. The brothels, two concrete barracks each containing a bar, band-
stand, and sixty curtained-off compartments where the women lived and
worked, were located in fenced compounds guarded by military police,
compounds that included restaurants and other recreational facilities for
the soldiers. During the Korean War, some three hundred politically suspect Korean women, members of the communist party and leaders of people's committees, were confined by the U.S. military to a warehouse in
Seoul and repeatedly raped by U.S. soldiers. In Okinawa, U.S. military
personnel recruited twelve- and thirteen-year-old Okinawan girls,
placed them in cages on the U.S. base there, and forced them into sexual
service for the soldiers. In the Philippines, commanding officers in the
U.S. military actively promoted prostitution, some of them even owning
their own clubs and managing their own groups of prostitutes. And in
Korea during the 1970s, military buses were used to transport as many as
two hundred prostitutes a day from the camptown of Tongduchon into

nearby Camp Casey.[22] In each of these cases, commanding officers either tacitly condoned such activities or actively participated in them.

These are just a few of the examples culled from historical records and eyewitness testimony. Although some of them may be dismissed as aberrations, the system of militarized prostitution developed by the United States in Asia suggests otherwise. While Japan, which has no troops stationed overseas, no longer has the opportunity to engage in its version of militarized prostitution, America's comfort women still exist today in the camptowns outside every U.S. military base in Asia.[23] In Okinawa, South Korea, and the Philippines, the U.S. military directly and indirectly regulates clubs and the hostesses-prostitutes who work there, ostensibly to ensure that U.S. soldiers are protected from venereal diseases.[24] In Korea, the system of militarized prostitution is so pervasive and so central to the U.S. presence, that Korea scholar Bruce Cumings calls it "the most important aspect of the whole relationship (between the United States and South Korea) and the primary memory of Korea for generations of young Americans who have served there."[25]

America is not the first country, of course, to use Korean women for the entertainment of its soldiers. The sexual exploitation of women by the military, particularly the exploitation of a subjugated country's women by the conquering country's men, have gone hand in hand throughout history.[26] Indeed, the history of prostitution in Korea is intimately linked to Korea's political and military subjugation by foreign countries, first Japan and then the United States.[27]

Before the twentieth century, wandering bands of entertainers occasionally bartered sex for money or goods, and *kisaeng*, women trained in music and the arts who entertained upper-class men, sometimes engaged in sexual relationships with their patrons. Ruling elites of past centuries have used the bodies and sexualized services of women such as the palace ladies-in-waiting, *kisaeng*, and young maidens sent as tribute to Mongol kings, in order to advance their own interests.[28] But prostitution as an organized, commercial endeavor was first introduced to Korea by Japan at the turn of the century. As Japanese power over Korea gradually increased, eventually culminating in Japan's annexation of Korea in 1910, Japanese troops became a common sight. So did single Japanese men who came to Korea for the economic opportunities offered by this nascent colony. It was for them that Japan created the first legalized prostitution quarters in 1900. The largest were located in Pusan, a southern port city, and Seoul.

Illegal prostitution was also deliberately encouraged by the Japanese government, which undertook a policy of transforming bar waitresses and *kisaeng* into prostitutes. Bar waitress and *kisaeng* became euphemisms for prostitute, and what used to be the *kisaeng's* occasional sexual relationship with a favored patron, better characterized as an illicit love affair often accompanied by love letters and poetry than as sex-for-money one-night stands, became obligatory commercial transactions. Japanese troops and government officials formed the customer base for many brothels and bars, while high-ranking Japanese military and government officials frequented the more expensive *kisaeng*.[29]

Many of the young women working as prostitutes were sold by destitute families, while others were kidnapped. As this soon became a social issue, the Japanese colonial government in Korea instituted "placement agencies." These agencies ostensibly brokered employment for young women, especially those from poor rural families who came to urban areas seeking work. (Japanese colonial policy dispossessed many Koreans of their land, turning small farm owners into impoverished sharecroppers. The sons and daughters of many such families sought work in urban centers.[30]) But in fact the agencies placed the women in brothels, bars, and *kisaeng* houses. Once "dirtied" in such a way, patriarchal mores emphasizing female chastity made it difficult for them to find other employment or lead "respectable" lives.[31]

This legacy of Japanese colonialism remains a strong presence in South Korea. Placement agencies have existed throughout the decades since Japan left the Korean peninsula in 1945, and they have played a significant role in tricking young Korean women into prostitution, including work in the camptown clubs serving U.S. soldiers. Contemporary red-light districts are often located in the same areas where Japan created legal prostitution quarters. *Kisaeng* tourism, a form of sex tourism, draws thousands of Japanese men to Korea each year.[32]

Militarized prostitution in Korea formally began in 1937 with the advent of Japan's expansionist war with China. Japan began mobilizing Korean workers for the war effort, drafting laborers to fill the manpower shortage in Japan and in Japanese settlements in Manchuria, Russia, and

Southeast Asia. The mobilization soon expanded to include women, first as manual laborers and then as "comfort women," sexual slaves in a system of brothels organized and maintained by the Japanese government for the exclusive use of the Japanese military. Brothels were established in the war zone in the South Pacific, Southeast Asia, and China, as well as in bases located in Korea. Some of the youngest and prettiest women, usually girls just in their early teens, were sent to special camps in Japan where they were first offered to high-ranking military officials and then, their virginity soiled, sent to the war zone brothels to service rank-and-file troops. Some two hundred thousand Korean women, some girls as young as eleven, were sent to work in these brothels. They were recruited by teachers, local administrators, and anyone else in a position of authority within the Japanese colonial government in Korea. The government issued quotas that had to be met by each locality, and when girls couldn't be recruited with the promise of earning money in Japanese factories to support their families, they were simply kidnapped.[33]

With Japan's defeat in World War II came Korea's official liberation from Japanese imperialism. But emerging Cold War realities divided the nation in half at the 38th Parallel, with Soviet troops entering the north and U.S. troops entering the south. In his first proclamation to the Korean people, General McArthur announced that the troops were occupying forces and that the U.S. military would be taking over both the functions and the property of the departing Japanese government. Soon thereafter, the U.S. military government was formalized. The southern part of Korea was now little more than a colony of the United States.[34] As if to symbolize this, Yongsan Garrison in Seoul, once the headquarters for the Japanese Imperial Army, became the headquarters for the U.S. military. Other Japanese military installations, such as posts in the port city of Pusan, also became U.S. military installations.

The Camptowns: A Brief History

The U.S. entry into Korea and the establishment of camptowns were virtually simultaneous. U.S. forces landed in the southern part of Korea on September 8, 1945, in the west coast port city of Inchon. By the end of that year, a nearby town called Bupyong had become the first camptown. Soldiers stationed at Inchon sought liquor and girls for recreation. Poverty-stricken women, some of them prostitutes who had catered to the Japanese, others part of the rural and urban poor, gathered to fill the soldiers' desires in the hope of making a living. Soon simple frame houses sprang up in a neighborhood called Shinchon. These clubs and brothels housed about a thousand women. Few, if any, spoke English, and they were compensated for their services not with money, but with U.S. military supply items such as rations, cigarettes, and jackets.[35] These prostitutes were dubbed *yang galbo* (Western whore). As militarized prostitution, U.S. style, expanded throughout Korea, other terms were added: *yang gongju* (Western princess) and *yang saeksi* (Western bride). The use of "princess" and "bride" to describe these women can be seen as a rhetorical gesture that acknowledges the material comfort and glamor symbolized by the United States while ridiculing the women's efforts to achieve it by selling their bodies to American soldiers.

During the Korean War (1950–53), the number of camptowns expanded. The camptown centered around the Shinchon neighborhood in Bupyong doubled in size, as an estimated two thousand women gathered in the area's clubs. Makeshift camptowns sprang up wherever bases were located, only to be torn down as troops retreated or advanced. Since troop access to civilian villages was strictly controlled during the war, women carrying blankets made deals outside the villages and did their business in the mountains. This was the beginning of the so-called blanket squad, groups of women who followed the troops from place to place. After the war, blanket squads followed soldiers to annual training maneuvers held deep in the Korean countryside. These squads still exist today, organized by pimps with the aid of U.S. military personnel who provide detailed information on the dates and locations of annual training maneuvers. Largely composed of camptown women, the squads follow troops into remote rural areas where the soldiers conduct war games. There, each woman services thirty to forty men a night.

The development of camptowns transformed and often destroyed once peaceful rural farming villages throughout South Korea. The 1990 novel *Silver Stallion* describes this process, linking it to the social demarcation between virtuous and unvirtuous women. Set during the Korean War, the novel begins with the appearance of U.S. troops in a small farming village, apparently checking the area for enemy soldiers. They set up base not far from the village. One night, a widow living alone with her two children is raped by U.S. soldiers. She is shunned by the villagers, who are simultaneously stunned at her misfortune and ashamed at her loss of female virtue. They are also terrified that a similar fate will befall them as well, and they set up night patrols to watch for marauding soldiers. On several occasions, soldiers ransack houses looking for women.[36] Soon, however, prostitutes begin to gather near the base and a small camptown is established. Although distressed at the proximity of such filth, the town heaves a collective sigh of relief, for at least the village women will be safe from the sexual violence of the foreign troops.[37]

The novel's separation between "virtuous" women and "dirty" women mirrors that of Korean society, where women who work in the camptowns are social pariahs, but are also seen as a necessary evil since their existence safeguards the chastity of the "virtuous" women. Camptowns and *yang gongju* became a permanent fixture in Korean society after the Korean War, and the camptown woman became the archetypal "fallen woman." Because the war ended not with a peace treaty but with a truce, the U.S. military has continued to maintain troops in South Korea. As a result, the number of camptowns increased with the number of military installations, as did the number of *yang gongju.*

In addition to Bupyong, some of the earliest and largest camptowns include Itaewon, areas of Pusan called Hialeah and Texas, Tongduchon, and Songtan. The camptowns in Pusan were among the most stable, as U.S. soldiers were stationed there throughout the war. (This was possible because Pusan, a port city located at the southeastern tip of Korea, left UN control only briefly during the war.) The U.S. military used Pusan as a landing port, and the camptowns of Hialeah (next to Camp Hialeah) and Texas soon appeared. Hialeah remains a camptown today, while Texas (located next to the Pusan train station) has become a camptown serving not only the U.S. military but also sailors and other itinerant travelers passing through the port.[38]

The 1960s were the heyday of the camptowns, when more than thirty thousand women earned their living entertaining some sixty-two thousand U.S. soldiers stationed in virtually every corner of South Korea. The Paju area northwest of Seoul, militarily important due to its proximity to the DMZ[39] that serves as the truce line between North and South Korea, contained the highest concentration of U.S. troops until 1971. Nick-named the "GI's Kingdom," the area was home to the 1st Marine Division and the 24th, 7th, and 2nd Infantry Divisions. The largest camptown during this period was Tongduchon, nicknamed Little Chicago and lo-cated just east of Paju and north of Seoul. When Camp Casey was estab-lished as the main infantry base at the end of the Korean War, Tongdu-chon was transformed from a remote farming village into a chaotic world of drugs, sex, crime, and black market deals in PX goods. During its height in the mid-1960s, some seven thousand women in Tongduchon worked as prostitutes serving the U.S. military.[40]

Because U.S. bases were one of the few, if not the only, sources of in-come in the poverty-stricken years of the 1940s through the 1970s, the camptowns attracted not only poor women, including war widows and orphans seeking to make a living, but also entrepreneurs and criminals. In collusion with GIs, Korean civilians smuggled military supplies and PX goods out of the bases, selling them for a handsome profit on the black market. Pimps and madams established clubs catering to the sol-diers, hiring women at starvation wages to work as hostesses-cum-pros-titutes. Villagers opened laundries, restaurants, stores, and other busi-nesses serving the more mundane needs of the soldiers and the camp-town women. The *Dong-A Ilbo*, one of South Korea's major newspapers, reported on the development of these camptowns, using as a model Ui-jongbu, a camptown just north of Seoul but south of the larger Tong-duchon. Before the war, Uijongbu had about ten thousand residents and one silk mill as its sole industry. But with the war, hundreds of un-employed people, UN forces, and criminals literally invaded the town, bringing with them various underworld activities. About two thou-sand women worked as *yang gongju*, and the small town was suddenly filled with cabarets, bars, tailor and dress shops, and other stores. By the 1960s, an estimated 60 percent of the sixty-five thousand Koreans in Uijongbu were engaged in some form of business catering to the U.S. military.[41]

With the construction of U.S. military bases came not only the trans-formation but also the literal destruction of Korean villages. In July 1951, Songtan, about an hour south of Seoul by bus, was invaded by the bull-dozers of the 417th Squadron of the U.S. Air Force. The squadron built an airfield, causing five thousand people (one thousand families) to lose their homes. These families had farmed the same plots of land in Songtan for generations, making their living from the annual rice harvest and the charcoal they made from the wood they chopped in surrounding forests. As they left their ancestral lands, each family held a piece of paper from the U.S. military promising monetary compensation in neatly typed Korean and English. The promised compensation, which was much less than the market value of the land, never materialized despite years of legal battles.[42] Over the years, more residents were displaced as Osan Air Force Base expanded to become the largest base in Korea and the second largest Air Force base in Asia. (Since the 1992 closing of Clark Air Force Base in the Philippines, Osan is now the largest.) Journalist Oh Yun Ho describes the transformation of Songtan:

> Oblivious to the local residents' resentment, the airfield was completed at top speed within six months. The surrounding area became the land of the stars and stripes. Thatched-roof houses gave way to all kinds of stores with English signs, aluminum cans replaced gourds, and a village full of shy maidens with their long braided hair instantly became a village full of *yang gongju*.[43]

With the construction of the airfield, Songtan became home to a major hub of U.S. military activity in Asia and a thriving camptown. When the United States began to reduce its land forces in 1971, army camptowns such as Tongduchon suffered, but Songtan grew as the United States continued to emphasize airpower. An air squadron is stationed there, and soldiers from other units regularly fly in from Okinawa for weekend training sessions.[44] Songtan today is one of the largest camptowns, with about one thousand five hundred prostitutes. The projected move to Osan of the Eighth Army and USFK headquarters (currently located at Yongsan in Seoul) is sure to make Songtan Korea's camptown capital.

American Town is a camptown developed with the collusion of both the South Korean and American governments. Built by a South Korean general and a landowner in 1969 during the height of the Park Chung Hee regime, American Town turned farmland in North Cholla Province into a sanctioned red-light district for U.S. soldiers. Distinctly marked off from the nearby civilian town of Kunsan and the surrounding countryside by chain-link fences, American Town at first was wholly owned by the two developers, but later became a corporation with shareholders. During the 1970s business was so good that the clubs opened even during the day and a fleet of buses ferried soldiers between Kunsan Air Force Base and the town. Today (2001), two buses operate daily between the camptown and the base. The town includes dormitory housing for the women, about twenty clubs, a dozen stores, and a government-run health clinic where the women receive mandatory testing for sexually transmitted diseases.[45]

These camptowns perform crucial social functions for both South Korea and the United States. Both governments seem to consider camptowns a necessary evil. For South Korea, the camptowns hold the promise of containing unhealthy American influences, protecting "virtuous" women from the threat of rape, and—especially during the early years of economic development—earning foreign exchange.[46] It is also a way for a subjected government to cater to the dominant country. For the U.S. military, camptowns provide a release for the troops and help to maintain troop morale. They also help to keep unruly soldiers away from "normal" civilians and thus reduce tension with the Korean public at large. While the U.S. military officially decries prostitution as an unhealthy influence on its soldiers, it also lets the soldiers know that frequenting prostitutes in Korea is acceptable behavior. As one military chaplain says,

> In Korea, the guys are inundated with prostitutes. And the U.S. forces and the American government are saying "Hem, hem—be tolerant." . . . Where we could make a difference is, where we could take the rules, the strictures like in Germany or in other nations where they are stricter, where this kind of thing doesn't go on, and apply it to Korea, we could fix this problem in 20 minutes. . . . But in Korea, we just say, "Aw, it's the culture" and wink at what goes on.[47]

Both the South Korean and U.S. governments, however, do more than simply "wink at what goes on." For the South Korean government, these camptowns and the regulation of camptown women have been crucial to maintaining smooth relations with the U.S. government. Katherine Moon points out that making sure that camptown women played their proper role as entertainers and sexual playmates who would foster goodwill toward Korea among American soldiers was an essential aspect of the South Korean government's strategies for national security. The United States, for its part, takes it for granted that its soldiers "need" paid sexual companions for high morale and demands that camptown women be kept free of venereal disease so that soldiers do not become infected. Thus, as Moon demonstrates, the South Korean government and the U.S. military have engaged in a decades-long collaboration to regulate camptown women and their behavior. In the process, they have subtly, sometimes overtly, promoted the sexual exploitation of Korean women. The women are doubly victimized: betrayed by their own government and virtually sold as a kind of war booty to the United States, and exploited by a foreign government interested only in the women's usefulness as sexual diversions for the ostensible purpose of maintaining troop morale.

The U.S. military has also long regarded prostitution as a moral and health issue, however, sometimes worrying that it damaged U.S. reputations in the eyes of the local civilians. But despite official hand-wringing over the moral state of "our boys," the United States has never seriously attempted to eliminate prostitution around its military bases in South Korea. This is in contrast to its efforts to eliminate prostitution around its European bases, as the chaplain quoted above notes. Although soldiers are officially forbidden any involvement in prostitution, unofficially they are given a wink and a nod. A 1965 report conducted by the Eighth U.S. Army frankly admitted that "fraternization (in the form of prostitution) is near the core of troop-community relations here." It also found that most soldiers believe that such "fraternization" endears Korea to the soldiers, making them more willing to fight, and that "most officers believe that fraternization is generally a constructive force." In the end, the United States adopted a "boys will be boys" policy toward camptown prostitution in South Korea.[48]

Before the 1970s, the U.S. military engaged in sporadic efforts to regulate clubs and club women, primarily to control the spread of venereal disease. U.S. medical officers intermittently checked camptown women for sexually transmitted diseases, military authorities unilaterally declared as off-limits clubs that were deemed problematic because infected women worked there, and military police went on patrol through the towns. Bases also instituted VD contact identification systems, pressuring soldiers to identify those they had patronized. Club women identified by soldiers were summarily taken to military medical centers where they were tested and medicated. But such regulation contradicted the official position that the military had nothing whatsoever to do with prostitution. U.S. officials therefore continually pressured the Korean government to regulate the camptowns and the prostitutes.

Although reluctant to take systematic action, the Korean government did take steps toward regulation. The first step was to set up official districts where "entertaining" foreigners was the main business. Thus, even as prostitution was officially outlawed in 1961, 104 areas were designated in 1962 as special districts of prostitution. By 1964, that number had increased to 145, all of them camptowns. Since 1972, about 72 such districts have remained in operation. The highest concentration has been in the area surrounding Seoul, which includes the Paju area, Tongduchon, Uijongbu, and Songtan.[49] Women who work in the clubs were registered as hostesses and required to join "women's associations" with names like the Rose Club and the Dandelion Club. Government-run medical clinics and private clinics on government contract were established in each district for mandatory VD testing and treatment of the women. But due to a lack of finances and initiative, regulation was lax. Venereal disease remained a constant complaint by the U.S. military, along with repeated requests that the Korean government do something about the problem.[50]

The South Korean government did little until 1971, when troop reductions under the Nixon Doctrine caused the Park Chung Hee government great anxiety about the stability of U.S. support. By then, official U.S. rhetoric about the immorality of prostitution had faded to the background and health issues, namely, the spread of venereal diseases and the effect this would have on the combat-readiness of the soldiers, moved to the forefront. Prevention and treatment of disease and the control of the local prostitute population became the primary concerns. One sailor described how the ship's medical officer would gather the men before docking in a Philippines or Korea port, give them a quick briefing on health precautions, and hand out condoms.[51] The message to the men was clear: Go ahead, but don't catch any diseases. In 1971, spurred by American complaints about conditions in the camptowns and feeling a need to forestall reductions in the U.S. commitment to Korea's defense, the Korean government joined with the American military in a five-year cleanup campaign.

The cleanup campaign, initiated by the U.S.-Korea Status of Forces Joint Committee,[52] intensified and expanded existing efforts to control VD to include improving civilian-military relations, improving sanitation and the physical infrastructure, reducing crime and black market activities, and teaching club owners and hostesses how to equitably treat black and white soldiers. At each step of the way, the U.S. military prodded the Korean government into action, providing advice, medical supplies, and other forms of support, but almost always keeping American officials in the background. This creates the illusion that it is primarily the Korean government that regulates prostitution and the camptowns, but in reality such regulation is demanded and orchestrated by the American military, with a weak Korean government able to do little but acquiesce.

The Korean government was motivated primarily by its belief that American military assistance was vital to its national security. The perception, whether justified or not, that North Korea would attack the moment that U.S. support of South Korea faltered fueled this belief in the necessity of U.S. military aid. This partially explains the Park Chung Hee government's strategy of using patriotic rhetoric and the communist threat to persuade camptown women to cooperate in the cleanup campaign. Throughout the 1970s, Korean government officials gathered camptown women into town halls for monthly lectures on patriotism. The women, the officials would say, were patriots because their work with American GIs helped the national defense and earned foreign exchange for the development of the national economy. Thus, their full cooperation in the cleanup campaign, and the expectation of better relations with the U.S. military plus increased business for the camptowns, were posited as a form of patriotism. The women, according to this logic, were performing the supreme sacrifice for the good of their country. However, few, if any, women believed this rhetoric. As camptown women told interviewers, sex work was just dirty, there was nothing patriotic about it.[53]

In addition to controlling venereal disease, the U.S. military also wanted to allay increasing racial tension between black and white troops. Although this tension was a reflection of racial tensions back in America during the 1960s and 1970s, U.S. military authorities blamed camptown women and camptown practices of segregated clubs. Camptowns were segregated along racial lines just like American society. Most clubs catered to white soldiers, while a few clubs, usually with inferior facilities, catered exclusively to blacks. The women themselves were categorized as those who catered to whites and those who catered to blacks. One black soldier bitterly complained to the *Overseas Weekly* (4/71) that "I ask a girl to go to bed and she says no. My money is as green as anybody's." Club owners and camptown women countered that it was the prejudices of white soldiers that dictated camptown segregation. Clubs who allowed blacks lost business from whites, and women who serviced blacks found that whites avoided them.[54] Since white soldiers were more numerous, losing their business meant losing profits. Instead of trying to educate their soldiers, the U.S. military authorities turned to camptown women to smooth racial relations among their troops. "Educating" the women to treat black and white soldiers equitably was a major aspect of the cleanup campaign.

The U.S. military's regulation of prostitution in the camptowns was conducted at the highest levels. The commanding officer of the Eighth Army in Yongsan personally visited clubs in Itaewon, the nearby camptown, to ask club owners to educate the women about proper behavior toward black soldiers. Continued discrimination by the women against black soldiers, he warned, would result in the military placing the club off-limits, and thus in reduced revenue for the clubs. The military produced posters, banners, coasters, and other paraphernalia for use in the clubs, all emblazoned with antidiscrimination mottoes. Also produced were brochures telling the women that a failure to treat black and white soldiers equitably would result in a loss of morale among the soldiers, thus endangering Korea's security.[55]

Efforts to control VD soon became the focus of the cleanup campaign. The efforts, however, targeted only the women. The soldiers themselves were given warnings, education, and treatment if found infected, but were never regulated. The U.S. Surgeon General, in a report to the commanding general of the Eighth Army, emphasized that "control of infection in the prostitute reservoir [is] of primary importance," and recommended that the USFK "encourage growth of ROK diagnostic ability."[56] In practice, this meant increased regulation of the women. The number of women registered as club hostesses rose, and conditions for registration became more stringent. Registered women were required to carry

VD identification cards. Invalid cards resulted in fines, being summarily taken to detention houses (known among the women as the Monkey House) where women who tested positive were held and given medication until the infections cleared. Testing as often as twice a week was required, and women were routinely harassed by both U.S. military police and Korean police for proof of registration and testing. Failure to register meant that the women could not work in the clubs, recognized as the locus of camptown prostitution.[57]

The number of U.S. military police patrolling the camptowns as well as the frequency of their patrols increased. This was ostensibly intended to monitor the behavior of the soldiers, but it effectively served as another means of regulating the women. The U.S. military police, for example, engaged in surprise visits to the clubs, demanding to see the women's VD identification cards. The military police also rounded up women identified by infected soldiers as the source of their infection. A camptown woman was never given a chance to verify that the soldier who had identified her had in fact had sex with her. There was no such thing as medical confidentiality for the women, while the military kept in strict confidence the identities of infected soldiers. Many women, therefore, never found out which soldiers had identified them. For the women, these control methods posed both mental distress and financial burdens. They found the police harassment and the exams, especially when performed by U.S. medics, to be deeply humiliating as well as an affront to their sense of national pride. What, after all, were U.S. officials doing harassing and examining Korean citizens in Korea? The women were also required to pay for the mandatory testing and treatment. On their meager earnings, this was often impossible. Many were forced to borrow from their club owners (essentially pimps) and were thus thrown into greater debt and under the tighter control of the club owners.

The women were also required to wear numbered tags so that the soldiers could better identify who they slept with, and the soldiers were expected to write down the names of these women on slips of paper kept at the club. Each base also kept photo files, books filled with the names and photographs of the registered women, along with their numbers, to make identification easier. In cases where soldiers did not remember the numbers and had failed to write down the names, the military police escorted them to the clubs and had the soldiers point out the offending women.

The women were then taken to medical clinics or detention centers, usually on the spot and with little explanation. Because the soldiers often had difficulty remembering whom they had slept with, they often identified the wrong women. Nevertheless, even women who tested negative after such identification were often medicated anyway.[58]

Much of this system remains in place in the twenty-first century. Korean officials and U.S. military officials together make routine tours of camptowns to check registration and VD identification and otherwise keep an eye on the camptown women. The military police still accompany soldiers on identification missions, and the women are still required to pay for and undergo regular testing for venereal disease.[59]

The Road to Camptowns

Who are the camptown women and how do they end up there?[60] For the vast majority of the women, prostitution is a last resort and is often an occupation which they are tricked into entering. In the early years of the U.S. military government period and the Korean War, the women were often war widows or orphans, some may have been former prostitutes during the Japanese colonial period, and some were victims of rape by UN or U.S. forces. Although generalizations are hard to make, the available evidence indicates that poverty plays a leading role in camptown prostitution. Over the years, camptown women generally have had low levels of formal education, have come from poor families with either one or both parents missing, have often been financially responsible for the upbringing of siblings or the care of sick or unemployed parents, and in many cases have been the victims of rape, incest, or irresponsible and/or abusive boyfriends or husbands. Most have worked in factories, as domestic laborers, or in odd jobs as waitresses or store clerks. Camptowns may also not be the first place where they entered prostitution, whether it was as a last resort or as a result of being tricked or kidnapped. Some women are sold to camptown club owners by their current pimps.

For many camptown women, the path to a camptown club began when they answered placement agency ads. Placement agencies, already well established under the Japanese colonial regime, got into the camptown business almost as soon as camptowns first appeared. As camp-towns became established, they worked vigorously to persuade, coerce, and trick poor women seeking employment into working as prostitutes. After answering ads promising work, room and board, and sometimes even an education (although education in what was never specified), the women were usually raped, beaten into submission, and then sold to a Korean brothel or a camptown club.

Outright kidnapping is also a common method. Pimps seek out young girls from the country arriving in big cities such as Seoul and promise them employment, food, and shelter. The girls are usually poor, seeking work, and may be runaways. If they believe the promises, they are usu-ally raped and then sold as prostitutes. Sometimes women who have lost their virginity will voluntarily walk into camptowns. These women are often the victims of male cruelty or irresponsibility. They may be victims of rape or incest trying to escape from difficult family situations, or have had coercive sexual relationships with men who later left them, or are fleeing abusive husbands, or have been abandoned by husbands or boyfriends. They are usually poor and often have to support siblings or children. Finding themselves with few options for making a living, they turn to sex work in the belief that since they have already been "dirtied," they might as well use their bodies to support themselves.

Once the women enter this line of work, regardless of how, it is very difficult for them to return to "normal" work and "respectable" society because of the social stigma. Other factors that make escape from the camptowns difficult, however, are the club system itself, which keeps the women in a form of debt bondage, and the reality that with little ed-ucation and few skills, few forms of alternative employment are open to them. For those women who do learn skills such as taxi driving, beauty salon work, or dressmaking, jobs remain hard to find.[61] As a result, many women simply grow old and die in the camptowns. The more fortunate among them may perhaps become club owners themselves, while the less fortunate may end up spending their elderly years as streetwalkers, so-liciting drunk soldiers young enough to be their grandsons in order to eke out a meager existence.

The club system generally dictates the lives of camptown women.[62] The women usually start by borrowing money from the club owner to buy a bed, sound system, dresser, and other items necessary to furnish the room they are assigned. This is the room where they are expected to receive customers, thus the need for a Western-style bed and sound system. Many clubs have rooms in the back for the hostesses. Room and board are deducted from their earnings. This initial debt is usually the beginning of the women's debt bondage to the club owner. Because their earnings often cannot cover all their expenses, particularly for women who are supporting children, siblings, or parents, they are forced to continually borrow from the club owner, their sole source of credit. In addition, the placement fees charged by employment agencies or the body price charged by traffickers (essentially the price the club owner has paid to purchase the woman) are usually charged to the women's accounts. In this way, women enter camptown life with substantial debt which they must pay off if they wish to leave. For most women, paying off the debt proves impossible.

Some clubs have a meager base salary, while others make the women work solely on commission. The workday begins in the early evening. Their job is to make small talk with the GIs who come to the club, dance with them, and make them buy drinks. Every drink the GI buys for a hostess results in a small commission, less for plain juice, more for an alcoholic drink. To earn more money, the women must have sex with the men. Although in theory a woman might choose never to engage in prostitution, in practice her employers and the weight of her debt effectively render that choice impossible. A "short time" means just an hour or so, while a "long time" means overnight. It is common for the women to have regular customers, and a regular customer can also turn into a contract live-in arrangement. In such an arrangement, the pair sets up house and the man pays monthly living expenses. It is usually within such an arrangement that promises of marriage are made and children born. Such relationships usually end with the GIs' tour of duty, if not before, and the women are forced to return to the clubs to earn a living.

America, America

American soldiers, camptowns, and *yang gongju* are inextricably intertwined for Koreans. They also hold dual meanings. On the one hand, they are despised for immorality and their corrupting influence. GIs and *yang gongju* frequently appear in Korean novels and short stories, for example, in story lines and descriptions that leave little doubt as to the cruelty and crassness of the GIs and the tawdry, tragic lives of the *yang gongju*. As one middle-aged man who grew up in rural southwestern Korea notes, "We all knew about the *yang gongju*, but it wasn't part of our lives. We just knew that they were dirty. Everyone knew that." On the other hand, they can be imbued with an alluring glow by their link to America's material abundance. One camptown woman explains how her longing to enter the luxurious America pictured in the movies and on television led her to naively seek out a camptown in the 1980s:

> When I watched TV and the movies during my youth, I wanted to go live in America. When I was a little older, I wanted to have some luxuries, but that was impossible in our poor household. So I came to the camptown to meet Americans and earn lots of money. But once I got here, I found that many things were different from what I had expected. I never imagined that I would have to do this kind of work. And it doesn't even earn lots of money. If I had known that it was this kind of place, I would never have come.[63]

Similar sentiments are expressed in *Gobbi*, a novel that traces the lives of two half-sisters, both of whom become *yang gongju*. The heroine Chongin's childhood during the Korean War and her impressions of America are described as follows:

> American soldiers camped in the orchards of her grandmother's brother. The child [Chongin] grew up in the midst of endless talk about the war. To her, the war wasn't fearsome or a terror, but a thrill, an impression, an excitement within which was always embedded the sweet scent of chocolate and American soldiers. So the child liked the war and the American GIs because she could go to the orchard everyday and receive chocolate. She couldn't understand Pilsu's father, who got so angry at the GIs when they asked to borrow his wife. If he had lent them his wife, he would have received a barrelful of chocolate and delicious cookies. . . . And then there was Wonja, whom she saw by chance. . . . On a hill behind the orchard, several American soldiers

made the village maiden Wonja lie down and then took turns riding on her belly. As soon as the American soldiers left, Wonja struck the ground repeatedly with a hoe as she cried. A year after she disappeared, she came home to visit wearing stylish high heels, perhaps proving true the rumors that she had become a *yang gongju*. Seeing how Wonja had turned into a stylish woman, the child believed that the act of American soldiers riding on a maiden's belly was a wonderful magic that turns maidens into beautiful women.

. . . Young girls on tiptoes and with sashaying hips would sing merrily:

Yang galbo (Western whore), ttong galbo (dirty whore), where are you going? With my high heeled shoes, I'm going to the *yangnom* (here used as derogatory slang for American soldier).

Chongin sang that song until she was ten. Each time, she wanted to wear high heels and run to the American soldiers like Wonja.[64]

In both the fictional character's reminiscence and the camptown woman's testimony, the realities of sexual assault, poverty, and camptown life are glossed over with a naive, awed view of America's material luxuries and pleasures. In the early years, food figured prominently among the luxuries. Food items were among the most important in a long litany of never-before-seen material goods that American soldiers brought to an impoverished and literally starving Korea: Taster's Choice coffee, ham, Spam, Oscar Mayer hot dogs and bologna, hot cocoa, marshmallows, peanut butter, butter, cheese, jam and jelly, Oreo cookies, Ritz crackers, Jello pudding, potato chips, and of course Hershey's chocolate. An army ration staple that GIs often tossed to Korean children, chocolate symbolized the abundance and generosity of America. Not only was America so rich that it could provide its soldiers with a candy like chocolate, but Americans were so generous that they simply gave it away to the children they saw. Americans, the saying went, were so rich that they had meat at every meal, and not just bits lost in the soup or stew, but whole great hunks of it, one for each person. The culinary trappings of middle America, items like the ones listed above, were rare delicacies affordable only by the rich and only if one went to the black market. Even after South Korea prospered, American food items remained luxuries.

American foods such as Spam, for example, are imported and sold in fancy department stores as gourmet delicacies, while Oreo cookies, Cheese Whiz, Kraft singles, and the like are still spirited out of the nearest PX and sold in black market corners of neighborhood grocery stores and outdoor markets.

As the South Korean economy prospered and the nation industrialized, the luxuries of American life were conveyed to Koreans through Hollywood movies and the daily broadcasts of AFKN, the U.S. military's television network in Korea.[65] During the 1980s, for example, the prime-time melodrama *Dallas* conveyed the portrait of a glamorous, high-living America. But American soldiers, as the most visible, palpable American presence in Korea, remained the primary symbol for American material abundance and the luxurious life of plenty. Soldiers also conveyed the impression, unlike *Dallas,* that even ordinary folks led lives of plenty in America. A rank-and-file soldier seemed to enjoy greater material plenty than even upper-class Koreans. Stories of golf courses, bowling lanes, movie theaters, large houses with expansive lawns, swimming pools, and restaurants serving steak at half the going price spread among Korea's urbanites. These were the amenities found on large bases such as Yongsan, where family housing faithfully mimicked suburban America, complete with schools, parks, sports leagues, and PTAs. If one became a *yang gongju,* one would get to know GIs and have access to America and its luxuries. Becoming a *yang gongju*—although what that entailed was unknown to the innocent—is thus seen by impressionable youngsters as the clearest way to achieve this life. The magical lure of America obscures the reality of its presence in Korea.

The lure that America exerted (and to a large extent still exerts) on Koreans is a consequence of the unequal relationship between the two countries. It is the lure that the metropole exerts on its colony. It is all the stronger because America was seen as a liberator, not a colonizer. Under the dominant discourse of America as the savior who rescued Korea from Japanese imperialism and then saved Korea from communism, American heroism and generosity joined with American material abundance into an image of utopia. The same Korean man who spoke of everyone knowing that camptown women are dirty continued by saying, "But America was like our big brother, our ally. And we felt gratitude to the soldiers for helping us defend our country." Although a countering image of

America as a corrupting influence has run parallel with this image of utopia, the positive image has been dominant. The power, wealth, and modernity that America symbolizes overshadow the negative consequences of America's dominance over Korea. Indeed, America's image began fraying at the edges only after the 1980 Kwangju Massacre, a brutal crackdown on prodemocracy protesters in which the United States has been implicated.[66]

But even as America's allure held sway, most Koreans despised camptowns and the *yang gongju* who worked there. Traditional patriarchal mores emphasizing female chastity and a centuries-old pride in what Koreans consider a homogeneous culture and people have meant that prostitutes serving foreigners were relegated to the dregs of society. Those who, like the camptown woman quoted above, came to camptowns seeking the America of their dreams were quickly disillusioned by a reality they never imagined. In this light, Korean government exhortations to camptown women that they were patriots working on behalf of their nation can be seen as empty rhetoric justifying the exploitation of these women.

But neither patriarchal mores nor extremes of cultural and racial pride can account for the contempt heaped on camptown women and military brides. Those same mores and that same pride kept the issue of comfort women under Japanese rule a secret for decades, but they are now held up as innocent victims of an imperialist aggressor while camptown women remain pariahs. Indeed, former comfort women themselves disdain any links with camptown women. What can account for this difference? Part of the answer lies in the identity of the aggressor. Japan is seen as a former colonizer who has yet to fully come to terms with its history and who may yet have designs on its former colony. The United States, however, is still primarily seen as an ally and a friend who deserves thanks, whose freedoms and material abundance are ideals to be envied and emulated.

To see the camptown women as victims of militarized prostitution and as modern-day comfort women, would be to shatter that vision of America. It would force Koreans to confront the myriad humiliations and brutalities committed by Americans and the U.S. military, incidents tucked away in small print in obscure corners of the newspaper, hidden in half-forgotten memories. Land seized by force and farmers forced out to make room for U.S. military installations; American troops firing into small groups of unarmed civilians peacefully demonstrating against the division of their country and against the U.S. military government; workers thrown out of factories they had begun to operate on their own after the Japanese owners left in the wake of Japan's defeat in 1945; countless Korean civilians murdered or brutalized by American soldiers who are given little more than slaps on the wrist by U.S. military authorities. Numerous such incidents, painstakingly researched by journalist Oh Yun Ho, testify to an America that is imperialist, cavalier, and ruthlessly self-centered in its dealings with "junior partners" such as South Korea. In addition, recent revelations about not only the 1980 Kwangju Massacre but also the 1948 Chejudo massacre and the Nogunri massacre during the Korean War reveal an America brutal in its treatment of Korea.[67]

It is an image that directly contradicts the dominant thinking. But more to the point, seeing camptown women as victims of U.S.-sponsored militarized prostitution would shatter a self-conception of Korea as a sovereign nation. It would force a realization of the ways in which the United States oppresses Korea and Koreans, of the fact that Korea is at best a junior, a very junior, partner, and at worst a victim, even a pawn, of an imperialist America. The U.S. military presence in South Korea has meant, for example, that whole towns have grown economically dependent on the local U.S. military base, their fortunes waxing and waning with the size of the troops. In short, towns such as Uijongbu, Songtan, and Tongduchon are economically dependent on decisions made thousands of miles away by the leaders of a foreign country. But if such realities are faced, a national self-identity as a sovereign nation in partnership with the United States would be in tatters.

This self-identity as a sovereign nation is a distinctly masculine one. To keep itself masculine and sovereign, it must banish the feminine and the subordinate. Camptown women, as prostitutes servicing the soldiers of a foreign power, are emblematic of the feminine and the subordinate. They serve to symbolize all the humiliations that Korea suffers at the hands of the United States. Indeed, political radicals in South Korea are increasingly using the image of the camptown woman as a metaphor for a nation brutalized under imperialism. Novelists have long utilized this metaphor, portraying *yang gongju* in Korean literature for decades as a metaphor for the subjugation of the Korean people as a whole.[68] But for

Koreans in the mainstream, it is necessary to condemn these women as whores and/or cynically praise them for patriotism as civilian ambassadors and earners of foreign exchange, all the while relegating them to the shadows. Only by doing this can the realities of the situation between the United States and Korea be ignored and denied, thus allowing the officially sanctioned belief in Korean sovereignty and American benevolence to remain dominant. America's golden image is left relatively untainted while Koreans despise camptowns and camptown women. In effect, the realities of U.S. influence on Korean society are interpreted as individual depravity: the women are prostitutes not because of Korea's circumstances and relations with the United States, but because the women are morally corrupt. The logic of national pride requires this interpretation.[69]

This simultaneous condemnation and shunning of *yang gongju* and glorification of America can help explain why camptown women who have no illusions about camptown life have so often clung to dreams of marrying an American soldier and living in America. They are well aware of their pariah status in Korean society. Interviews with camptown women conducted by My Sister's Place, a community center for camptown women run by camptown activists, and by researchers Saundra Pollock Sturdevant and Brenda Stoltzfus show that these women believe that they too have rights as human beings and should not be condemned for being prostitutes.[70] But most, if not all, view coming to the camptowns as a mistake. For camptown women, the concept of sex work as a legitimate profession is literally foreign. Many dream of a "normal" life as a wife and mother, and since this life is impossible to achieve with a Korean man due to Korean society's ostracization of camptown women, they dream of marrying an American soldier. How to survive and how to escape the camptown is the daily concern of most camptown women. The historical and social conditions underpinning camptown prostitution render largely irrelevant the arguments of some Western feminists and activist prostitutes who claim that prostitution can be an empowering occupation and a way out from patriarchal domination.[71] The converse is true in the case of militarized prostitution in Korea: The camptown women live under extremes of patriarchal domination literally practiced on their bodies by both Korea and the United States.

In addition, the negative experiences that many camptown women have had with Korean men—abusive relationships, experiences with pimps, sexual assaults, and the like—often lead women to believe that all Korean men are untrustworthy and do not treat women well. In such a situation, the pervasive lure of America becomes even stronger. American men, even the crass GIs, can be viewed as "better" than Korean men.

Novelist Kang Suk-kyung, who lived in a camptown as preparation for writing about camptown women, describes them in her 1983 short story, "Days and Dreams":

> When you think about it, a camptown is like an island floating between Korea and America. Neither mainland nor sea, just an island. And just as an island is just an island, the women here are nothing but foreigners' whores. Temporary honeys for the American GIs, shunned by their homeland, they are called only by that name.
>
> . . . Because it is a rootless island, the women who live here cannot lay down roots either. Women either depend on their pimps or long to go to America because they know all too well the hopelessness of this island life.[72]

In the dreams of a camptown woman, camptown life may be miserable, but surely among the GIs there will emerge a Prince Charming who will sweep her away to a wonderful new life in the American paradise. This Cinderella dream, however, appears to have waned considerably as younger camptown women hear about their elders' experiences with American soldiers and as women who have left camptowns for America return with tales of horror.[73] Nevertheless, marriage to an American soldier remains one of the few paths out of the camptowns.

It has been a narrow path, however. Most women in the camptowns have stories about GIs who promised marriage, only to desert them once their tour of duty ended. Women who succeed in marrying a GI and immigrating to America constitute a small percentage of the tens of thousands of women who have worked in the camptowns during the past half-century. It is not uncommon for women to trust GI promises of marriage and give birth to children rather than abort unexpected pregnancies. When the promises are broken, the women are left with mixed-race

children to raise alone, a task made more difficult by poverty and the
double stigma attached to illegitimate mixed-race children.[74]

Working On-Base

As emphasized earlier in this chapter, camptowns are not the only places
where Korean women and American GIs meet. Another common locale is
the U.S. military base itself. Ever since the U.S. military first came to
South Korea in 1945, it has employed Korean nationals in a variety of
jobs, ranging from interpreter to janitor. Jobs that have been open to
women include dishwashers, cooks, or waitresses in on-base restaurants,
mess halls, bars, and clubs; clerks, receptionists, or secretaries in various
offices; and cashiers at the PX or commissary. Many of the women who
gathered around U.S. bases during the 1940s and 1950s were probably
hoping for jobs of that kind, only to find that such jobs were difficult to
obtain without some knowledge of English or a personal connection.

Several women I interviewed for this study spoke of working on U.S.
bases and of having met their husbands there. One worked as a dish-
washer and vegetable peeler in an on-base restaurant, most likely a mess
hall, judging by her description. Another worked as a clerk in a supply
office. Her job was to type records of inventory and disbursement of supplies. Although she knew only the English alphabet and had no typing
skills, she did her work by memorizing the spellings of the various items
that were disbursed through the office. Base jobs such as hers were obtained mainly through personal connections. One woman, for example,
obtained her job through a Korean military official, a close neighbor.

Working on a base, especially a PX or an office, puts Korean women
into a primarily American environment which inevitably leads to an opportunity to make comparisons between Korea and America. If camptowns can be compared to islands, neither here nor there, then bases can
be compared to peninsulas, extensions of the American mainland in-
truding upon Korean territory. The language is English and the woman's
coworkers are American, as are her customers and other people she must
deal with in the course of her work. The work culture, the way of inter-
acting with other people, even the tools of the work and the material

goods encountered through the work (typewriters, pencil sharpeners, dishwashers, flush toilets, ovens, and most especially the consumer products in the PX, the commissary, or the Sears catalog) are American. If she works in a large base such as Yongsan, she may see military housing reminiscent of suburban America, each house with its own lawn and backyard. Every time she steps through the gates of the base, she is stepping into a world very different from the one in which she lives. A camptown woman described the difference between Korean society and the base as follows:

> When you go to the U.S. Army base, everything is automatic. They can use as much electricity or water as they need. Meanwhile, the government tells us to save electricity and water. It's a world apart.[75]

This was the situation in the 1990s. Again, the primary contrast is between scarcity and abundance, deprivation and privilege. How much starker the contrast must have been in the past, when even parts of the capital city had no running water or electricity, or when the entire country lay in ruins after the Korean War.

America was, indeed, a world apart for Koreans, and yet it was a world that reached into their lives in profound and unsettling ways. America influenced not only the political situation and economy of South Korea, but also the personal lives of countless Koreans.

CHAPTER 2

American Fever

In addition to the dreams common to any engaged or newly-wed couple, Korean women who married American soldiers had aspirations for a better life in a new land. Like other immigrants, they sought a new start in America, the fabled land of plenty. Their hopes for a better life were shaped by war, poverty, Korean patriarchy, Japanese colonialism, and American imperialism. The narratives of the nine women whose stories are presented here illuminate how and why they decided to marry American military men.

The stories are organized chronologically into three sections, each of which highlights some of the major themes of the period that pertains to the marriage and emigration of Korean military brides. A fourth section briefly discusses some common themes that tie the narratives together.

Out of War

After thirty-five years under Japanese rule, Korea was liberated in 1945, only to be cut in half as differing ascendant world powers occupied each side of the 38th Parallel, the Soviets in the north, the Americans in the south. Literally torn between opposing ideologies regarding its future, Korea was soon engulfed in a bitter civil war in which each side was supported by foreign powers engaged in their own struggles for international dominance.[1] Armies advanced and retreated throughout the length of the Korean peninsula, leaving hundreds of thousands of refugees in their wake. Among them were three young women. Unknown to each other, each would eventually make her way to the United States as the wife of an American soldier and settle in the same urban region of the American East Coast. Their stories reveal some of the ways in which colonialism, national division, and foreign domination affected the lives of Korean women.

Cho Soonyi came first, leaving for America in 1951, barely a year after the Korean War broke out. Growing up in colonial Korea, she had always longed to escape what she saw as a backward, stagnant country. First she longed to go to Japan, a country that her teachers described as a veritable heaven on earth. With liberation in 1945, the Japanese colonial government was replaced, in the southern half of Korea, by the American Military Government. Having left her rural hometown in a southern province for Seoul several months before the Pacific War ended, Ms. Cho witnessed the entry of Americans into Korea. With the help of a hometown friend who was a nurse at the U.S. Army Base, she landed a job working at the PX. For Ms. Cho, this was the first step in her dream of escaping from Korea.

I wanted to . . . get out . . . Korea. Least I want to go live Japan. That was my dream. I want to least go to Japan to live. Fine. I don't want to stay Korea because there is no future. Not much future. You know, a small country, [it] doesn't have everything developed. Always other country take care of. I don't know today how things are. But anyway my dream is I want to . . . move out, move out Korea. Go foreign country. Japan, America, don't matter. So I, I, that's, that was my wish so, only way you can come to America is you have to marry.

When asked how she came to hear about foreign countries, she seemed to think it a stupid question. *"Well, Japan,"* she laughed, *"you know,* Japanese teachers teach about it in school, so why wouldn't I know about Japan?" As for America, she said, "Well, the war ended, *ah, Second World War* ended, and Americans, they all entered Seoul, didn't they? And so, *they control everything."*

Her desire to live in Japan was quickly replaced by a desire to live in

America, and learning the language of these newcomers who, in her words, controlled everything, became her obsession.

I came to think about this, because, well, in the old days, you know, our parents didn't know Japanese that well, and so they were like fools, and when we didn't want them to hear what we were saying, we would speak in Japanese. So because of that, *I, I think I have to learn English*. Because I felt that *I must learn English*, I would read books, like the *dictionary*. *I, I learn, I look, I read, . . . I [as]sociate with American soldiers. I can learn speak, enough. You, you,* that is, we have strong *accent,* right? Speaking doesn't come easily. So I grit my teeth and *I have to learn, I have to, must learn English*. At night, *I study. I study with a dictionary.* During the day, *you pick up each day different words, with a,* because you have contact, you have contact with Americans, so you have opportunities for conversation. So *you can, you can learn each day. When you young, you learn real fast.*

Ms. Cho's memory of parents and older Koreans being treated as ignorant fools by their own children who would speak in Japanese to keep secrets from them seems to have inscribed for her a connection between language and power. In addition, she recalls that her brother's fluent Japanese gave him access to education in Japan, something that only well-educated children from wealthy families could afford. She didn't want to be in the position of the fool who could not understand and was cut off from the world of the powerful. But with Japan defeated and replaced by America, her Japanese language ability no longer had the potential to carry her into the better world she was seeking. She was thus driven to study English with something akin to desperation.

She came from a well-do-do family. Because her father, a local government official during the Japanese colonial period, and her mother both died when she was a child, she was raised in the family of her uncle, her father's younger brother. Her older brother died in Japan during World War II when his dormitory was bombed. This lack of immediate kin may also have been an influence in her desire to leave Korea.

But no matter what, the more I thought about it, no matter how good they [her aunt and uncle] were to me, in my mind, *I always want to go foreign country. . . . Uh, I want to get away from small town,* [go to] *big city and step by step,* I got away [from my small town and Korea].

Ms. Cho explained that one reason she wanted to leave Korea was that she did not like Korean customs regarding male and female roles. In Korea, she said, *"Everything is* for men. *Cater, King Kong.* Women are, it's not like this anymore, but back then, women just cooked, they lived in the kitchen. . . . umm . . . that kind of thing. *I didn't like* [those kinds of] *customs."*

She also didn't like the taunting she encountered on the streets of Seoul for wearing makeup and Western clothes. In the 1940s, most Koreans, especially women, wore Korean clothes and no makeup. Only women who worked in camptowns or otherwise associated with Americans used cosmetics and wore Western clothes. To most Koreans, therefore, these embellishments marked a woman as a prostitute and, more importantly, as somehow tainted by foreign influence and thus beyond the control of Korean mores and social structures. Such women were considered fair game for curses and insults. This kind of thinking only increased her dislike of Korea. The best thing about America, she said, was freedom from such behavior. *"You can walk street, nobody say nothing. There's nobody who curses* at you. *You have freedom,"* she said. *"In* Korea, it's unthinkable that you could walk down the street with an American man. *Everything's secret, secret. I don't like that.* . . . Even in Japan, it's not like that. *You have a lot of freedom. Nobody say nothing. They look* . . . [but that's all]. Even Japan, *very very modern."*

Korea, in contrast, was a backward, undeveloped country that either relegated women to the kitchen or cursed them for leaving it. Her childhood dream of Japan was replaced by a dream of America, but in both scenarios leaving Korea was her solution. The only way to get to America, however, was to marry an American. This was much easier said than done. Although, by her own account, there were many Americans who wanted to marry Korean and Japanese women, such marriages did not give the Asian brides the legal right to enter America. For Ms. Cho, that made marriage pointless: *"You can marry,* but, *you marry, you cannot come with your husband. So why, why should you get married?"* Even after American immigration laws were revised to allow Asian military brides to accompany their husbands to America, red tape made the process difficult.[2] Besides, meeting a suitable American man wasn't easy either. It was only a series of lucky breaks, she said, that made it possible for her to leave Korea.

> *All I know, I was very lucky. Each step by step, I was very lucky. Lucky to come over Seoul, lucky to I met the nurse, my best friend, she's very very beautiful woman. And I was a lucky enough to meet nice young man, you know. I met and I come over Japan and got marry. Ah . . . everything was just like I planned. I got very fortunate, lucky.*

While working as a sales clerk at the PX, she began to date a white American soldier, an enlisted man. In 1949 he was transferred to Japan. The Korean War broke out the following spring. With the help of another friend, she was able to board a ship in Inchon, a port city near Seoul, and flee to Japan. There she managed to find her American boyfriend. In February 1951, they married in Tokyo. At age twenty-one, Ms. Cho became Mrs. Linburg.

Asked why she married him, she seemed surprised by the question. "*Well, we, we, love each other.* Of course, *why, why anybody wants to marry?*" When I probed further and asked why they loved each other, she broke out in laughter.[3]

> Everyone, *you meet somebody, oh——! I like to get to know him. You know, you, you love feel, you, you love, you love the person, your heart your heart your face your body you learning to . . . fall in love. Why? Why anybody fall in love? You know,* everybody when they're young, *umm, you fall in love when you young, everybody's fall in love somebody.*

When Mrs. Linburg sought to leave Japan for America, she discovered that she first had to prove that she had the right to be in Japan. Having fled in the midst of war, she didn't have the proper documentation. She also needed a passport and an emigration visa issued by the Korean government—documents which were not easy to obtain. Korean Embassy officials in Japan gave her a hard time when she applied for the necessary papers. Then she discovered that the consul there was an old acquaintance from her days working at the U.S. military base. With his help, she obtained everything she needed for her emigration to the United States.

"Because of him," she said, "thanks to him, *they, they permit* my marriage. *That a give me a visa.* He made one for me, in other words. If he hadn't, *who knows? Maybe I didn't get* [the necessary papers]."

With her husband, Mrs. Linburg went to Yokohama. There they boarded a ship bound for America. According to Mrs. Linburg, the ship was under contract with the U.S. military and carried many American passengers. After fourteen days, they docked in Seattle. It was late summer 1951 and Mrs. Linburg was to become one of the eleven Korean women who entered the United States that year as wives of American citizens.[4]

In that same year, 1951, Yi Kyung-Ja was a war refugee. She had grown up in Seoul in a middle-class family. When the war broke out, her extended family gathered to live in one house. Her grandmother had reasoned that it was the only way to stay together during the confusion of war. The house was bombed, however, and everyone died. Ms. Yi, who was not home at the time of the bombing, survived, but she had nothing. And with the opposing army poised to occupy Seoul, her only choice was to flee.

I had a friend, and we left together. It was summer then. You know what malaria is, don't you? I got sick with that. It was summer. It's what you get when you get bitten by mosquitoes, malaria. That's what I had, while we were living on the road. And so my friend, {silence}, umm, {long silence, sigh, crying} I'm sorry. {crying} Daegu, Daejun, there were too many people. There was nowhere to go. {silence, sigh} So we stayed for about two days, and then we couldn't stay any longer. There were so many people, and you couldn't drink the water. So {crying} we went back to Daejun. {silence} And then, after that, well, we won, right? The Chinese retreated. So then we returned [to Seoul]. My friend worked at the [U.S.] military base and she knew my husband. And then because we, well, you know, we got married. That's how it all happened. {silence} I left out a lot. {laugh}

Ms. Yi did not reveal much more about how she met her husband or about her life in the years immediately preceding her arrival in America.

After the war ended, the mother of another friend took her in as a surrogate daughter. Together with the surrogate mother, her friend at the base introduced her to an American soldier, apparently with the explicit purpose of marrying her off to an American. When asked if she herself wanted to marry an American, she was briefly silent and then replied, "Yes, *I guess so. Maybe better life, maybe. Yeah, better life. Yes.*"

But like Mrs. Linburg, she also emphasized that hers was a love marriage. When asked what she thought would be better in America, she replied, "Well, that kind of thing wasn't so important. He loved me, so, you know." And elsewhere in the interview, when asked whether she wanted to go to America, she replied, "Of course. I had nobody. And at that time I loved him very much." Her two main concerns were whether her future children would be discriminated against for being half-Asian, and whether American men were faithful to their wives. Assured on both counts by her boyfriend, she agreed to his marriage proposal.

From a young age, she had determined not to marry a Korean. Growing up watching her mother suffer due to her father's adultery was a decisive factor in her decision. He had a series of mistresses, including one whom he set up as a sort of second wife in a house not far away from where he lived with his legal wife. This mistress would often visit and otherwise humiliate Ms. Yi's mother. Since Ms. Yi's grandmother, who lived with them, supported her son and told her daughter-in-law to be a better wife, Ms. Yi's mother was isolated and left with no recourse.

Unlike her father, however, American men "weren't so dirty like that. If they married, when they married, they didn't fool around with other women or live with other women, that's what I thought," she said.

> I heard that when people here [in America] get married, if there's a problem, they would just get divorced. They didn't have to endure things like that. Isn't that right? So, I decided then that I would never ever marry a Korean. My father had so many mistresses, you see.

So Ms. Yi welcomed the offer of an introduction to an American soldier. The soldier in question was a white enlisted man from the East Coast. They dated for two years. Although they couldn't fully communicate, since he knew no Korean and her English was minimal, Ms. Yi said that wasn't much of a barrier. When people are in love, she said, things like that don't really matter. Besides, she said, he didn't seem to have much trouble understanding her English. They decided to marry and began preparing the necessary papers, which included permission from his military commander. Permission obtained and his tour of duty in Korea finished, they flew from Seoul to Japan, spent one night in Tokyo, and then flew to San Francisco. From there, they flew to his hometown on the East Coast, where they spent a few weeks before transferring to his next post, a base in Kentucky. When Ms. Yi, now Mrs. Grant, arrived in San Francisco, she became one of the 288 Korean women who entered the United States in 1957 as wives of American citizens.[5]

The simultaneous liberation and division of Korea in 1945 put Bak Hye-Young on a long journey that led her away from her hometown in the northern province of Hwanghae, passed through Seoul, and ended in a semirural suburban area on the eastern coast of the United States. The journey was to take some fifteen years.

Ms. Bak grew up in a prosperous family. Her father made a handsome living trading fish for Manchurian rice. After failing the junior high school entrance exam, she went to a two-year vocational school and then worked as an office girl for a Japanese firm. As a product of a Japanese colonial education, she spoke, read, and wrote Japanese like a native, but she barely knew the Korean alphabet and her verbal ability was that of an unschooled youth. She was just fifteen when the Pacific War ended, the Japanese left, and the communists took over.

The police regularly visited her home, for as a businessman who had prospered under the hated Japanese her father was politically suspect. Rice, which was plentiful in their home, was routinely confiscated. There was one policeman, however, who would poke his head up in the attic and into the storage sheds, and come out saying, "Comrades, there is no rice here today." This endeared him to her father, and when he asked to be boarded in the spare room, her father gave his permission despite the objections of Ms. Bak's mother. The boarder lived with them for nearly a year. According to Ms. Bak, he had spent a lot of time in Japan where he had apparently read a great deal of Marxist literature. He then made his way to northern Korea where he joined the communists out of political conviction. But he became disillusioned. This got him in trouble and he was once thrown in jail. Ms. Bak's mother was also jailed briefly on charges of harboring a political degenerate. Unless their boarder fled to the south, his life would be in danger, Ms. Bak said. But unknown to her, he'd decided that he wanted to take her with him, as his wife.

> One day I was in the back, playing with jacks like this, when he came home. We spoke only in Japanese then, so he calls me, "Michiko, Michiko." So I said, "Yes." That is, I said, "*Hai*." And he asks me if I want to go south. So I said, "Sure, why not?" I was so young then, you know. "I'll go, sure," that's what I said. I didn't know anything about the opposite sex or anything. We never had a *date*. I never went on a *date* at all. So you know, I was so naive and innocent. At that time, they said that in the south the lights were bright and sparkly, and young couples would go on dates and that everything was just so peaceful and lovely. In the north, we couldn't listen to the radio, we couldn't turn on the lights, so as a *teenager*, you know, it was just. . . . If we wanted to listen to the radio we had to go under the covers and listen secretly and the only thing on was the news broadcast from the south. So when he asked, of course I said I wanted to go. But I, *I don't mean to be his wife*. I didn't mean that at all.

When the confusion was cleared up and her parents refused his request to take their daughter with him, he threatened suicide, Japanese-style. In Korea, it is said that great misfortune visits a house if a man commits suicide on account of that family's daughter. So Ms. Bak's mother told him to leave. He went to the seashore, which was not far from their home, and prepared to commit suicide there. Unable to let him die and thus wreak misfortune on the family, Ms. Bak's mother relented and sent her daughter to the south with this man, who was some fifteen years her senior. It was 1946, and the border—barely a year old—was not yet heavily guarded. Like nearly everyone else who crossed, whether going north or south during the five years between division and war, the couple traveled on foot.

> So that's how I came south. But it was scary, when we went south. We had gone about halfway, and I was shaking so hard and it was so scary, you have no idea. So I said, no, I want to go back north, I have to go

back to my mother. But he bulged out his eyes and looked at me like this, so I couldn't do anything, not a thing. And also part of me was curious, part of me wanted, just a little, to go and see what the south was like. So I thought that when I go south, I would search out my uncle. I never considered living with that man.

Once they reached the outskirts of Seoul, they found the inns were swarming with refugees who had fled the north. Exhausted, her feet bruised and bleeding, and her legs swollen, she pleaded with him to stop at one of these inns. She intended to sleep there for a night, and then take off alone the next morning in search of her uncle. But he refused, and forced her to keep going. "He got mad, you know, and by that time I was scared of him, ever since he threatened *seppuku*, I was scared of him," she said. He took them to a quiet inn inside the city. There, he raped her.

I found that he had spread out the blankets side by side, so I said that wasn't right and I separated them. And you know what he did? He threatened to kill himself! He took out his white clothes and started to change into them. That day I cried and cried so much, pleading with him, telling him not to die, asking him why he was doing this. I knew nothing about sex or anything. I just pleaded with him. I had come south and didn't know anyone and I thought if he died then I would be put in jail and it was just so incredible that such a thing could happen, so I just begged and begged and you have no idea how much I cried and cried. So I cried and cried and finally I said that I would do whatever he wanted, just don't commit suicide. And you know, I didn't know anything about sex or anything, and maybe it wasn't really rape, but *you know force into really, he did* and so, well, that's how at such a *young age* I had a child.

With that, she became his wife. After a brief stay in his hometown, a city in the southeastern provinces, they settled in Seoul. Like so many other Koreans of that era, they were desperately poor. In the aftermath of Japanese colonialism and the chaos of national division, Korea as a whole was a poor country.[6] From the late 1940s through the 1960s, the South Korean economy depended heavily on foreign, primarily American, aid and many South Koreans made their living by providing goods and services to the American military stationed in South Korea. As Korea scholar Bruce Cumings puts it, "creative enterprise in the 1950s . . . quite reasonably consisted of sucking the American teat for all it was worth."[7] That strategy was one of many that Ms. Bak implemented in her struggle with poverty. Over the years, both she and her husband worked at U.S. military bases and she also sold U.S. goods through a well-developed, thriving underground economy.[8]

Her husband's stint at a U.S. military base was brief. She said he quit because he couldn't stomach toadying to the Americans. He was unable to find other work and, with his level of education, was too proud to accept manual labor. He also forbade his wife from working at the time, for it would have been an embarrassment to him. Ms. Bak's family—like the families of many other landlords, professionals, and businessmen from the north—were also fleeing to the south, and they met their daughter in Seoul. It was her mother who discovered Ms. Bak's pregnancy. She herself knew nothing about such things and had not been aware that she was carrying a child. With the help of her mother and a midwife, Ms. Bak, only sixteen years old, gave birth to a baby girl. For a time everyone lived on the salary that Ms. Bak's elder sister earned working at a factory. Ms. Bak also resorted to selling her silk clothing, part of the wedding dowry that her mother had carried from their hometown all the way to Seoul. Sell a skirt, and buy rice for dinner. The next day, sell a blouse, and buy rice for that day's dinner. Once she found a bird and kept it in a makeshift cage. When she sold it, it brought enough money for the family to eat for a whole month, she said, speculating that it must have been some kind of rare bird that flew away from its previous owner. She also sold roasted yams on the streets. If the yams sold, she would buy some rice and make porridge for dinner that night. If not, the yams were fed to the child and the adults went to bed hungry. Like many others who suffered hunger during that time, she recalled picking fallen produce at markets:

In Mapo, they sell cabbage [for the winter putting-away of kimchi], and they count off, it's a one, it's a two, as they hand them over [to the housewives who come to buy] and when they do that, the outer leaves fall off. So, I was so young then, I went to pick up those leaves, and I would think, who are these people who have so much money they can actually buy so much cabbage? But me, *I couldn't even afford one head of cabbage*, back then. And I would pick up the leaves, far from the sellers, and you know, the older grandmothers would go right up next to them and pick them up as they fell, and so the sellers would throw the leaves in my direction. I was so young then, and picking up cabbage leaves like that.

She became pregnant again, but this time she gave birth alone as they had no money for a midwife. It was winter, their room was drafty, and the baby boy caught pneumonia. With no money for medicine, much less a visit to a doctor, she turned to her mother. But her mother rebuffed her request to buy medicine for the baby, saying that she had never bought medicine for any of her children and they had all turned out fine. Ms. Bak's son died when he was just ten days old.

> I cried so much. If I had been able to take him to the doctor even once, to feed him some medicine, before he died, I wouldn't still have this here in my heart. {puts hand on chest and sighs} But I wasn't able to. So now I think, there is nothing but money, money, money, money money money . . . That's all I could think of. . . . So I thought, I have to get a job. I can't live like this. So now, *I don't care what he say, I'm going to get a job*, that's what I thought. It was the first time that I really felt that I couldn't live like that. When my baby died, I realized that there is nothing you can depend on except money, not your parents, no one. They didn't buy medicine when I asked, and so I felt that I didn't have any parents or any siblings or anyone. When I die, I just wanted to die with a big pile of money, like this.

By this time, her husband had become an invalid, and she was no longer scared of him. Indeed, she resented and despised him for his tyrannical ways, but most of all for his inability to earn a living. She went out and got herself some American clothes that came in as relief goods, and became a street vendor, selling cigarettes, candy, and other sundries near the Han River. But life was still hard, and she resolved to kill herself, reasoning that once dead, there is no need to eat and therefore no hunger. She put her daughter on her back, and went out to the river, intending to jump in together. But she could not bring herself to do it, and resolved instead to try harder to find a decent job. Their landlord was an officer in the Korean Army, and she asked his wife for help. He got her a job at a U.S. military base outside Seoul, doing payroll for the Korean soldiers attached to American units. In a month or so, she was transferred to a clerical job working with Americans.

At first this terrified her, for she knew no English and was sure that she would be fired. But the new job turned out to be relatively simple. She received handwritten vehicle inventories indicating that such and such vehicles had arrived and she was responsible for typing the information onto a form. The vocabulary she needed to do this job was limited to words such as truck and jeep. The most difficult part, she said, was deciphering the soldiers' handwriting. But under the tutelage of soldiers in her office, she learned the English alphabet, how to type, and how to read American cursive handwriting. She also studied American elementary school reading primers. She was the only Korean woman working at this base and said, with a tone of pride, that because she wore a badge on her traditional Korean blouse, the military police never bothered her. In other words, she was never mistaken for a camptown woman and her right to enter the base was never questioned.

The soldiers there offered to order goods for her through the Sears Roebuck catalog, and she also ran into a Korean woman who offered to buy them from her. Since the "wholesale" price in Korea was more than double the catalog price, this was very lucrative. Ms. Bak earned enough money to build a house and looked forward to quitting her job. But her husband rented out the house, became unable to pay the real estate taxes, and ended up selling it. This was apparently the last straw, and she divorced him.

She later quit her job at the base, and operated a beauty salon and other businesses. She began to date a soldier whom she had met while working at the base. Eventually they married.

Why did I marry him? Well, he ordered a lot of stuff for me, and he was *honest*. He didn't skim money from me. Of course, when I was working at the office, no one skimmed money from me. But he always asked, *"Can I order for you more, more?"* and he was so *kind*. And so also, if I marry him, he asked me to marry him, so if I marry him, he has a job, so I wouldn't be hungry. There wasn't any love, but I just married him. I just did it. I thought there was love, but there probably wasn't, not much. I was just *simple*. I couldn't tell a man that I loved him, it was just that at the time, I liked him, so I married him. Isn't that the way it is? Otherwise, how can you marry someone? Isn't that right?

After answering my question about his military rank (master sergeant), she added:

I thought everyone in America was rich. {laughs} I thought everyone was rich. (What made you think that?) *Well, first of all,* Americans all have cars. If you look at pictures, they all have cars. That means they're rich. In Korea, who can afford to have a car? In my time, no one had a car of their own. So you see that, and you think, wow! They must be rich, everyone has their own cars. And the houses are big and high, but *main thing is he's honest, honest,* and he loved me.

It was October 1960 when Ms. Bak, now Mrs. Mulligan, arrived in America with her teenage daughter and her four-year-old son, the child of her American husband. That same year, 648 other Korean women also entered the United States as wives of American citizens.[9]

Shadow of the Camptowns

If national division and war marked the lives of women who immigrated to America during the 1950s, then it was the camptown that marked the lives of women who immigrated in later years. As U.S. troops settled in and became a permanent fixture in South Korean society, so did the camptowns. Even as Korea's economy improved during the 1960s and 1970s, poverty remained widespread and there were plenty of desperate young women who were easily tricked into working in the camptowns.[10] Among the women who told me their life stories, three spoke of working there. But even those who had no direct experience with camptowns felt their presence, for the image of the prostitute who marries an American becomes etched in the collective consciousness of Koreans. The shadow that looms over the lives of Korean military brides begins here, in the camptowns, precedes them across the Pacific, and sometimes even arcs back to Korea, reflected in the opposition of American parents to marriages to Korean women.

Bai Juhyun was the middle child of a respectable family in a small rural town in central Korea. After she graduated from the local girls' high school, she heard that applications were being accepted for typist positions at U.S. military bases in the area. She went to take the exam. It was simple, she said, since she had already learned how to type both Korean and English. She was assigned to a missile base in a rural area some distance from her home.

In 1967, an officer was transferred to her base. They took a liking to each other and began to date. They went to on-base movies and spent time at the officers' club talking. Just before his tour of duty ended, they decided to marry. She was twenty when she told her parents that she wanted to marry an American military officer. Because she was not yet twenty-one, she needed their permission. But they were adamantly opposed. When she brought her fiancé to meet the family, her father refused to meet him. The whole family was in an uproar because marriage to an American, especially a soldier, would disgrace the family. As Ms. Bai explained her family's opposition, her speech stopped and started and became disjointed.

> *Well,* at that time, uh, marrying an American is, getting parental approval is, *you know,* people's image of it wasn't that good. So they said no, absolutely opposed, and *you know,* about, *I will say about 80 percent, 90 percent* of those who marry . . . *I don't know how to say. . . . I don't want to . . .* Because I myself married an American, the same, women who marry Americans, *I don't want to put them down.* It's because I don't want to do that that I'm speaking like this. At any rate, the image isn't that good, so parents oppose it.

Ms. Bai felt the shadow of the camptown, but could not bring herself to explicitly discuss it. She started to say that some 80 to 90 percent of military brides were former camptown women, but then stopped, unable to find a way to say this without, in her view, putting down women who married Americans. It would be an insult to herself as well, since, as she noted, she too was a military bride. Although it was clear that she set herself apart from those responsible for the bad image of military brides, at the same time she felt she was one of them. This sense of a shared image, of collectivity, was expressed by every military bride I encountered.

Opposition was strong on the man's side as well. As the son of a prominent East Coast Jewish family, her husband was expected to meet and marry a Jewish girl from an equally prominent family, not a gentile who wasn't even white. At the request of his parents, a relative who wielded some political clout wrote a letter to the U.S. Embassy in Seoul, asking that Ms. Bai's request for an immigration visa be denied. Stereotypes of Korean women as wily prostitutes and poverty-stricken desperadoes who con innocent American men into marriage may have been a factor in the opposition. As Ms. Bai put it, using a common Korean expression for a loose woman: "They probably thought that I was a woman who had rolled around everywhere."

But despite such active opposition from both sides, the young couple persisted. He extended his tour of duty for four months, so that as soon as Ms. Bai turned twenty-one and no longer needed parental permission they could get married. But in the end, her mother gave in.

I guess I was determined. I guess I wanted to get married. So I just threw everything off, and at the time I was working at the base, and so for the time being I didn't go home, I just stayed at the base. You know, it was far from home, the base, so for the time being I didn't go home. Then my mother, resigning herself to losing a child, came to see me, to tell me that she would give permission. She brought me the necessary papers, a copy of the Family Register[11] and stuff. You needed that to get married, and she brought me those papers. *That's how we started.*

In November 1968, they married and Ms. Bai became Mrs. Weinberg. Although she had many close friends, she told none of them about her marriage and had no contact with them for some ten years. When asked why, she replied, "*Well, I guess because I married an American guy.*"

In February, Mrs. Weinberg arrived with her husband in Seattle, where he was officially discharged. They proceeded to his hometown, a major urban center on the East Coast. Mrs. Weinberg was one of 1,954 Korean women who entered the United States in 1969 as wives of American citizens.

Kim Myung-Ja was among the 80 to 90 percent of women that Mrs. Weinberg considered responsible for the bad image of military brides. Ms. Kim made a living by entertaining the U.S. military for most of her youth, first as a member of an orphanage song-and-dance troupe, then as a camptown prostitute. Neither occupation was by choice, but as she said, "When you are so poor, and so ignorant, and bad people trick you, what can you do? It must have been my fate."

Born to deaf-mute parents in Seoul, she was the eldest of five children. Her earliest memories were of wealth, but the Korean War reduced the family to abject poverty.

> After the war, I went begging with my mother. We went secretly so that father would not know. Rice, barley, money, *kimchi,* anything people would give we accepted. Father would not eat what we brought back. He made mother sick at heart.

Unable to support the children, Ms. Kim's parents sent her to a convent orphanage that housed some two hundred orphans, children born of Korean mothers and American soldiers, and children from poor families. Part of the orphanage's operating expenses, according to Ms. Kim, came from money earned by a handful of children who sang and danced on TV shows and performed for the U.S. military. Ms. Kim became a member of that troupe, and said she was proud to be able to contribute to the orphanage and happy to be singing and dancing rather than begging for food.

> We entered many shows, because if we placed we would bring back prize money, money we used for our living expenses. President Rhee Syngman held many shows featuring children's songs and dances. We always placed within the top three. We were usually first, and if we placed third we would cry. Sometimes we would go on KBS-TV. But

every Saturday we went on the American military's TV station, and the money we got from that was used for our living expenses too. We also went to each military unit's shows, and on Wednesdays different units would come to the convent to see us sing and dance. From all these things we would earn money for our living expenses.

Ms. Kim lived at the orphanage for twelve years. When she was nineteen, she was sent away and she returned to her family. Adjustment to society was difficult. Confined to the strictures of convent life, she had never taken public buses or handled money. Eventually she found work as a secretary at a hospital in downtown Seoul. There she began to date an impoverished construction worker. The romance bloomed until her family arranged for her marriage to a rich man.

The man I was to marry came from a rich trading family. He said he had seen me at the hospital. I didn't want to marry him. He was so skinny nothing was left but ribs and he looked like he was going to die any minute. But our family needed his money. Daily life was difficult for us. My mother was happiest that he was going to take care of all of us. But I didn't want to marry him. I wanted to see my lost love. My family made wedding plans anyway.

Ms. Kim ran away to her lover on the morning of the wedding day. They spent a few days together in the company barracks that housed construction laborers.

Those few days with him were like a dream. The rooms next to us were filled with twenty or thirty men, and the walls were thin. We whispered, and we were happy. Even if all we ate was thin barley gruel and soured *kimchi*, it was delicious because I was eating it with him.

He died, however, in a midnight brawl at the barracks. Ms. Kim returned home, was soundly beaten by her mother, and then tried to find work. Answering a help-wanted ad, she ended up being sold to a brothel catering to American soldiers in Tongduchon. But Ms. Kim did not know that the place the employment broker had taken her to was a brothel.

They asked if I knew English. I said yes. I went to Tongduchon. They
said I would earn a lot of money there. I ended up a *yang gongju*. But
the brothel madam had a problem with me. Even when she brought
over an American, I was just quiet. When the American soldiers discovered I knew nothing, many of them just laughed and left. I learned
later that the soldier had to take off his clothes in order for me to make
money.

Ms. Kim had fallen into one of the traps set by brothel operators. She became a *yang gongju*, one of the approximately thirty thousand Korean
women working as camptown prostitutes during the 1960s, with a rotating population of sixty-two thousand U.S. soldiers stationed throughout
South Korea as the primary "customer" base.[12] Those were horrifying
years for Ms. Kim. A rather unprofitable *yang gongju*, Ms. Kim was sold
from brothel to brothel during the mid-1960s by madams who found her
a burden rather than a moneymaker. Although at first bewildered and
dazed, she soon learned what military camptowns were all about.

I discovered there were many women selling their bodies to support
families. One woman supported her younger brother through school
and he eventually became a member of the National Assembly. He then
denounced her as a dirty woman and cut off all ties. She killed herself.
I learned that only the women bear sorrow.

During this time, Ms. Kim met the soldier who was to become her husband. She became pregnant several months before he was to leave Korea,
and in a panic she aborted the pregnancy. She left Tongduchon and went
to work at a motel in Yongsan, a neighborhood near the main U.S. Army
headquarters in central Seoul. The soldier, an African American veteran
of the Vietnam War, wrote to her from the United States and from Okinawa, his next post. In his letters, he suggested getting married. Ms. Kim
was unsure what to do, and was especially worried because he was
known as a philanderer and a drinker.

I consulted my mother. She told me about my father. When they were
brought together by the nuns, he had been a smoker and a drinker. As
a condition of marriage, he agreed to quit both. I had never seen my

father touch either tobacco or alcohol. So his vices could be changed, my mother said, and furthermore, because I had been a *yang gongju* in the past, I had no hope for a future in Korea. So I agreed to marry him. We decided to marry in December.

His "vices" showed little sign of changing, however. He continued to womanize and drink. But her past as a camptown prostitute left her with little hope for a future in Korea, and so Ms. Kim married him anyway. It was a loveless marriage from the start, and it was unclear why he proposed at all. Perhaps, Ms. Kim speculated, he just needed a woman around. According to her account, her married life consisted mainly of keeping house for him, being beaten by him, and being humiliated by his stream of girlfriends.

I never told him about my past, and I never asked him about his. We just met, had sex, and then got married. We were a couple who knew nothing about each other.

The couple's honeymoon was perhaps the most peaceful time of their married life. After a simple civil ceremony, they went to a motel in Tong-duchon.

He says to me, "*I'll be back*," and goes out. Well, he didn't come back, and I stayed up all night talking with the motel woman. She kept me company, because it was my wedding night and it wouldn't do for me to be alone. He shows up in the morning, and quietly lies down next to me. I pretend to be asleep. In a little while he gets up and says, "Let's get breakfast." So we ate. And then again he says, "*I'll be back*," and leaves. He didn't return by evening, so I went back to Seoul by myself, thinking that it would be better for me to at least work. Three days later, he showed up, hopping mad. Without saying anything, I sent him back to his post in Okinawa.

Once her papers came through, Ms. Kim, now Mrs. Goldin, joined her husband in Okinawa. After his tour of duty was over, they entered the United States together with their infant son. After briefly stopping in his hometown, an eastern suburb, they moved to his next post in Texas. It was 1972, and Mrs. Goldin was among the 2,148 Korean women admitted to the United States that year as wives of American citizens, and among the approximately forty thousand Korean women who married American soldiers during the 1970s.[13]

Noh Soonae was the only child of a comfortably stable family in a small town in southeastern Korea. But when she was in the fifth grade, her family was thrown into poverty. To this day, she says, she does not know what happened. But suddenly, there was no money for food or housing, much less her tuition for middle school. It was the mid-1960s, and she began to work as a street vendor and then in factories, becoming so emaciated that she would often collapse from hunger and exhaustion. This was the period of South Korea's big push to industrialize, in which young women like Ms. Noh served as the foot soldiers. In dimly lit warrens, they sewed clothing and stamped out sheet metal, producing hundreds of different consumer and industrial goods for export.[14] The majority of these workers came from rural areas and were seeking to escape increasing rural poverty. Instead, they found themselves caught in urban poverty.[15] No matter how hard she worked, Ms. Noh said, there was no escape from hunger and poverty:

> There was no end to it. You'd work and work and there was no end to it. You'd work at night and extra hours and work and work and there was no end in sight. There was just no end to it. And so when you hear that if you go [to Seoul] and work that hard, you get paid more and there's hope for a better life, well, you fall for it. You fall for it and that's how you get sold into it. There are innumerable numbers of Korean women even today who get sold like that, and want to escape but can't get out. There are too many women like that in Korea.

What the women get sold into is prostitution, and this is what happened to Ms. Noh. Seeking a better job, she answered an employment broker's ad in a newspaper. The address was near Seoul Station, but when she arrived, they told her that there were no jobs available that day. So she called the number given in the ad, and the person who answered the phone told her to go to such-and-such a street and stand on the pedestrian bridge there, holding the paper with the ad. She did so, and a man met her there. Together they went to a motel room on the grounds that it was already late and the broker's office was closed. At the motel room they talked about job possibilities. He told her that there was a job opening as a live-in maid. Then he asked her if she had eaten. When she said no, he ordered dinner. She later found out that this became part of her debt, but at the time she was grateful for what she thought was kindness. He asked her if she had a place to stay, and invited her to stay at the motel. There, he tried to rape her. But desperate for a decent job and still believing that he would at least get her the job he promised, she followed him the next morning. They took the subway, transferring several times, and when they finally reached their destination, they were met by another man and a young woman.

When we arrived, [the two men] exchanged a big huge bundle of money. I didn't know why, I didn't know why he was giving him money. I just figured, you know, it must be something between them or something. Then they tell me to go over there, and the young woman takes me. Then what this *unni*[16] says is, "Do you know what kind of place this is?" So I said that I didn't, that I had come here to take a job as a maid. Then she says that I was sold. So I said, "What do you mean, sold?" And she says, "Didn't you see the money being exchanged? That's your debt." So I said, "What are you talking about? I came here to work as a maid, as a maid, and I'm just waiting." And she says that it isn't so. Then she tells me to wait until she tells me to go, and that then I should just go. And I told her she was a strange *unni* and asked her why she was like that. I had come to work as a maid, and she was saying all kinds of strange things. I couldn't believe what she was saying. But anyway, she kept insisting that when she tells me, I should hurry and leave. So I said okay. A little later, she tells me to hurry. She was showing me how to escape, this *unni,* she was helping me run away. So I ran, just ran. She told me to run as fast as I could, giving me money for bus fare and telling me to just take the first bus out, any bus. So I said okay and I ran as fast I could. But I couldn't escape. I was caught.

Both Ms. Noh and the *unni* were beaten. Ms. Noh was taken to another camptown and the *unni* was also sent elsewhere. It was 1975, and Ms. Noh was not yet twenty.

> I went to Seoul to get a job, and out of nowhere, incredibly, I was sold to a camptown. There I experienced suffering that shaves away at your very bones. Tears of blood, they invented that expression for precisely this, it was tears of blood, tears of blood.

She recalled her first night on the job:

> It was an American, an American, I can't forget his name, Bobby, it was Bobby. He was an absolutely huge person, so tall. Anyway, they tell me that this is my room and tell me to go in. So I went in and sat down. Then the madam brings over this man and tells me to do whatever he says. No matter what he says to do, just do as he says. By that time, several days had passed and I had already been beaten several times, so I was already just numb, I was in a frozen state. So, it's the first time that I'm really raped, by this man. He had given money and bought me, but for me, it's not like that, you know. The bedsheets were soaked with blood, my legs, I bled for four days afterwards, because I was all torn up. And so that's how, you know, it was completely stolen from me that day.

Ms. Noh spent some three years working in camptowns. At first, she continued to run away, only to be caught each time, beaten to within an inch of her life, and transferred to another locale. In the end, she gave up. But the work never got any easier. "I just couldn't stand it. It's, my body wasn't my body, you know?" she said. "It's twenty-four hours, twenty-four hours. My body wasn't my own."

The first places she was sold to catered to both American soldiers and Koreans. Later, she worked in clubs where only American soldiers were allowed. In one of those clubs, she met the soldier who would pay her debt and get her out. They became close, so close, she said, that the club owner tried to separate them. When he learned that she was kept there in debt bondage, he decided to help her escape. He had money sent from America, and as she watched, he counted out the bills to her "employer."

Her debt paid, they left the camptown together and rented a small apartment. A few weeks later, his tour of duty over, he left Korea. For some time after that, he continued to send her living expenses, but the remittances gradually stopped. She shrugged as she discussed this, saying that they must not have been fated to be together. But, she said, she still remembered him as the one who saved her life.

She earned a living by running a small gift shop catering to American soldiers, working as a waitress, and occasionally entering into contract live-in arrangements with soldiers. "Well, I wasn't a virgin anymore, you know, and if you keep house for one of these soldiers, you can earn a lot of money. Five hundred dollars a month was big money then," she said.

With her background as a camptown woman, she knew that she had been relegated to the bottom of Korean society. She decided to go to America and entered into a contract marriage with an American soldier:

With this body, I could never get married to a Korean man. And it wasn't like I had lots of money and could live enjoying the power of money. So, since they said that if you go to America, you can just pick up money off the ground, well, since my body is ruined anyway, let's earn some money. Let's go to America. So I said to my mother, "Mom, if I go to America, only three years. Just wait, only three years until I get my citizenship. When I get my citizenship, then Mom, come to America and we can live together, in America. Because they say you can just pick money off the ground. So let's wait for just three years." That's how I came to America, telling her that. But not even three years, within one year she died, of cancer. I couldn't go to Korea, of course, all I could do was stamp my feet in grief and cry, in America. I couldn't go to Korea.

She paid the soldier $1,500 in advance and $1,500 when she received her permanent residency two years later. He left for America first, and when the papers came through, she joined him at a military base in Texas, where they lived as husband and wife until she received her green card. It was August 1980 when she arrived as Mrs. Edson, and in that year, more than four thousand other Korean women also married American soldiers.[17]

Looking for Adventure

By the late 1970s, American goods had long been flooding South Korean black markets, carrying with them intimations of prosperity and modernity. Mass emigration to the United States was well on its way, spurred by Park Chung Hee's emigration policy and the 1965 revision of United States immigration laws.[18] The American fever, *migug byung*, was epidemic throughout South Korea.[19] It was the desire to escape crowded, tiny, repressive Korea for expansive, freedom-filled America, to escape the ordinariness and the poverty and seek one's fortune in a land where, it was rumored, money really did grow on trees and anyone could become somebody.

Some Koreans were also beginning to seek limited encounters with American soldiers, primarily to learn English, which continued to increase in importance as a prerequisite for success. Colleges throughout South Korea, especially in the Seoul area, organized English clubs where Americans, often soldiers, were hired to teach conversation. Sometimes Koreans would deliberately seek to make friends with an American, with learning English the motivation and the goal. At other times, it was simply the desire to experience a piece of America, its glamor and its glitter. But Korean society still drew the line at women dating and marrying American men, especially soldiers. This retained its stigma, even as the number of Korean women marrying American soldiers rose to approximately four thousand a year in the 1970s and 1980s.[20] Although the assumption, as always, was that they all came from the camptowns, many did not.

For Moon Kyunghee, college was her cherished dream. There were so many things she wanted to learn, an entire world to discover. But in her junior year of high school, her father's business failed, and she was told to forget about higher education. The family barely had enough resources to survive, much less pay for college. So when she graduated from a Seoul high school in 1975, she got a job as an office clerk at an American electronics company. There, she felt intimidated whenever she encountered a foreigner, even though her job duties did not entail associating with them. She decided that she needed to improve her English in order to succeed at her job. But she had no money to hire a tutor. So she and a like-minded friend decided to seek out American friends in order to practice English conversation. They went to Itaewon, a camptown and foreigners' area in the heart of Seoul, the only place they could think of where Americans congregated. But they failed to strike up a friendship with Americans, and after a few more attempts they gave up the idea.

One day the two friends were at a coffeehouse far from Itaewon when two American soldiers sat down at the next table. Just when they had given up, they thought, here was their chance. Ms. Moon approached the soldiers and pretended to take an interest in the portable radio one of them carried. The soldiers responded eagerly and proceeded to come over to the women's table. One of the men asked them if they attended church, and said that there was an American church nearby. The men took the women to the church, and urged them to keep attending.

> Their motive was to evangelize, that's why they told us to come to the church, but we had a different motive, we wanted to learn English conversation. So that's how we all became friends. They asked if we could meet again the next day. We thought that was great. We'd be able to learn English for free.

The women continued to meet the men. The man with the radio took an interest in Ms. Moon and he asked her one day if she would be his girlfriend. She agreed, unaware of what the word really meant.

> The word *boyfriend*, you know, it's just *boy* and *friend*, so I just thought it meant a friend who was male, I didn't know that it meant a lover. So when he asked me if I wanted to be his *girlfriend*, why don't you be my *girlfriend*, I just said, *Oh, of course.* . . . And then after that he starts to *kiss* me and stuff.

After a month or so, he told her that he only had six months left in Korea, and that if they wanted to be together, they should get married. He urged her to decide right away, because the process would take at least three months. Although she wasn't in love with him, she did like him and the thought of never seeing him again spurred her to accept his proposal. She added:

> I was too young. In a way, it was a kind of adventure, and a kind of rebellion. . . . And there was a curiosity and, well, the thought that it might be better if I went to America and lived in a wide-open land. Here [in Korea], no matter how good a person you meet . . . so it wasn't because I loved him, I wasn't following someone I loved, rather, it was a kind of adventure, half and half. And also, because my parents were so opposed to it, it was a kind of rebellion.

Her disappointment that her parents had been unable to send her to college only made her more resistant to their opposition. In America, she thought, she would be able to go to college. "No matter how well I marry in Korea, how well can I really marry?" she said. "That's what I thought. I'd rather go to a big country and do all the studying that I want to do. That's what I thought."

So against her parents' wishes, Ms. Moon married her American boyfriend, an enlisted man in the Army. She was twenty-one and it was 1978. They went straight to his next assignment, a base on the American East Coast near his hometown. Ms. Moon, now Mrs. Ferriman, was among the approximately seven thousand Korean women who married American soldiers in 1978. It was the largest number recorded in any one year.[21]

Chun Myungsook grew up accustomed to the sight of American soldiers. She lived in a rural area near Uijongbu, a region directly north of Seoul and home to two U.S. military bases. Her father farmed a few plots of land, and her mother ran a small grocery store. Because of its proximity to the bases, American soldiers were frequent customers. After high school, Ms. Chun stayed home, helping out at the family store. She was the second of four children, three girls and a boy. The family had little money and so could not afford to send her to college. Anyway, she said with a laugh, she didn't do well enough in school to get into college. Compared to other farming families, however, Ms. Chun's family was relatively well off, for they had the income from the store to offset low yields, low crop prices, and other farming misfortunes. So Ms. Chun, unlike tens of thousands of other young rural women in Korea, was not compelled to seek work to help support the family.

From an early age, she said, she had compared Korean men unfavorably with Americans. She speculated that her early exposure to Americans at the store and through the mass media may have been a factor.

Ever since a long time ago, for no good reason, you know, I just liked Americans. So maybe that was an influence, a factor in my marrying an American. You could see Americans on TV, in the movies. And at home, you know, we were right near the base, so a lot of Americans came through here for training. And so since we have a store, they all came through here and stuff. And so for no reason, even in my opinion, for no good reason, I just came to get a good impression of Americans. And so when I heard that my friend was working there, you know, I went to see her. It was my first time in that kind of area, you know, and it was all bright and shiny. So I began spending time with her there, just having a good time, and that's how it all came about.

Curious about Americans, Ms. Chun sought out her friend, a classmate from junior high school, when she heard that she worked with Americans at a club in Tongduchon, a larger camptown further north. There the streets were lined with bars, clubs, restaurants, and shops catering to U.S. soldiers. Every night, the streets sparkled with neon and pulsed with the rhythm of American rock and roll. It was a sight that impressed the young Ms. Chun as glamorous and exciting. For her, the camptown seemed to be a sort of playground, a place where a restless young woman could break loose and have fun. When I asked her about the women who worked there, she did not seem to have much knowledge about the actual working conditions, the system of prostitution and debt bondage, and the constant regulation that the women undergo. Her experience seemed to have been limited to partying.

Ms. Chun's friend lived there with an American soldier from nearby Camp Casey. Ms. Chun followed her friend to the clubs, where within weeks she met an enlisted Army man. As she spent more time with him in the clubs, she began to stay in Tongduchon for the night instead of returning home. Fearing her father's wrath for such behavior, she started living with her friend. That soon turned to living with the Army man.

At home, her family was frantically searching for their missing daughter. Her sisters scoured the area, showing people her picture and asking if anyone had seen her. Several months later, they finally found Ms. Chun. She went home that day and told her parents everything. The proposed solution was marriage.

> My mother said no, she was opposed. But my father said, well, if that's what you want, get married, but why of all things does he have to be _black?_ Anyway, since I had already starting living with him, you know. . . . So I brought him home to meet my parents.

For Ms. Chun, the fact that she had already started living with him seemed to make marriage an inevitability.

> There was nothing else to do but marry him. At that time, I didn't know anything about marriage or anything. It was just that I had already started living with him, and my parents had met him, so the thought of switching to another man was like, well, it was like I was strange, you know, like I would be a dirty woman or something.

Asked why he married her, she smiled, and then said that he had always told her that she was a good woman. He would say that she reminded him of Sheena Easton, a popular singer of sultry dance tunes.

They were married in 1986, barely a year after the two had first met. Ms. Chun was twenty-four years old when she became Mrs. Peterson. They lived in Korea for a few months. During that time, Mrs. Peterson prepared for her life in the United States by attending the U.S.O. Brides School.

Organized in 1971 through the U.S.O. office in Seoul as one of its intercultural programs, the school is aimed specifically at Korean women engaged or married to American soldiers. The curriculum covers a broad spectrum of basic information about life in the United States, such as how to open a checking account, keep a household budget, shop for groceries and cook American food, as well as some conversational English. The course also covers military lifestyle, American customs, history and geography, healthcare, education and employment, and legal rights and responsibilities. Many of the class materials consist of handouts prepared by instructors and the U.S.O. staff and are written in both Korean and English. The three- to five-week course is offered several times a year. During the 1970s, the U.S.O. offered the course not only in Seoul, but also at different bases around South Korea. About three hundred women a year enrolled in the program during the 1970s and 1980s, but by 1997 when I visited the U.S.O. office in Seoul, the number had dropped to about seventy a year. The goal of the program is not only to prepare the women for life in America, but also to prepare them for the realities of an intercultural marriage. There is no corresponding program to prepare the husbands for an intercultural, interracial marriage.[22]

Explaining that her husband preferred to send her to such courses rather than teaching her himself, Mrs. Peterson said that the Brides School was worth attending. "When I think back on it now, I'm glad I went there," she said. "They give you a lot of materials, books, and pamphlets and stuff, and sometimes I look through them and they are useful."

In December, Mrs. Peterson and her husband arrived in the United States. First they went to his hometown, a suburban area on the East Coast. From there, he went to his next assignment, a base in Kansas, while she stayed with her parents-in-law for another month until family housing on-base became available. Mrs. Peterson was among the more than three thousand Korean women who married American soldiers in 1986.

In 1986, Huh Miyoung was in her second year at a university just south of Seoul. Of the some hundred and fifty military brides I met in the course of my research, she was the only one with a college education. She had grown up comfortably middle class in the capital. Her father was a banker and her mother a housewife. She described herself as a carefree young woman who spent much of her time with friends and enjoyed college life. Eager to learn English, she joined a student English club during her freshman year. Club dues paid for an instructor, usually an American from nearby Osan Air Base. They met weekly at a local church. During Ms. Huh's sophomore year, the club's tutor introduced her to a friend stationed at the same base.

> At first, I was just meeting him out of curiosity, and so that I could have more opportunities to speak English. . . . We met about once a

week and gradually we began to meet more often. Six months passed, and then a year and I began to get the sense that this is the one. So from then on I began to think more seriously about our relationship.

As it turned out, she said, it was his second tour in Korea and he was looking for an Asian wife.

From the beginning my husband wanted to marry an Asian woman. Because, well, my father-in-law retired as an officer in the Air Force, and so even though they didn't live overseas, they lived in different bases in the United States and they came in contact with many Asians. And so he had a good impression of them. And now that he was stationed at Osan, you know, well, there are many low-quality people there and he wanted to meet educated people. He heard about our club, and so he started coming to our meetings and that's how we met.

Asked why her husband wanted to marry an Asian woman, she responded with an anecdote from her mother-in-law.

She says that while they were in Kansas, they were living on-base there, there was an Asian woman with her daughter walking by. My husband saw them, they were wearing pretty clothes and walking by, and he called for his mother to come and look. So she came out to look, and my husband is telling her that Asians are really, really pretty. And at that time, she thought, aha, he has a lot of interest in Asian women. Anyway, each time he was sent to Korea, it was the same, he just had a lot of interest in Asian women.

The couple kept their relationship secret from their families and from her college friends, including the English club. Indeed, she said, club rules forbade such dating and particularly frowned on female students dating Americans. When she first joined the club, the tutor, also a soldier at Osan, asked her out to dinner. Unsure what to do and extremely nervous in the face of this sudden invitation, she called over an upperclassman to translate her refusal. The upperclassman told the tutor that such behavior was unacceptable. The tutor, who had been with the club for quite some time, was fired on the spot.

Ms. Huh said that she considered this an invasion of individual rights. Regulating who could go out with whom, she said, crossed a certain line. Further, she said, she felt that Korean students looked down on Americans, especially soldiers.

In my opinion, it's simply using the person. Using the American to learn English. After you use him, and you don't need him any more, then you just throw him away, it's like that. So, it's not that I was interested in that person, but it seemed to me that they crossed a certain line and invaded an individual arena. So I was very disturbed by this. Thus when I started to date my husband, I stopped going to the club, we both did. That was in my junior year, from then on we didn't participate in the club.

She also recalls that anti-American sentiment was high on her campus, just as it was in most campuses throughout South Korea during the mid-to late 1980s. Details about the 1980 Kwanjgu uprising for democracy and the subsequent massacre of civilians by the military were being circulated.[23] Chun Du Hwan, an Army general and the fourth president of Korea, had consolidated his power through that massacre and was becoming increasingly unpopular. Many students reasoned that since the United States held supreme command over the Korean military, Chun could not have unleashed specially trained forces on Kwangju citizens demonstrating for democracy without the approval of the United States.[24] The fact that Chun was Ronald Reagan's first official state visitor only served to confirm this belief. Students held demonstrations frequently, clashing with riot police. A number of students were killed. Others committed ritual suicide protesting the Chun regime. Ms. Huh recalled that whenever students in Seoul demonstrated, so did students at her campus. But Ms. Huh was not interested in what she called "politics" and said that activist students seemed rather extreme.

At the time, there were these suicides. Such things happened at our school too. But when I saw such things, I couldn't understand. When that student stood on the roof and poured kerosene all over his body and threw himself off the roof, in the name of the country, is that really, I wondered if that is really valid and worthwhile. Not even thinking about his family. I don't know. From the standpoint of activist students, people like me are no help, but is it really, is such an act really worthwhile, throwing one's body off the roof like that, I couldn't really. . . . Of course, students have to get together and demonstrate to express their opinions occasionally. That I agree with.

Anti-American sentiment continued to spread among students and demonstrations became more and more frequent. Even the prosperous middle class joined the call for democratization and an end to military dictatorship. Although Roh Tae Woo, Chun's handpicked successor, agreed to democratization and open presidential elections in his famous June 1987 proclamation, students continued to demonstrate and labor unrest was severe.[25] Roh, after all, had been Chun's partner in the Kwangju massacre. American troops were on constant alert throughout this period.

This was when I was dating my husband. When the news came that there would be a demonstration, that they were demonstrating in Seoul, then, in the case of the Air Force, a command would immediately be issued. *Emergency* or something like that, and everyone who was outside the base had to return. After that, warnings were issued in advance, that there are going to be demonstrations, so don't go outside, don't go running around outside the base. So because of this— when we went on a date, we always went to Seoul, because my family lives there—when that happened, then my husband would call me. He would tell me that he couldn't leave the base.

Ms. Huh said she carefully screened her behavior while dating her husband. They always went to Seoul where the sight of foreigners was more common. Usually, she said, they went to places like Myungdong, a fashionable, upscale section of Seoul. They avoided the area near her school for fear of running into her classmates and also because of her experience with certain incidents.

There's this general image that dating Americans is bad, a vague, general image that it's bad. In some cases, well, in the evening when our club meeting is over the Americans would walk us to the station, to the subway station. Then people who pass by, people who are drunk, they curse at us. (What do they say?) You know, there are some really bad curses. I can't even remember now. Especially when female students are together [with Americans]. Is it okay to say this kind of thing? (Yes, it's okay.) Umm, the people who work in clubs, they call them *yang galbo* [yankee whore], right? So that's how they curse us. At night, and when that happens we are just stunned, after all, we're just students.

Neither anti-Americanism nor the bad image associated with dating an American deterred Ms. Huh. She continued to date her soldier. As she faced college graduation, they began to think seriously about marriage and each of them approached their respective families. Ms. Huh's family was at first opposed. They knew no one who had married a foreigner, and their first reaction was shock and worry. How would their daughter live in a foreign land? What if this foreigner abandoned her? Aside from the threat of family disgrace, these were typical concerns for parents whose daughters wanted to marry foreigners. Ms. Huh admitted that she too had harbored such worries. What allowed her to trust him, she said, was a combination of his family background and his character. He grew up in a conservative Italian-American extended family, living in the same house as both parents and paternal grandparents. To Ms. Huh, this seemed more like a traditional Korean family than like the American families she had heard about, the ones riven by divorce, strife, and instability.

It wasn't because he came from a well-off family, but because he came from such a warm and stable family. And when I talked with him, I could sense that he was a responsible person. His sense of responsibility was very strong. So I thought, aha, he must be the one.

A man from such a warm and stable family, one with such a strong sense of responsibility, surely would not abandon his wife, Ms. Huh reassured her parents. But before they would consent to the marriage, they insisted on consulting Ms. Huh's aunt and uncle, who had lived in the United States for some twenty years. Her parents thought that Ms. Huh's aunt and uncle would be able to give sound advice on this matter because they were successful and well-educated immigrants familiar with American life. The aunt and uncle opposed the marriage on numerous grounds, the primary one being that not only was the proposed groom a foreigner, but he was a soldier and merely an enlisted one at that. They had heard too many stories about failed marriages between American soldiers and Korean women. In addition, they felt, married life on a soldier's salary would be economically difficult. They did not want their niece to suffer such difficulties or to become yet another Korean military bride with a difficult and lonely life. Despite such opposition, however, Ms. Huh's mind was made up, she said.

> My belief that this person was the one for me was so strong that I insisted that this person was the one I would marry. When I made up my mind in this way, my parents dropped their opposition.

Opposition from the husband's family was minimal, according to Ms. Huh. Their view was that while they preferred a white daughter-in-law, as long as their son did not bring home a black woman they would not be openly opposed.

Ms. Huh finished her last set of college exams in December 1988 and graduated the following February. That summer, she and her husband-to-be participated in a mandatory three-day marriage seminar for soldiers and their Korean fiancées. There, Ms. Huh was exposed to other military brides for the first time.

> There were thirteen couples, thirteen couples came and among them, with a few exceptions, really, they were all the kind who worked as dancers downtown and stuff. When you look at them, their clothes, it was summer then, but their clothes were just so revealing and really, anyone who saw them would know immediately that they came from that class of society. So being with them together, it was really . . . It was very, of course I realized then that I was really a special case, but really, because they were like that, as I saw these not-so-good examples of military brides, I felt that that's why people curse and look down on [military brides]. I felt that it was a real shame, and I myself became ever more careful.

Feeling the stigma, and wary of being painted with the same brush, Ms. Huh had censored her behavior from the time she began dating her husband-to-be. She took extra caution to dress and behave modestly, for example, lest others see her as a loose woman. Her experience during the marriage seminar only increased her wariness and her caution.

After a long and complicated process, the twenty-four-year-old Ms. Huh became Mrs. Orellana in November 1989. The newlyweds lived in Korea for a year and a half. Mrs. Orellana was issued a military dependent's ID card and she began to take a slew of courses at her husband's base in order to learn about America and to improve her English. These courses included G.E.D. preparation, English language courses, and cooking classes. She credits this education with helping her adjust more easily to American life. In the early summer of 1991, urban, middle-class, and college-educated Mrs. Orellana entered the United States with her American soldier husband. After stopping at her husband's hometown, a medium-sized city in the east, they moved to his next post, a base in central Florida.[26]

Seeking America, Seeking Modernity

Although Korean military brides immigrate to the United States under different circumstances than do other Korean immigrants, these women still share with their ethnic kin the belief that going to America means a better life. To a remarkable degree, Koreans in the decades after World War II saw America as a paradise on earth.[27]

When Korean women chose to marry American soldiers and leave Korea for America, they were doing so in situations that were often not of their own making. These choices—efforts to make the best of their circumstances or even to overcome them—demonstrate agency, albeit one that was constrained, and resistance to those forces that the women perceived as oppressive. In their struggles to forge better lives for themselves and throw off the shackles of poverty and what they saw as backwardness and burdensome traditions, the women were reaching toward modernity. And to them America represented modernity.

For Koreans, modernity is inextricably entwined with colonialism and foreign domination. Experiences with Japan and America developed an awareness that made Koreans feel not only excluded, but also inferior.

Although Japanese colonialism and American imperialism are histori-
cally different, they share some broad characteristics. One of these is the
conceptual organization of the world into a hierarchy in which the imperial power is at the top and the dominated country is at the bottom. To
use a different image, the imperial power situates itself as the center and
the dominated peoples on the margins. J. Blaut calls this "the colonizer's
model of the world," and it has a profound effect on the colonized and
dominated.[28]

The stories of women who experienced Japanese colonialism, division, and war before entering the United States in the 1950s and 1960s
reveal layers of foreign domination permeating their lives. Cho Soonyi,
for example, spoke of yearning to escape from Korea for the wondrous
Japan described by her Japanese teachers. When the Japanese were defeated, and the American victors occupied the southern half of Korea,
this was quickly replaced by a longing to go to America. After all, "*they
control everything.*" She recognized the center of power and longed to go
there. This recognition and longing have been noted by Frantz Fanon,
Aimé Cesaire, and others as classic to the colonized mind.[29] Ms. Cho also
recognized shifts in power, and adjusted accordingly. Her understanding
of the power of the Japanese language during the colonial period facilitated her grasp of the linguistic consequences of the American occupation of southern Korea. She also displayed a keen sense of national hierarchies. When she discussed the benefits of American freedom, for example, she said that "even Japan" was very modern, in clear contrast to
both Korea and the United States. Her speech indicates that she placed
the three countries she had experienced within a hierarchy of modernity,
and thus of attractiveness: America was first, followed by Japan, with
Korea trailing at the bottom.

When Bak Hye-Young talked about the ill-fated conversation with her
family's boarder, she noted that they always spoke in Japanese. Recalling
how she replied when he called out her Japanese name, "Michiko,
Michiko," she could not produce that reply in Korean, even though she
had been speaking primarily in Korean throughout her narrative. Instead, she used the English *yes* and then the Japanese *hai*. What is remarkable here is not so much that she vocalized the Japanese that she
used then, but that she remembered her Japanese answer first in its English equivalent, a language that she learned only years later. Her tongue

failed to recall the Korean *nye* even in her remembering. Years of living with foreign languages and cultures more powerful than that of Korea are revealed in this brief rendering of an old memory.

Those years had direct linguistic consequences for these older women. Ms. Bak noted, for example, that there was no language in which she could count herself as truly fluent and literate. Foreign domination had literally left these women with no language to call their own. Far from being a liberating, transnational, and multicultural experience that allowed them to cross borders at will and revel in the interplay of multiple tongues, their contacts with multiple languages had been painful, frustrating, and even humiliating. Ms. Pak said that she had largely forgotten the Japanese she once knew like a mother tongue; her Korean ability was that of an uneducated country woman and her literacy remained shaky; and English would always be a difficult foreign language. For this reason, she generally avoided conversation with well-educated Koreans and with most Americans, preferring to limit her contact to family members, other Korean military brides, and the Amerasian families she sponsored to the United States. While Ms. Pak was an active, confident woman who founded and led a highly visible association of Korean military brides, she deliberately limited her circle to that community for fear of humiliation.

Many of these women found that there was no language in which they could fully express themselves. Ms. Yi noted that when she began going to meetings of military bride organizations some thirty years after she immigrated to America, the other women gently teased her for her Korean. It was halting and stilted, for she had rarely used it until then. She told me that sometimes she couldn't say what she wanted to say in Korean, so she just said it in English. But even then, she said, the English often didn't come out right, because she wasn't fluent in that either. Although she spoke it more often than Korean, she said that English remained a foreign language to her. Sometimes, she found that she had no language with which to express herself.

The prominence of English, felt so keenly by Ms. Cho, was echoed in the experiences of women who came after her. The link between English and economic survival, and between English and professional success, began nearly the moment U.S. troops set foot on Korean soil in 1945.[30] Young Korean men with only a cursory knowledge of English could earn a decent living as translators. Their English language ability could later be parlayed into scholarships to study in America. Knowing the phrases "do laundry," "one dollar," and "tomorrow" meant that a woman could earn a living by taking in soldiers' laundry. Learning how to type English, as Ms. Bak discovered, could mean getting better paid work. It was not only Ms. Cho who pored over a dictionary and grit her teeth to learn this new language. Ever since 1945, countless South Koreans have been driven to learn English as a means of economic survival and upward mobility.

The virtually overnight dominance of English was institutionalized with the establishment of English as a major component of Korea's educational system in 1954, when English was included among the major school subjects for which the government developed mandatory textbooks.[31] English-language courses became a requirement throughout junior high and high school. When Korean girls in high school learned how to type, they learned to do so on both Korean and English typewriters. Thus in the mid-1960s, Ms. Bai's ability to type both English and Korean was taken for granted. English became entrenched in Korea's education and employment reward systems, constituting a major portion of college entrance exams as well as employment and promotion exams for large corporations, newspapers and broadcast stations, the civil service, and other fields. Thus in the 1970s, Ms. Moon felt that she must improve her English to succeed at her job, even though her duties as an office clerk did not necessitate substantial contact with foreigners.

As time progressed, the drive to learn English only intensified. Even those who had little need to learn the language felt somehow left behind, less educated, and less sophisticated if their English language ability seemed deficient. By the 1990s, early English education was in vogue, and parents rushed to teach English to children who could barely command the Korean language. In the name of international competitiveness, English became a required subject in elementary school in 1997. Sometimes more hours per week are devoted to English-language instruction than to the Korean language. College students from Korea's top universities have long been able to earn a handy income tutoring high school students in English and math, the two essential subjects in college entrance exams. Native English speakers, especially Americans, can earn even more by tutoring students in conversational English. Korean Americans

visiting Korea often find that friends and relatives clamor for personal-
ized English instruction, help with English homework, and editing of
papers written in English. Schools specializing in English language instruction proliferate throughout Korea's urban areas. Most colleges have
one or more English language clubs, which offer conversational English
taught by Americans. As in the case of Ms. Huh's English club, the instructors are often American soldiers.

The power of English, its ability to confer status and distribute
awards, is directly tied to the power of America. Ms. Noh started her narrative by saying that everyone knew that you could literally rake in the
money if you went to America, that in America you could live like
princes and princesses. But America has not been the only place where
lucrative potential beckoned. Ms. Cho's first step in 1945 on her way out
of backward Korea was Seoul, the big city being preferable to the countryside. By the 1970s, when urbanization and industrialization were pro-
ceeding apace in Korea, Seoul was the place to go to earn money. Thus
Ms. Noh began by leaving the countryside for Seoul in search of a better
job, and noted that this was how many young women were tricked into
prostitution. A mass exodus from the countryside to urban centers like
Seoul was propelled by increasingly desperate rural conditions and the
potential for earning money. As America was the bright shining land for
Koreans, Seoul was the bright shining city for rural dwellers. Connections between prosperity, modernity, and the urban are revealed in this
multilateral web of relations.

Associated with wealth is freedom, such as the freedom to buy whatever you want. Said Ms. Cho: *"Oh! You have money, you can buy whole
world, you know, you can buy everything! Anything you want."* In 1940s
and 1950s Korea, money did not confer that privilege because consumer
goods were not readily available. When asked what was the best thing
about America, Ms. Cho unhesitatingly replied, *"Freedom!"* Not only
freedom to buy, but also freedom from the restrictions of Korean patriarchy. Her discussion reveals that she was talking about individual freedoms such as dressing as one pleases and seeing whom one pleases without being criticized. She also said that she didn't like the restrictions
that Korean culture placed on women. Several other women explained
that they felt that they would be free from burdensome obligations to in-
laws if they married an American rather than a Korean. Ms. Yi said she

believed that American men would not humiliate their wives by having mistresses. Negative experiences with Korean men—fathers who abused mothers, forced or abusive marriages—and just plain unwillingness to submit to Korean male dominance encouraged many women to look elsewhere for marriage partners. The American presence meant that they could look to American men, who were perceived as more handsome, better mannered, and kinder to women. Many women said they were impressed by the saying "ladies first," and believed that in America men treated women like queens. They spoke of Korean culture as sexist but American culture as equitable. That they may have escaped from one form of patriarchy only to be enmeshed within another was a realization that came only after years of American life. Even so, many women continued to believe that life was more equitable for women in America.

America was also equated with opportunity, which seems directly related to size. America was perceived as a grandly large country, while Korea was perceived as miserably tiny. Ms. Moon cited adventure and the prospect of getting a college education as some of the reasons she agreed to her American soldier's marriage proposal. When asked why she thought she could get a college education in America, she replied that she didn't know, but that everyone knew that America was full of opportunities. She referred to America as a "wide-open" country where a person could stretch and stretch to the fullest potential. Another women said that after having lived in America one could not return to live in Korea, because after tasting life in broad, wide-open America, one could no longer tolerate narrow, restrictive Korea.

Wealth, freedom, opportunity, and a grandness of scale were all associated with modernity. In the minds of many women, Korea was backward and America was modern. The perception of Korean sexism and American equality only underscored this difference.

The camptowns lurked as a pervasive presence for all the women, although not always for the same reasons. The curses directed at Ms. Cho for wearing Western dress in the late 1940s were echoed in the curses directed at Ms. Huh and her fellow club members for walking with an American four decades later. The only cases in which parents did not oppose marriage to an American were those involving women with experience working in the camptowns. Marriage to an American was partially propelled by the shadow of the camptown itself. As the logic went, it was impossible to marry a good Korean man because one had been "ruined" and so one might as well go to America and seek out a decent life there. For women without such backgrounds, parents opposed marriage to an American precisely because they did not want their families to be tarred with the camptown brush.

The shadow of the camptown has also made its way across the Pacific, for Korean immigrants bring their prejudices with them, as do American soldiers who have spent time in Korea. Stereotypes of Asian women as prostitutes, with American men as their clients, have become common in the United States. Thus Ms. Bai, reflecting on her in-laws' opposition, pointed out that they probably thought she was just a loose woman.

For women like Ms. Noh who directly experienced the camptowns, a great deal of their anger was directed against Korea and Korean men. Stating that it was Koreans who ran the clubs, Korean men who procured, beat, and raped the women, Koreans who lived off the money that the women earned, and the Korean state that left its people in poverty, she said, "Koreans made the camptowns." Americans, in contrast, were seen in the favorable light of the American soldier who helped her leave the awful camptowns, rather than the American soldier who raped her.

Although statistics are not readily available, anecdotal evidence suggests that the current number of military bride marriages may well remain at the approximately four thousand per year average of the 1970s and 1980s.[32] Have these women found the America of their dreams? What have they wrought of their immigrant experiences?

CHAPTER 3

Immigrant Encounters

From Resistance to Survival

Korean military brides did not find the fabled streets paved with gold and for the most part, their Prince Charmings didn't remain charming forever. Too often, their encounters with America brought them deep disappointment and an acute sense of dislocation. They left familiar hardships in Korea for hardships they never imagined they would find in America, including poverty, sexism, racism, divorce, and intense loneliness. As immigrant women of color, as non-native speakers of English, as interculturally and interracially married women, as workers in the lower tiers of the economy, they found themselves consistently faced with a wide variety of demands, indignities, and humiliations inflicted by both society at large and the people closest to them.

Throughout their lives, their responses to these difficulties, although varied, have included a complex mix of compliance and resistance. In many cases, the resistance has been subtle and fashioned out of seeming compliance. Their struggle has been not only for physical survival, but for emotional and cultural survival as well. It is a struggle for the survival of the whole self, intact with dignity, history, and self-respect.

In order to protect themselves, Korean military brides in the United States employ the only tools available to them. Their resistance takes place on the small stage of everyday life, often in the home, in personal encounters and relationships with husbands, children, in-laws, supervisors, neighbors, the children's teachers, and the cashier at the local grocery store. It is rarely overt or hostile, and it is rarely accompanied by an articulated critique of the conditions under which they live. Like the Malaysian factory women studied by anthropologist Aihwa Ong, they display few, if any, signs of Western-style oppositional consciousness, and rarely do they engage in demonstrations or blatant demands for their rights. Ong argued that this approach did not mean that the Malaysian factory women were not critiquing and resisting the domination they faced. Rather, they were expressing their discontent and their desire to improve their condition through the inventive use of their own cultural practices, which in their case included spirit possession.[1] For the Malaysian factory women and for Korean military brides in the United States, disguised resistance is often the only viable option.

Many of the problems that Korean military brides face are directly related to their relationships with close family members on whom they are dependent or whom they love. These women usually do not have sufficient power—economic, cultural, social, or personal—to engage in blatant struggle without incurring heavy penalties. Furthermore, they may not wish to treat husbands and other family members as enemies and aggravate strife within their households. As women, many have been socialized to value harmony in human relations above their own personal needs. Thus military brides use strategies that can be characterized as infrapolitics, which James C. Scott describes as "a wide variety of low-profile forms of resistance that dare not speak in their own name" and "practices that aim at an unobtrusive renegotiation of power relations."[2] Among military brides, resistance is characterized by an outward deference to the authority of husbands, in-laws and American culture accompanied by an insistent, backstage privileging of their own desires and opinions and of Korean culture and identity. This strategy is expressed in conversations among the women when they criticize their husbands and children or make jokes about American ways, in subversive opinions they will never change even though their outward behavior is designed to conceal these strong feelings, and in thousands of everyday acts performed in the face of opposition from the people closest to them.

The domination that military brides faced came at all levels, from the most personal to the most public, from the very subtle to the blatant. It inflicted upon them continual humiliation, degradation, and marginalization that stemmed from an assertion that all that was superior was male, American, and English-speaking. As the following pages illustrate, marriage to an American and immigration to America left no aspect of their lives untouched. Korean military brides faced struggle in virtually every aspect of their lives.

Stranger in a Strange Land

When I arrived here, I was so scared. I was so scared that at the airport, I threw away my *bag* and just ran to my husband who was just visible over there. I just ran, just ran, and someone from *customs* calls me, he calls me and tells me to take my *bag*, but there was nothing to inspect, even. Because I ran away like that, he was telling me to take my *bag*, but when I came, I just brought some clothes, a cross, and a small statue of St. Mary in my *bag*, that's all I had. So the people at customs, when they opened the bag and that's all there was in there, some clothes and this stuff, they were startled, I think. And then I flung the *bag* away and ran away, so, {laugh} they were calling to tell me to take my bag. But I was so scared then and I didn't know what to do.

This was the beginning of Mrs. Crispin's answer to my half-formed opening question, "Perhaps we could start by talking about how you came to immigrate . . . ?" Her answer encapsulates many aspects of military brides' first encounters with America: fear of the unknown, the husband as the only contact in a foreign world of strangers, the unfamiliar state of being alone, and a sudden dislocation of perspective. To Mrs. Crispin, immigration began when she arrived alone at Los Angeles airport in 1965. A sea of foreign faces awaited her. The entire procedure of entering a foreign country—presenting papers and answering questions to prove her right to enter, opening her luggage for inspection, and so forth—was a stressful experience that emphasized both her act of crossing borders and her foreignness. As she later noted, seeing Americans in Korea was very different from seeing them in the United States. In Korea, she had categorized them as foreigners. When she arrived in the United States, she quickly realized that she was the one who would now wear this label. In fact, she was worse than a mere "foreigner," for the U.S. government had labeled her an "alien." Although she couldn't shake off her own perspective of America and Americans as foreign, she became painfully aware that she lacked the power to assert that perspective. The trauma of simultaneously arriving in a foreign country, a new world of unknowns, and being named a foreigner seemed to be at the root of her fear. In her eyes, the only person to whom she could turn was her husband. Thus the moment she glimpsed him waiting on the other side of customs, she abandoned her belongings and ran to him—the first familiar person she had seen since stepping on the plane that had winged her away from her homeland.

After that first instance of panic, homesickness, loneliness, and a persistent sense of dislocation set in. The country left behind became the country yearned for. "Very lonely, no matter how poor a hometown you came from, you miss your hometown," said Mrs. Bugelli of her first years after arriving in 1957. For those who came in the early years before the 1970s, the absence of other Koreans accentuated their homesickness with a sharp awareness of being alone in their difference. Said Mrs. Bugelli:

> When I first came, it seemed that people looked down on me, there was some discrimination. . . . Um, see, I'm not an American. Discrimination, there was some of that. Even if they don't say anything, it's there in their minds. And also there weren't many Koreans. Even though it was so difficult in Korea, I missed Korea.

It wasn't just the home country that was missed; it was the feeling of belonging. Mrs. Mullen recalled how the stares from Americans, black and white, made her feel literally like an alien from outer space:

> Back then in the 1950s, it was very, really, very difficult to see an Asian person, *very far in between*. *Only Chinese restaurant, few Chinese people*, otherwise there were no Asians at all. So, when Americans see an Asian, well, they stare and stare as if, what, *they look at you like you out of the space*. That's how extreme it was, extreme, *they stare at you. They*, oh, it was just incredible.

This sense of not belonging was imposed by the very environment in which these women lived. Regardless of exactly where they began their lives as immigrants, they were keenly aware of being different, and painfully aware that this difference was linked with inferiority. Like other military brides, Mrs. Bugelli understood that it was a matter of her being "not an American," that is, not white. For Mrs. Mullen, the experience was even more traumatic, for the stares made her feel that others viewed her as nonhuman, as if by not being American she wasn't even part of humanity.[3]

This kind of treatment falls under the broadly understood definition of racism, a singling out of difference that results in exclusion and intimations of inferiority, expressed in everyday acts large and small within a matrix of power inequalities. It can be as obvious as stares or a racial slur, or as disguised as a husband's opinion that American women are uppity; it can be recognized and named, or it can be mistaken for praise and appreciation. Few military brides dwell on this, some don't even mention it, and fewer still seem to fully recognize its Orientalist face, that is, its connection to racialized stereotypes of Asian cultures and peoples. Yet many talked about it as something that dwelt just below the surface, rarely openly acknowledged or directly fought, but often recognized and privately battled.

Although race is a fluid, dynamic social construct, it is a powerful one with profound, far-reaching consequences.[4] It is also tenacious, for while racial categories and meanings may change, they have yet to go away. Defining race primarily in terms of skin color and facial features, American society continues to privilege whites as superior.[5] Korean military brides encounter racism not only among strangers but also among their closest family members. Even the quotidian practices of cooking food, raising children, keeping house, and having a marital spat are infused with race. Their experiences also show that while the civil rights struggle of the 1960s and 1970s may have eliminated much of legalized racial discrimination, it was less successful in eliminating racism at the microlevel of everyday experience. Women cited incidents from the 1990s which they felt were racist as readily as they cited incidents from the 1950s. This lends experiential evidence to sociologists Michael Omi and Howard Winant's theory that racism in America simply changes form and adjusts, but does not go away.

Although many women did not use the term racism, others named their experiences as such, even if the racism was difficult for them to pinpoint. The content of a stare, the tone of a voice, slow service from clerks, and other experiences added up to a feeling that racism was at work. Mrs. Crispin recounted an experience from 1966 when she was subtly but persistently denied access to public restrooms at a highway rest stop:

> Between Kansas City and Chicago, it was racial discrimination. When I asked (for the restroom) at the *gas station*, they told me to go to the restaurant; when I asked at the restaurant, they told me to go to the *gas station*. So I went back and forth, back and forth, like a *yo-yo*. After about two times, I realized, aha, this is what they call racial discrimination. I woke up to this, and next time I had my husband ask and find it for me. So he would go and ask and find it, and then tell me, and then I would enter and go to the restroom without bothering to ask the workers there. So there was racial discrimination, and it wasn't a good feeling.

When Mrs. Weinberg tried to describe her experience with racism, she noted that it was hard to explain, because it was so subtle. Finally she asked, "Haven't you ever experienced this? You, yourself?" When I answered affirmatively, she began to discuss a recent incident. The week before our February 1996 interview, her husband had won an award from one of his biggest clients, a large corporation. Mrs. Weinberg described the awards banquet:

> Because it's *more like business people*, the women are all dressed very grandly. So, *I don't know, that's* . . . maybe it's just me, but when I have to go to these functions, *sometimes I don't talk much*. I just keep my mouth shut and stay silent. Just say hello and that's it. I really hate going to these things. (Why?) It's just the way I look and maybe because of that, it's *just like*, I'm Asian. I just feel like *I'm not fit it in there*.

Her own grand clothes and upper-class status apparently do little to ameliorate her sense of not belonging in a roomful of Americans. Mrs. Weinberg is aware that in American society, racial difference from whiteness confers inequality. Her response is to be as unobtrusive as possible.

That she is apparently unable to openly resist the racism she faces may be due in part to a lack of support from her husband. Notice that it is only after she receives affirmation that I too have experienced racism that she is able to describe what she feels. While she credited her husband with always taking pride in her as his wife, saying that that is probably why their marriage has worked out for so long, she also said that he considers her feelings of encountering racism to be nothing more than oversensitivity on her part. Whenever she complained that his secretaries did not seem to treat her with due courtesy and were too abrupt or even rude, he would dismiss it as a cultural difference between America and Korea, she said. But, she added, there is a difference between casual American manners and rudeness and she just couldn't completely accept her husband's interpretation. As she discussed her sense of being looked down on and of not belonging, she often seemed unsure of both her own conclusions and of her husband's dismissal of them. Thus she ended by saying, "But whenever I tell him that someone did such and such, he always says, It's just because you think that, no one did such a thing. *I don't know . . .*"

Mrs. Weinberg's sense of discomfort among Americans is echoed by other military brides. Their position as Asian wives of American men does not give them an entrée into American society and help them "fit in." Instead, it seems to further expose them to Orientalist prejudices regarding Asian women. Mrs. Crispin noted, "They call us *Oriental, Oriental girl* and so forth. . . . Americans ask us, What's your special skill? Why do our people marry you girls?"

Mrs. Crispin said she senses hostility in these questions, as if the questioner views her and other military brides as having somehow "stolen" American men away from American women. The idea that Asian women possess a special sexual allure and docile Oriental femininity constitutes a whole body of Orientalist stereotypes that categorize Asian women as submissive, erotic, docile, and hyperfeminine, stereotypes that are often called the Lotus Blossom image. In particular, Asian women have been portrayed as eager for the attentions of Western men.[6] The immigration of Asian war brides and their depiction in the American media only served to reinforce such stereotypes. In addition, stories told by returning soldiers about Asian women in military camptowns gave the Lotus Blossom image a hint of the Dragon Lady, with depictions of Asian women as not only exotic and willing sexual playmates, but also as morally depraved and always scheming to catch a soldier as a ticket to America. These stereotypes can be found in a diverse sampling of American popular culture, including the movies *The World of Suzy Wong*, *Year of Living Dangerously*, and *Welcome to Paradise*, the television drama *M*A*S*H*, and the Broadway play *Miss Saigon*.[7] In each, one or more Asian women serve as the feminine, submissive, exotic, and sexually available foil for the desirable, masculine white man.

In such an environment, many military brides felt the heavy burden of representation and a special responsibility to combat such stereotypes. During her years in Chicago, Mrs. Crispin would find herself in the dead of winter walking home with heavy groceries. With her fingers frozen and ready to fall off, she would feel the urge to just abandon one or two of the heavy bags. But, she said:

> If someone saw me, since I'm Asian, they might say that they saw an Asian woman just leaving her groceries in the street. So because I was afraid that people might say this, I would grit my teeth and carry it all home. The minute I closed my door behind me, the tears would just come and I would think, why did I come to America only to work so hard and freeze my hands off and to live like this? And the tears would threaten. So on those days I would make myself a good meal.

For Mrs. Crispin, living "like this" includes both the burden of feeling singled out for racial difference and the burden of being a representative of all Asian women. This sense of living within a society that is not one's own only intensifies the physical hardships of her immigrant life. The incident she recounts here is not so much the cause of her tears as the trigger that threatens to unleash all the hurt and sorrow accumulated while living in America. She refused, however, to be overwhelmed by her tears. On these occasions she reproached herself for complaining about her life and for allowing herself to be weak. Admonishing herself to be strong like a man, she would treat herself to a good meal, complete with all the formalities of a fully set table.

The stereotypes that military brides like Mrs. Crispin feel obliged to combat are part of the shadow of the camptown. Military brides often feel that they are seen not only as Asian women, but also as former camptown women. The two stereotypes are closely intertwined, for the Orientalist image of sexually available, submissive Asian women correlates with the image of the Asian prostitute, especially for Americans and their families in the military. Mrs. Morgan, who immigrated in 1983, stated that many Americans would tell her that at first they just saw her as another former "working girl" who had snagged a soldier as a ticket to America, but after getting to know her they came to realize that she was different. It saddens her, she said, that people see the stereotype and not the real person. Her white neighbors at one military base, for example, were unfriendly at first. After a few months, they told her that they had been dismayed to find out that an Asian woman was moving in next door. They had heard too many bad stories, they said, about Asian military brides. But when they saw that she was a good wife and mother, they were impressed and came to think more highly of Korean women. They even told her that they went so far as to look up Korea on the map, and that they were happy to have such a woman for a neighbor. Mrs. Morgan said that this made her feel proud, because she had always tried to live up to her brother-in-law's parting admonition never to forget the dignity of Korean womanhood. Knowing that Americans look down on Asian women, especially on women married to soldiers, makes her all the more committed, she said, to showing them through her actions that Korean women, if not all Asian women, should be respected.

For some military brides, overseeing their own behavior is not enough. One woman who arrived in the mid-1970s said that she couldn't stand to see Korean women whose behavior lends credence to stereotypes of military brides. So she cajoles, threatens and chastises them, showing them how to dress modestly and how to keep house, helping them learn to drive, enrolling them in English classes, and helping them find jobs. Even if they did come from the camptowns, she said, they should leave all that behind and behave in a manner befitting their new status as wives and mothers. She shook her head, sighed, and then said, echoing the words of many other military brides:

Well, they just don't know, some of them. So when someone takes the time to show them, they learn quickly. There are a lot of diamonds in the rough among military brides, women who could really make something of themselves if someone would just help them out a little.

"Suddenly, I Was Deaf and Dumb"

Language was one of the most profound and difficult cultural differences Korean military brides faced. In a largely monolingual environment where English is the ruling language, lack of fluency in English means not only the inability to fully communicate, but also the inability to function with confidence and to command the respect even of children, much less other adults. The simplest tasks—making a telephone inquiry, reading a utility bill, asking for directions, even answering the phone— are stressful and rife with the potential for failure. Language barriers make it difficult to become close to neighbors and in-laws. To speak English is to leave oneself open not only to misunderstandings but also to ridicule. Just as the women are made to feel inferior due to their racial difference, they are also made to feel inferior due to their lack of English fluency.

The general view they encountered was that the problem consisted of their inability to speak fluent English, rather than a mutual inability to speak each other's languages. It's a view that many women unconsciously adopt, for there is little support for the voice that points out that while the women are able to communicate in English, however "broken" and "accented" it may be, the overwhelming majority of the Americans in their lives, including husbands and children, do not possess a comparable level of Korean ability. Social service providers, for instance, who recommend English-language courses for the women as a solution to communication difficulties that lead to marital problems, do not even mention the idea of Korean-language courses for the husbands. Indeed, many husbands and other family members say that Korean is too difficult a language to learn and therefore impractical, conveniently overlooking the well-known difficulties of learning English as a foreign language. In other words, the burden of adjustment is placed almost entirely on the shoulders of the women. This is true not only for language, but also for virtually every area of daily life, including food, child rearing, housekeeping, and work.

Perhaps the weight of that burden can partially explain why every woman I met somehow felt obliged to comment that her English was poor. These comments were not merely expressions of a lack of confidence in their English skills, but a kind of apology, as if limited English competency were some kind of flaw or even a sin. Even women with a high degree of English competency made such comments. Both Mrs. Mullen and Mrs. Bugelli commented that their English was not perfect, even though I observed that they had no trouble communicating with their neighbors and other American associates. Other women laughed ruefully and said that even living within American families did little to help improve their English because conversations were limited to expressions such as "Clean your room" and "Dinner's ready." Women who were busy with jobs, family, and other responsibilities called themselves "lazy" for not studying English in their spare time. Although this self-denigration can in part be attributed to the practical need for adequate English skills to function in American society, it can also be traced to the humiliation they experience as Asian women who are not native speakers of English. There seems to be the sense that, while the burden of racial difference cannot be changed, if they had studied more or tried harder, perhaps they could at least have achieved English fluency and escaped from that particular burden of difference and that particular source of humiliation. Many women pointed out that the children of Korean immigrants speak flawless English—"just like Americans," in the words of one woman—and are therefore able to compete successfully with Americans, something that they themselves could not do.

Linguist Rosina Lippi-Green argues that American insistence on the primacy of standard English, the obsession with correct grammar and pronunciation and the disdain for certain types of accented English, serve as disguises for racial discrimination. She notes that it is primarily Asian and Latino speakers of English as a second language whose accents are deemed unintelligible or incorrect, while European accents are often deemed glamorous. Likewise, black English or Ebonics is viewed as incomprehensible and a mark of being uneducated. American native speakers, she argues, shift the burden of communication onto Asians, Latinos, and African Americans by insisting that only standard English grammar and a standard accent are intelligible. Americans are thereby refusing to engage in the mutual efforts necessary for communication to take place. Lippi-Green persuasively argues that the problem is not whether or not these speakers of English are intelligible, but whether or not they appear to accept dominant American ideologies maintained by a white, educated middle class. In other words, whether or not they agree to be Americans on the terms set by mainstream Americans.[8]

Many military brides have an organic understanding of Lippi-Green's argument. Women expressed a certain resentment and a sense of injustice over the demand that they improve their English. As long as their English was passable, some women asserted, that should be good enough. One woman came to me after church service one day and asked if she was saying the following sentence correctly: "I need change for this dollar, please." When I said yes, she then asked if her pronunciation was too terrible to be understood. When I said that her pronunciation was understandable, which it was, she exclaimed: "I knew it! I always thought that Americans were deliberately being difficult when they tell us that our English isn't comprehensible!" When she had used this sentence at a convenience store, she explained, the white American cashier had looked at her blankly and then made her repeat the sentence several times before finally giving her change. "Americans, they give us a hard time for no reason," she said. Other women nearby chimed in their agreement and an animated discussion ensued. Said one woman: "They just assume that our English is poor the minute they see our faces, and when they hear our accents, they don't even try to figure out what we are saying." Remarked another: "Of course we need English, since we live in America, but I don't think that we have to feel inferior just because we are not fluent." Although they did not name it as such, these women were articulating connections between racism, language, and power, and refusing to shoulder the full burden of difference imposed on them.

Nevertheless, every woman I interviewed also cited English as one of the most difficult aspects of immigrant life. One woman said: "The minute I arrived in America, suddenly I was deaf and dumb. I couldn't understand what anyone said, and no one could understand me. I felt stupid and helpless." Some told me that they still hesitate to answer the phone for fear that the caller will be an American. Many women recounted numerous instances when they were made to feel somehow inferior due to their accent, a grammatical mistake, the misuse of a word or expression, or some other error in their use of English.

Mrs. Bugelli knew just enough English to communicate with her husband, but once she arrived here in 1957, she said, it was "*totally different, you know."* People thought it was funny, she said, that she couldn't speak English. They would laugh at her speech and her inability to understand what others said. Mrs. Dennison, who arrived in 1958, found that even little children felt free to take her to task and correct her English:

> When I first came to America, every time I opened my mouth I made a mistake. So I lived with my mouth closed. If my husband asked me something, and I said, *she* so on and so forth, then the nephews and nieces would say, no, it's not *she*, it's *he*. . . . So I lived without talking, for fear of making a mistake.

The non-native speaker is so powerless that even a child can correct her with impunity. The conventional authority of adults over children is humiliatingly reversed. While children correcting adults for their English is a familiar phenomenon among immigrant families in America and other English-speaking countries, there seemed to be a distinct difference between being corrected by one's own children and by the children of one's in-laws. Mrs. Brennan, for example, said that when her children corrected her English, she tried harder to get it right since she appreciated their wish to educate their mother. Besides, she noted, they never corrected her in public or in front of other people, only when they were alone. But those outside her family, she said, had no right to comment on her English, whether alone or in private, much less correct it. In drawing this line, she was asserting her dignity and refusing to accept the inferior status associated with limited English fluency.

Language differences brought more than ridicule or humiliation. They prevented women from receiving proper service, medical care, education, jobs, and other necessities. Mrs. Brennan recounted a story from her early days of living in New York with her husband and their first child, a daughter. While still a baby, the daughter became ill with dysentery and so Mrs. Brennan took the child to the doctor. Having seen other children become ill with the same disease, Mrs. Brennan knew what was wrong with her child. She wanted medicine. But she could not explain this to the doctor with her limited English. Every time she took the child to the doctor, he simply said there was nothing wrong and sent them home. But at home the baby would double up in pain, clutch her stomach, cry, and have bowel movements that consisted of little more than mucus. Mrs. Brennan said she was frantic as well as furious with the doctor. So she went back to the doctor one more time, carrying with her a sample of her baby's recent bowel movement. Showing this to the doctor, she mimicked her baby's behavior at home. Pointing to her baby, she doubled up, clutched her stomach, and writhed as if in pain. Once again examining the baby's stomach by simply pressing his hands on her abdomen, the doctor shook his head and said there was nothing wrong.

I was so frustrated, I just yelled. I just yelled but that probably didn't help much. Even now I can't speak much English, think how bad it must have been then. So, I yelled, "*that little stomach, okay?*" That's what I yelled. "*That little stomach, okay?*" I was saying, that little stomach, so I yelled, "*that little stomach, okay?*" . . . And I kept talking to him, yelling, telling him that just because he can't find anything doesn't mean that the baby isn't sick, I just kept talking. Well, he probably didn't understand a word I said, but here I was, I kept bringing the baby in saying that there was something wrong with her stomach, so he had the nurse give me some baby aspirin. But did I know what that was? I didn't even know what it was. Anyway, they said to give her half a tablet. And so, since this was the first medicine they gave her, you know, I had dragged her to the doctor so many times and they never once gave me any medicine for her, so since this was the first, well, try it and see. So I cut it in half with a knife, crushed it with a spoon, mixed it with water and fed it to her. And what do you know, she got better after eating that.

American Family, Korean Wife

Most other immigrants are able, at least, to create a cultural haven out of their homes. Military brides do not even have that luxury. Their own family becomes the terrain for intercultural encounter, struggle, and negotiation. Just as the women are named foreigners in American society even as they are pressured to assimilate, they also become cultural outsiders within their own families. This is reflected in the identities assigned to family members. The husband, the biracial children, and the

family itself are defined as American, while the wife, however accultur-
ated she may be, is defined as Korean. But even as she is defined as Korean, attempts are made to contain that Koreanness[9] and erase that difference. Without this kind of containment and erasure, the contradiction
of having a crucial family member, the wife and mother, defined as Korean while the family itself is defined as American would become untenable. Thus defined, contained, and erased, many military brides are culturally and sometimes psychologically isolated within their own families.

Often, in-laws and husbands pressure the women to Americanize. In
a random survey of military brides in Oklahoma in 1975, nine out of ten
reported that their in-laws tried to remake them into "all-American"
women. They were told not to associate with other Koreans and to "renounce" their cultural past.[10] Unless the husband supports his wife,
which seems to be rare, the women are often alone in their struggle to express their Korean identity. But husbands generally expect wives to participate in building American families, as defined by the husband. In
most cases, this meant minimal acknowledgment of the Korean culture
and identity of the women. Many husbands frowned on things Korean,
insisting that their Korean wives raise "all-American" children and stick
to "all-American" lifestyles. Women spoke of husbands preventing them
from socializing with other Koreans, teaching children the Korean language or dressing them in traditional Korean clothing, observing Korean
holidays, and cooking and eating Korean food.

The demand that women raise "all-American" children is fundamentally a directive that they participate in the social reproduction of Americans with primary loyalties to America and no substantive ties to other
cultures or identities. The expectation that all signs of any connection to
homeland cultures be erased has been particularly strong for Asian immigrants, and accompanies a persistent belief that Asians are the "unas-
similable alien."[11] America has a long history of viewing its members
from Asia as suspect, disloyal aliens, interpreting an affinity for their
homeland culture as disloyalty to the United States.[12] In the context of
the interracial and intercultural marriages of Korean military brides, any
expression of Korean identity on the part of the women or their children
is often taken as rejection of American culture and sometimes even as rejection of their American husbands and fathers. Several women noted
that their husbands seemed to take it personally when they or the chil-

dren expressed a preference for something Korean. Many also noted that husbands were particularly anxious that the children grow up American like them rather than Korean like their wives.

Language and food are two mediums through which Korean military brides are pressured to act American. English was the dominant language in the homes of the women I encountered, even in the few cases where the husband was able to speak Korean competently and even when the wife had minimal competency in English. Likewise, American food was dominant in most homes while Korean food was only minimally present. The predominance of English and of American food is not only for the husband's convenience or because it is "practical" and "makes sense" when living in America. It is also a way for husbands to assert their authority and preside over an "American" family, a way to contain the racial-cultural other that they have brought into the family through marriage.

Mrs. Brennan's husband spoke Korean quite well, so well that even though she spoke minimal English they had little trouble communicating. But, she said, once they arrived in the United States, he stopped speaking it.

> At first he spoke Korean because there was no other way to communicate. But later he wouldn't. When [we first arrived in America] and lived with his family, he would speak in Korean, because then we couldn't communicate in English. But once we arrived on-base, he stopped. If I struggled because I couldn't get what I wanted across, then he would say a word or two in Korean. So I asked him why, why doesn't he speak Korean any more? I'm blabbering in Korean all by myself. He said that if he continued to speak Korean, then I would never learn English. So that's why he stopped speaking Korean, so that I would learn a foreign language.

While she learned English, however, he forgot Korean. They have communicated almost entirely in English since those first months in America, and their two children are able to speak only a few phrases of Korean. Instead of becoming a bilingual family, they have become a primarily monolingual family. This was the case in every family I encountered. Indeed, Mrs. Brennan's husband was unique among the men I met, for most husbands were never able to speak Korean at all, and did not seem to feel any need to learn more than a few stock phrases such as hello and thank you. The expectation was always that the wives should learn English.

Husbands seemed to be particularly adamant that English become the children's mother tongue. The two women I met whose children were somewhat competent in Korean were both divorced and raising their children alone. In addition, their children had spent several years in Korea. Some women said that their husbands told them not to speak Korean to the children, as that would hamper their acquisition of English. Mrs. Orellana, who arrived in 1991, said that her husband wants English to be the first language for their preschool son. Since they are living in America and not Korea she agrees that this makes sense. With the exception of a few words, such as those identifying the Korean foods that he likes, she speaks to her son in English. Speaking English to the children is such an ingrained habit that even women with very limited English skills had no problems switching to English to address their children in the middle of a Korean conversation with someone else. During our interviews, for example, Mrs. Ferriman would repeatedly interrupt herself to address her toddler in English. One woman who arrived in the mid-1980s sent her children to a church-sponsored Saturday school for Korean children, where elementary school children are taught the Korean language and Korean songs and games. But when her husband complained that he didn't understand what his daughters were singing, she stopped sending them to the school. Another woman, who arrived in the late 1960s, recounted an incident early in their marriage. She was singing a Korean lullaby to her newborn daughter when her husband suddenly shouted, "No Korean! She's an American!" That's when she realized, she said, that her child was an American.

Like this mother, most women seemed to accept the definition of their children and their families as American. Their children, for example, are usually given American names. I encountered only two families in which the children were given Korean names. In one family, the eldest child was given a Korean middle name, which I never heard actually used, to follow her American first name, but her younger brother was given only an American name. In the other family, the eldest child was given a Korean name, while the other children were given American names. Although when questioned, mothers would say that their children were half-Korean, they would also define them as simply American, pointing out that the fathers were American and that the children were growing up American. Mrs. Kingston's response regarding her adult daughter, whom she raised alone after a divorce, was typical: "She's half-Korean, but she's American." The overlap of Korean and American patriarchal thinking regarding families and children—the woman leaving her natal family and entering the husband's family upon marriage, the husband as the head of the household, children taking the father's name, the family defined by the presence of the husband—may partially account for this acquiescence. The Western practice of taking the husband's name and giving that name to the children reinforces the definition of the family and of the children as American. When compared to Korean practice, in which the children are given the father's family name but the wife keeps her own family name, the Western practice also emphasizes the incorporation of the woman into an American family, for she has given up her Korean name in favor of her husband's American name.

Acquiescence has its price. Few women are able to speak English fluently and so the use of English as the family language means that they are unable to fully communicate with their husbands and children. Most women said that the greatest difficulty in their marriage stemmed from cultural differences, including language. Even those who said that they had little trouble communicating with their husbands also said that they were not able to satisfactorily communicate their innermost thoughts. No matter how well they speak English, they said, it just doesn't feel like their native language. Many women said that when they get angry or emotional, English becomes that much harder for them and Korean just spills out. They said that they often give in or give up in a conflict because they just don't have the language ability to argue their case in English. Mrs. Peterson cited language as the greatest difficulty in raising her seven-year-old son. Unable to effectively communicate with him, she has trouble disciplining him. She also feels that he does not respect her because he has begun to recognize her inability to fully function in American society. She cannot put together a perfect grammatical sentence and she is unable to help him with his homework. Other women said that sometimes they feel left out when their husbands and children speak to each other in English. "I don't really understand what they are saying, they speak so fast to each other," said one woman.

Many women also find that their ideas about child rearing are denigrated. Whenever they tried to assert their views they were told by both husbands and children, "This isn't Korea, this is America." The authority of place—America—is used to deny maternal authority. These words are also a rebuke that serves to highlight the women's displacement and isolation.

Like many other women, Mrs. Ferriman said that she still could not get used to having her teenage daughters "talk back" to her, but that if she scolded them for disrespecting their mother, they simply replied, "Mom, this is America." She would never have dared to speak her mind to her parents the way they do to her, she said. Other women talked about how they tried to tell their children not to date until at least college, or not to participate in senior cut day, a day when high school seniors deliberately cut class, only to be told by both husbands and children that such activities are normal for Americans. Said Mrs. Weinberg of her teenage children:

> They say what they think, and I say what I think, and that's how the arguing starts. (And your husband?) My husband is *more likely* to tell me to *shhh*. Or sometimes if yelling starts, he might tell the children to listen to their mother. (Do the children obey their father?) Yes, they do, but, I don't know. If they want to, they obey, but if not, they don't.

Later in the interview, she continued:

> I want to raise the children Korean-style, but if I try to do that my husband says I can't. It's America, he says, so don't keep doing that to the children. So . . . most of the time, I just give up. If I keep insisting on that, *you know,* in the end it just becomes a family fight. So now, I guess I've become a little *wise*. When I think that way, it's easier to understand the children, and as my husband says, this is America. And my husband grew up that way, so *what he sees the,* maybe he thinks I'm wrong. So there are many times when I *give up.*

Mother Love

Having raised them to be part of a foreign culture and often unable to fully communicate with them due to language barriers, some women said that they sometimes feel as if their children are not really theirs. "I love them, of course," said one woman, "but they are so different from me, it's hard to understand each other. Sometimes I can't believe that I really gave birth to such children." Nevertheless, every mother I interviewed expressed strong attachments to her children and emphasized her responsibility and status as a mother. They may not have been able to raise their children the way they wished, and they may not have been able to exert the kind of maternal authority they expected to, but they did feel confident that they had fulfilled their maternal responsibilities.

Mrs. Ferriman, for example, said that her backbreaking work as an agricultural laborer was bearable because of her daughter. She discovered, she said, that mother love can overcome any hardship. Mother love can even become the motivation for marriage and divorce. Mrs. Morgan said she struggled to avoid divorce in her first marriage, believing that her eldest son needed both parents. When her second marriage faltered, she hung on to make it work because she did not want her younger sons to also be deprived of their father. Mrs. Vaughn divorced her second husband because he abused her daughter, who was from her first marriage to a Korean man. When she felt that her son needed a father she decided that perhaps it was time to seek another husband even though she had no desire to remarry. Her third husband, she said, was the answer to her desperate prayer for a father for her son. In this emphasis on the mother-child relationship, the women were expressing strong Korean views about the strength of mother love and affirming their identity as mothers. Thus even though they could not raise their children to be Korean with Korean-style maternal authority, and even though they sometimes felt strongly about their children having a father in their lives, they defined themselves as Korean mothers with an emphasis on self-sacrificing mother love and maternal responsibility.

Several women also recounted stories of advocating for their children when they were unfairly punished at school. Invariably, these incidents were related to verbal abuse and racial slurs. And like other instances of racism, they were not confined to any one time period. Mrs. Weinberg, for example, said that her son was once suspended from junior high school for beating up another student. The other boy, however, was not. She found out that her son had beaten up the other boy because he had called him an "Oriental Jew" and other racial slurs.[13] She immediately went to the principal and, asking if the school condemned only physical violence while condoning verbal violence, demanded that either her son's suspension be revoked or that the other boy also be suspended. As a result, the other boy received exactly the same suspension. Mrs. Vaughn remembered that she was often called to school because her son would fight on school grounds. When she asked him why he fought so much, the boy replied that the other children made fun of him, calling him a chink and other racial epithets. The next time she was called to school she told the principal that he should first prevent his other students from making such cruel and ignorant remarks. Then she instructed her son to take his fights off school grounds. She was never called to school again, she said.

These acts of maternal advocacy are also acts of resistance toward racism and toward institutional and social authority that punishes physical violence but allows racist, verbal violence to go unchecked. Mrs. Weinberg's insistence that words can be violent is an expression of what scholars in critical race theory would, in the 1990s, begin to call "assaultive speech," "words used as weapons to ambush, terrorize, wound, humiliate and degrade." Scholars such as Mari Matsuda and Kimberlé Williams Crenshaw have argued that such speech includes racist speech and is not necessarily protected by the First Amendment. Just as the mothers emphasized the harm that racist speech inflicted on their children, these legal scholars emphasize the injury to victims and the infringement of the victims' rights that result from racist speech.[14] By standing up for their children against verbally expressed racism, the women taught their children resistance and self-esteem. Mrs. Weinberg said her son had been depressed and angry when he came home from school that day faced with suspension, but became proud and confident after her encounter with the principal.

Although some women reported that their children seemed to be ashamed of having Korean mothers, many more said that they never sensed such embarrassment from their children. Mrs. Weinberg, who has been a full-time wife and mother since her marriage, said that her children always volunteered her to chaperone school field trips and serve as class mother. Mrs. Brennan said that her children, especially her daughter, have always insisted that they are half-Korean because their mother is Korean. When other children called them "chink," they would be enraged not only for being insulted with a racial slur, Mrs. Brennan said, but also for being mistaken as Chinese: "'Mom,' they would say, 'they are so stupid, they can't even tell that I'm Korean. I'm not a chink, I'm Korean.'"

Refusing Erasure

Such stories reveal that efforts at definition, containment, and erasure are not completely successful. The taunting of school children forces recognition of racial difference even as it provides an opportunity to assert a particular ethnicity. A child's taste for rice and *kimchi*, a mother's eruption into Korean when angry, a wife's insistence on sending money to her family in Korea, these can all be reminders that the Koreanness of the wife and mother has not been erased and that the identity of the family must somehow take this into account.

In addition, military brides do not passively accept efforts to erase their identity as Koreans and to define their family as American. Mrs. Brennan recalled an episode early in her marriage after she and her husband first arrived in America. During an argument when she declared that she would take their daughter and go back to Korea, her husband pointed out that the daughter carried his last name and that therefore she was his daughter and his wife had no right to take her away. "So did I take that lying down?" Mrs. Brennan said. "No way. I raised hell, breaking everything in the house. Then he begged for forgiveness." The husband's claim to their daughter based on her last name can be read as an attempt to erase Mrs. Brennan's role and authority as mother, an expression of patriarchal thinking in which power is vested in the father, through whom descent is traced. Faced with this attempt to deny her claim to her daughter, Mrs. Brennan reacted explosively and ultimately won her husband's concession that she had just as much claim, if not more, to their daughter. Mrs. Brennan later said, "Is it so important that she has only the father's last name? When she marries, she will take another name. But I bore this child for ten months.[15] She is flesh of my flesh and bone of my bone, my blood flows through her veins. That cannot be changed the way a name can." Invoking the visceral, physical connection between mother and child as more permanent than a name that can be changed, Mrs. Brennan was resisting both the patriarchal privileging of the father and the privileging of an American identity over a Korean one.

Mrs. Ferriman recounted an incident during her first pregnancy. Her husband told her to stop eating *kimchi,* a spicy dish of fermented cabbage that is crucial to Korean meals, believing that it would be bad for the baby. Mrs. Ferriman, however, was flabbergasted. Koreans for hundreds of years had eaten *kimchi* with no bad effects on babies, she told him. If she couldn't eat the food she wanted to eat, then she wanted a divorce. Faced with this ultimatum, her husband backed down. Mrs. Brennan talked about cooking soup made from fermented soybeans. She fermented the soybeans herself to make what is called *chunggoogjang* and then used that to make soup with cabbage. The smell, she said, was very strong. When her husband came home from work, he walked through the door holding his nose and saying, "Oh, honey, honey." Mrs. Brennan immediately flew into a rage, asking him, "Well, didn't you know that I eat this kind of stuff? Didn't you know that?" Both Mrs. Ferriman and Mrs. Brennan are among the few women I met who are able to cook and eat in their homes whatever kind of Korean food they please.

Most resistance was not as overt. Many women treasure their links to Korea and savor them when alone, whether by eating meals of Korean food, watching videos of Korean television programs, reading Korean books, or meeting Korean friends. They keep an American house for their husbands, but bring out their Korean things when alone. Mrs. Weinberg, for example, kept an immaculate home with the material comforts of American upper-middle-class status, a home that could be found in any American suburb. But when she was alone, she often ate Korean food, chatted on the phone with other Korean women, and watched Korean videotapes. Another woman told an interviewer:

Whenever my husband is at home, my house is a typical American house. Everything is American. But when he is not home, my house

turns into a miniature Korea. I watch Korean videotapes mostly by myself and sometimes with other Korean friends.[16]

She accepts the containment of her Koreanness but refuses its erasure,
maintaining an "American" home for her husband while defining the
home as "Korean" when he is away.

My Prince Charming? My Lotus Blossom?

But even as husbands expect their wives to maintain American homes
and families, they also seem to want their wives to be "traditional" Asian
women. Believing the stereotype that Asian women are docile, submissive, self-sacrificing, and humble, many husbands anticipated this kind
of behavior from their wives. The women, for their part, believed that
American men were not sexist and treated their wives like queens, and
thus expected a certain measure of equality in their marriages. Each side
seemed to base their expectations on stereotypes about the other. One
survey of fifty Korean woman–American soldier couples found that con-
flicting expectations based on stereotypes regarding Asian women and
American men were a primary source of marital conflict.[17] The women
were searching for Prince Charming, while the men were searching for
Lotus Blossom. Often both sides were disappointed.

Mrs. Ferriman recalled that her husband expected her to always be
waiting on him, just like a maid, and didn't want her to work. But his frequent unemployment and the need to support a growing family rendered
his opposition ineffective. However, she said, the housework remained
her responsibility. Even if he is home all day while she is at work, she
said, he doesn't bother to even wash the dishes or fold the laundry. She
found out, she said, that men, whether Korean or American, are all the
same. This was a common remark among military brides I interviewed.
Many said that their husbands were initially attractive in part because
they believed that American men would not be as sexist and domineering as they had experienced Korean men such as their fathers to be. Some
were impressed by the chivalrous behavior of the American men, who
would open doors, pull out seats, and otherwise behave in a "ladies first"

manner while dating. Their marriages to Americans can be read in part as acts of resistance to the real and perceived sexism of Korean society.

Mrs. Morgan remembered meeting the American boyfriend of a childhood friend, and cited that incident as one reason why she was open to the idea of marriage with an American. During a late-1970s visit to the bowling lanes at the U.S. Army Base in Seoul, she was impressed by his manner:

> He was so good to my friend, you just couldn't find that kind of manner among Korean men. {laughs} And of course, we all believed that they were better than Korean men. We did. That everyone is different, that no matter what country they come from, they're all men, they're all women, men are the same, women are the same, and that every individual is different, we didn't know that. Only life experiences can teach that. So at that time, no matter what anyone said, we wouldn't have known any better.

Believing that they would escape the sexism of Korean men and Korean society, many women found another version of sexism once they married, one imbued with an Orientalist racism. Not only was the chivalrous behavior no longer in evidence, but husbands expected their wives to fulfill the role of a traditional Asian wife as the husbands defined and understood it. Several women remarked that their husbands seemed to think it natural that they, as Korean women, should serve their husbands and shoulder all household duties. As Mrs. Peterson said: "My husband thought that shining the shoes every morning for the husband was just part of Korean culture. He never appreciated my efforts." One woman said that when she told her husband he was taking her hard work for granted, he replied that as a Korean woman she should know that working hard for the family was the right thing to do and that it wasn't necessary to praise someone for doing what comes naturally. The women noted that they were responsible for all housework and childcare duties even when they also held down full-time jobs. To make things worse, many women found that when their husbands got angry, they would resort to insults about Korea, Koreans, and Korean culture as a way of putting their wives down.

Sometimes the conflict between opposing expectations was so severe that it led to divorce. Mrs. Morgan married her first husband in the expectation of a relationship in which she was respected and loved. During their courtship he had been considerate, kind, and attentive. But the longer they were married, she said, the more he changed:

> He was a very conservative person. . . . Just like a Korean, he thought that women should just keep house and that men shouldn't even go near a kitchen, that women should do all of that, that was his *style*. But me, you know, Americans are supposed to be so considerate and really good to their women. [That's how he was at first, and] those were the things that attracted me to him. But that wasn't his true nature, and so it was just too hard for him to keep up the pretense.

After years of alternately struggling to adjust and trying to convince her first husband to change, Mrs. Morgan divorced him. As a full-time housewife, she said, the issue was not so much that he refused to do any housework, but that he became domineering and refused to respect her as an equal.

Divorce and remarriage were common among the women I encountered and interviewed. The majority were divorced from the husbands they had married when coming to America, and a substantial number were remarried to other American men. The given reasons for divorce ranged from spousal abuse to the husband's infidelity. After divorce, many women were left to raise their children alone in a strange and unfamiliar country. In these cases, remarriage was often a survival strategy, and American men were envisioned as the only appropriate marriage partners.

Household tasks were a salient aspect of marriage life, and one that women dwelled on during their interviews and conversations with me. It seemed to symbolize for them their service to their husbands in their role as wife. Mrs. Crispin recalled starching her husband's military uniforms the old-fashioned way every day, with starch she made herself and kept in the refrigerator, and making sure that dinner was always ready at five sharp. Mrs. Peterson said that she felt guilty about not working, since she had heard that among American couples both worked, and so she worked that much harder in the home, making sure that her husband never wanted for anything and never had to lift a finger at home. She went so far as to shine his shoes every morning, she said. When she tried to get him to help with the housework after the birth of their son, she was completely unsuccessful. "He just assumed that all Korean women always do all the housework and take care of their husbands," she said. "He thought that was just the way it was, and he wasn't interested in changing it." She also remembered the pleasure her husband took in his friends' comments as she served them food and drinks whenever they came over to visit or watch sports on TV. They would exclaim that American women don't treat their husbands so well and tell him how lucky he was to have a Korean wife who knew how to treat her husband right.

Some husbands told their wives outright that they preferred Asian women. Mrs. Orellana said that her husband was searching for an Asian wife when she met him, and had always considered Asian women to be more attractive. Mrs. Brennan said that when her husband proposed, she asked him why he wanted to marry a Korean woman. He answered by saying that American women are uppity and arrogant and do not know how to respect their husbands. After they married, he initially opposed her desire to work, saying that women who work become uppity.

Most military brides are only vaguely aware, if at all, of the phenomenon of American men escaping from what they see as "uppity, liberated Western women" for the haven of "docile, submissive Asian women," sometimes through the use of various "mail-order bride" services.[18] Some women even seemed to take pride in their husbands' preference for Asian women, as if it validated the worth of Asian womanhood and compensated somewhat for the humiliation and contempt they often encountered from both Koreans and Americans.

Working Women

A dominant reaction upon arriving in America was disappointment. The America that had glittered so alluringly when viewed from Korea turned out not to be made of gold after all. In place of riches, military brides often found poverty. Their husbands' hometowns were often rural areas that in 1950s America still lacked running water, flush toilets, and electricity. It wasn't that different from rural Korea, and it was sometimes worse than urban Seoul.

When Mrs. Bugelli went to Kentucky with her first husband in the late 1950s, she found a military base in the middle of a poor, rural area. Unable to obtain base housing, they lived in a series of small dwellings that rivaled any in supposedly backward Korea. It was all they could afford on her husband's meager salary as an enlisted man. One home was little more than a one-room shack. They had no hot water and no electricity. Their toilet consisted of a bucket that Mrs. Bugelli would empty once a day.

Discussing her disappointment at encountering an America that seemed less modern than 1980s Seoul, an America where people lived from paycheck to paycheck in dingy trailer homes, Mrs. Morgan said: "When I first came, I was so disappointed. I didn't know the reality of America. There was no way for me to know. I didn't know. The America I saw on TV, the America we saw in dramas, that's all I knew."

But they had little time for disappointment. They had to adjust. That usually included improving their English, learning how to drive, and often, getting a job. But as immigrant women with few job skills and minimal English fluency, their options were limited. Numerous scholars have theorized about the ways in which the U.S. labor market has been and remains segmented along race, gender, and class lines.[19] Although the segmentation has taken different forms in different regions and different time periods, race and gender have been consistently used to relegate certain groups of workers to the lower tiers of the economy. Evelyn Nakano Glenn has shown, for example, that Japanese women, be they immigrants or native born, have been pushed into domestic work throughout much of the twentieth century. Similarly, Korean military brides found themselves limited to unskilled or semiskilled labor with little room for advancement. Often, they were limited to temporary jobs in the informal labor market or to seasonal labor. This held true regardless of when a woman arrived in the United States.

The military brides I met worked largely as unskilled or semiskilled labor in such industries as textiles, agriculture, electronics, confections, toys, and other manufacturing sectors. They had little experience with unions and found that they were often the first to be laid off. Some

women engaged in seasonal labor such as picking blueberries or mush-
rooms, or cleaning beach houses and condominiums for the tourist season. Others took in piecework for the textile industry, sewing clothes at
home for pennies per garment. Still others worked as maids in hospitals
or hotels, as dishwashers in restaurants, as laundresses at dry cleaning
factories, and in other minimum wage work. Those working in the service sector were largely limited to the ethnic Korean economy, mostly as
waitresses or clerks in Korean businesses with Korean customers, such as
restaurants or grocery stores. A few women worked as hostesses in bars
catering either to immigrant Koreans or to American soldiers, and a few
owned such establishments near military bases in the United States, leaving open the question of where the camptown begins and ends. A very
few were able to open their own businesses, operating gift shops, beauty
shops, dry cleaners, and other small stores. They escaped the dead end
of wage labor exploitation through the self-exploitation of small businesses. Most women I spoke with had worked a variety of different jobs,
many worked two or more jobs at once, and nearly all had experienced
layoffs.

In 1954 Mrs. Mullen began working in a candy factory. The men, she
said, made the candies. She recalled seeing them stir huge barrels. The
women wrapped and packed the candies in boxes. The factory made all
kinds of candies, including chocolates. Some candies had to be wrapped,
others had to be packed into boxes. It was a small factory with about fifty
or so workers. Two and a half years after she began working there, it
closed. Her description of the work sounds much like a scene from Char-
lie Chaplin's classic cinematic critique of industrialization, *Modern
Times*. "It was just incredible," she said. "I had never worked like that
before, like a *slave*." She would stand at her station in front of a conveyor
belt, while candies passed by.

> *You have to move fast. . . . You have so many, everybody has so many to
> pack.* You have to hurry, hurry, hurry. If *you, you miss*, then *everybody
> get the miss, then you get big trouble.* Oh, you get yelled at. Really, be-
> cause of that, I had to be on my toes. Yes, *you really work hard, you have
> to work hard.* You have to, you can't be slow. *You know, you can't have
> a job, you have to work everything fast. Everything fast, fast.* At first, the
> work there, when I first started work, I would be so tired when I get

up in the morning. *You stand up in the belt. You work eight hour, you have fifteen minute break, fifteen, ten minutes. Fifteen minute break. Twice.* When I get up in the morning, I would be so tired, my hands would be all swollen, my face all swollen.

After the factory closed, she literally pounded the pavement circulating job applications. She was accepted at a dental lab. Like the candy factory job, this too was minimum wage. The difference, however, was that she was able to learn a skill. She became a dental technician, specializing in making dentures. It took ten years, she said, to feel that she really knew what she was doing because new technologies were introduced and she was constantly learning new things. Besides, she said, *"every case is different, every mouth is different."* She worked there for twenty-six years until the family-owned lab was sold to a corporation. One of her supervisors then opened up her own dental lab and invited Mrs. Mullen to work there. Mrs. Mullen accepted the offer, working there for twelve years until her retirement in 1994.

Of the women I met, Mrs. Mullen had the most stable work history. She was also one of the few to acquire a skill. She herself seemed aware of this, noting that she was lucky to get into dental lab work. Mrs. Bugelli was also able to find stable work. She began in the informal economy by working as a baby-sitter and maid for a white family in the late 1950s, receiving eight dollars a week. Her mother-in-law found her the job. Soon, however, she needed to earn more. The family's husband got her a job at the same shoe factory where he worked. She worked seventy hours a week for seventy dollars. She went from factory job to factory job, making gas stoves, electrical equipment, and other consumer items. Sometimes she left a job for another with higher pay, but usually she was laid off. In the late 1960s, she obtained a job making baby swings, where she stayed for nearly twenty years until her retirement. Although at times she barely had enough money to cover rent and utilities, especially in the years between her divorce and her remarriage, Mrs. Bugelli was fiercely proud of never having taken what she called "a handout" or resorting to welfare.

Most military brides were not able to find steady, secure jobs. Instead, they went from one low-paying job to another. Mrs. Dennison, who arrived in 1958, worked a series of such jobs for several decades as she struggled to raise her children alone after her divorce. She worked everywhere from sewing factories to restaurants, doing everything from washing instruments at hospitals to scrubbing floors in office buildings. She remembered those years as a blur of aching bones, work, and children. Some women acquired a series of civilian jobs on the bases where their husbands were stationed. Mrs. Brennan, for example, worked mostly odd jobs after she came to America in 1975. She worked for three years at an on-base laundry, then for several months at an on-base restaurant. Later she worked at an electronics factory doing quality checks on electronic dictionaries. After a car accident left her arm too weak to grasp and lift even a cup, she began to receive disability benefits. But because the benefits were too small to cover living expenses, she continued to work, this time mostly in the informal economy. She baby-sat the children of other military brides. She also went with other women at her church on seasonal jobs, such as picking blueberries or cleaning beach-front condominiums.

Many women, especially those who were divorced and supported children, worked multiple jobs. During the 1970s, Mrs. Vaughn sometimes worked as many as three jobs at once to support herself and her two children after her divorce. During the 1990s, another woman worked at a factory making latex products during the day and at a dry cleaning store during the evenings and on weekends.

Virtually without exception, the women approached their jobs as a means to earn money and perhaps obtain crucial benefits such as health insurance for their children, not as careers, a means for self-fulfillment, or a way to occupy their time. The few women who said they worked to occupy their time were married to either officers or businessmen and enjoyed middle-class status. That did not, however, allow them to obtain jobs commensurate with their class position, for that position was linked to their husbands. In the labor market, they, like other military brides, were immigrant Asian women with few job skills and limited English ability. Thus they too worked in factories. Although the women generally did not expect to find stimulation or enjoyment in their work, they did want to be respected and they also sought work that gave them flexibility to attend to domestic and family responsibilities. Because they viewed their jobs as a means to an end—supporting their families—they

considered not only their earnings, but also the hours and work conditions as they sought jobs that best suited their needs.

As several scholars of women and work have shown, women must
often take into consideration family responsibilities when they work.[20]
Women with children stayed at home to raise them if they could, entering the labor market as their children entered school. Divorced mothers
depended on other women—the children's paternal grandmother, older
daughters, fellow military brides—to help them care for their children
and also looked for work that gave them flexibility. One woman's daughter lived with her paternal grandmother, seeing her mother mostly on
weekends. Mrs. Vaughn depended on her eldest daughter, old enough to
take care of her younger brother, so that she could work and attend
school. Likewise, Mrs. Ferriman depended on her two teenage daughters
to look after their preschool sister so that she could work during the day
and attend night school.

For women without access to maternal surrogates, the advantage of
home work in the garment industry was being able to work at home and
care for young children. It also served as a side job for women who
needed to earn more money than one minimum-wage job allowed. One
woman said she preferred home work to factory work because of the
flexibility. She worked at night while the children slept or during the
day when they were at school. It also allowed her to take seasonal or temporary jobs. What this meant, however, was that she was almost always
working, for when she wasn't sewing garments, she was doing housework, attending to her two children, or working a temporary job.

Women also wanted to be respected at the workplace. One of the difficulties of factory work, many women said, was being treated like an ap-
pendage to the machine or the conveyor belt rather than a human being.
They often referred to the frantic pace of always having to keep up with
the machine, the lack of freedom to even go to the restroom except during set breaks, and the drudgery of repetition. The advantage of seasonal
labor, despite its lack of benefits, its instability, and its low pay, was
being able to work with friends in a more humane environment. The
women who engaged in blueberry picking every spring and early summer in the 1990s, for example, treated it like an outing although in fact
it was backbreaking physical labor. Picking berries required them to

stoop for hours, and the women often complained of painful backaches and swollen legs and feet. Each Sunday during the blueberry season they would confer on the state of the berries and which fields on which farm needed workers. One woman usually served as an informal information liaison, bringing news from other women who had recently gone blueberry picking. After figuring out who could go and when, they organized car pools and went together, picking the same patch of fields and comparing notes on the way home. They were paid by how much they picked, not by the hour, so they could work at their own pace. Mrs. Brennan, for example, picked slowly due to her poor health and earned only a fraction of what healthier and younger women earned.

Some women actively resisted mistreatment at the workplace. Mrs. Brennan recalled that one foreman at the base laundry where she had worked in the 1970s was often verbally abusive. No longer able to endure it, she lashed out at the foreman and then complained to the supervisor. The supervisor berated the foreman then and there, she said. The verbal abuse stopped, but the foreman found other ways to make her life difficult, she said. For example, he would no longer tell her what needed to be done, forcing her to figure out on her own what work she had to do that day. In an environment where workers depended on the foreman for their daily work assignment, this was untenable. She soon quit.

Although the only jobs they were able to find were in unskilled or semiskilled labor, the women resisted being relegated to the most menial tasks and sought job satisfaction and recognition of their abilities. Soon after she took a job during the late 1960s making rocket parts for a dollar and twenty-five cents per hour, Mrs. Crispin realized that she was always given the simplest and most tedious tasks. She asked if she could try the work that she found most interesting, assembling a crucial part that involved a complicated series of delicate tasks requiring precision and skill and did not tie the worker to a conveyor belt or a machine. She assembled three parts during her lunch hour. The next week, when she asked if she could try the work again, she was told that she had ruined the three parts. Surprised, she asked if the parts bore her initial, for she had carefully written her initial on them. It turned out that the ruined parts had been done by another worker. The three that she had worked on were perfect. She soon came to be the resident expert, and had free rein to work on the parts as she pleased in a work space that became her own domain. She quit after two years because the commute was too difficult. When she returned to the same job several years later, she was given a standing ovation by all the workers and supervisors.

The women also expressed solidarity by helping each other find jobs *Community* and negotiate the difficulties of the labor market. The church women's annual excursions to seasonal labor picking blueberries or cleaning condominiums, for example, was their way of looking out for each other. Not only women from the church but also other military brides in the area had been going on these excursions for as long as the women could remember. They speculated that the excursions began in the early 1980s, but no one I spoke with was sure. In deciding who could take these jobs, they demonstrated a keen sense of fairness based on need. Women with husbands who earned steady incomes and did not need the extra money as much as others were rarely invited on these excursions, while those who were struggling alone to make ends meet were often cajoled into going. Women also informed each other of job openings at their factories or other workplaces. The local hospital, for example, was a regular source of employment for the women at the church. Several had previously worked there and several others were currently employed there as maids, dishwashers, orderlies, and other unskilled or semiskilled positions. An electronics factory and a latex factory were also sources of employment for several women. Many women joked that once a job fell into the hands of a Korean military bride, it would be filled by a succession of Korean military brides until the job itself was eliminated.

Sometimes the women helped each other even at long distance. A group of women sat together after church service one Sunday in 1996, discussing work possibilities. The talk turned to the garment industry, which they felt offered the chance to earn money without turning their children into latchkey kids. One woman had a friend, another military bride, who lived in the rural Northwest and took in garment work. Unfinished garments were sent in the mail to her friend, she said, who sewed them and sent them back. The friend had offered to send some work her way, and she was contemplating the offer. She had previous experience working in sewing factories, so she was certain she could handle the work. The only drawback, she said, was that she had to somehow find the proper sewing machine. She couldn't afford to buy even a used one. One of the other women offered to help her find one, saying that it might be possible to borrow a machine from another woman. Thus, through help from women in disparate geographical locations bound by commonalities in their situation as Korean military brides, the woman was able to find work.

The Joy of Learning

Despite finding themselves dumped into the lower tiers of the economy, many women strove to improve their lives. Some succeeded by learning a skill or scraping together enough money to start a small business. Others pursued an education, hoping to study their way into better jobs. In this way, the women reached for the dreams they had carried with them when they first came to America, dreams dashed by the harsh realities they had encountered. Despite their difficulties, many interpreted their ability to work toward their goals as a blessing, deliberately adopting a positive attitude as a shield against difficulties. As one woman said,

> I could complain about all my hardships, about how awful American life has been. But it's not going to get me anywhere or help me change anything. If I think positively, however, then I can give myself the encouragement to work harder and maybe improve my life. I have to think about the good things so that I can build on them.

Mrs. Ferriman was bitterly disappointed when she arrived in America in 1978. She had hoped for the college education that poverty had denied her in Korea, but in America she found not only poverty but also the burden of supporting a family. Living in a trailer home with an intermittently employed husband and a baby on the way, she felt that she had no choice but to work. Her husband, however, opposed her working, she said, preferring that she stay at home as a housewife. But with economic realities forcing them to near-starvation, she overrode his opposition. Soon after the baby was born, she took a job at a large farm growing Chinese cabbages and radishes. After working all day in the fields under a blazing sun, she would come home to cook dinner for her husband and care for the baby. It was backbreaking work. She spent hours crawling or stooping along endless rows, weeding, thinning, and doing other work as the progression of the season demanded. Each day when she came home and showered, the dirt from the fields would run black, sometimes reddish brown, off her body, often clogging the drain. Her love for her child and her sense of maternal responsibility sustained her: "But I laughed and said, I'm learning stuff I couldn't learn even if I paid for it, I'm not working at Continental Farms, I'm going to Continental Agricultural College."

She continued to work at various jobs for the next fifteen years or so to support herself, her husband, and their children. Her third pregnancy in the early 1990s was difficult and she was unable to work for five months. She seized the opportunity to obtain her G.E.D. With a high school degree in hand, she began to attend night school. At the time of our interview, she was working full-time at a factory and attending college at night. She was studying to become a nurse, and her dream was to become a medical missionary once the children were all grown. She spoke of her expectations about working as a nurse:

If I get to work in a hospital, then surely the kind of people I come into contact with will be different, more educated. And so I'll learn more too. There will probably be a lot of stress too, since I'll have that much more work to do. But I think it'll be rewarding. So I'd like to work in the emergency room, someplace where I can really use the skills I learn. I can see all kinds of cases, broken bones, injuries, all kinds of things. That way I can gain experience. And then, my dream is, when the children are grown, although it's still a long way off, when they are all grown and they've gone to college and everything, I'd like to go somewhere as a medical missionary, go to another country and work as a medical missionary, spend the rest of my life doing good works. I'd like to spend the rest of my life doing something rewarding . . . that's my dream.

Mrs. Ferriman persisted in her studies despite discouragement from her husband. Although he didn't prevent her from going to school, she said, he would complain that she was wasting electricity by studying late at night. With a full-time job and three children, however, late at night was the only time available for studying. She was still learning to ignore his discouraging remarks, she said. Studying also brought her newfound confidence. As she struggled over the difficult vocabulary in her chemistry and biology courses, she had been afraid of failure. How could she possibly compete with native speakers? But she received good grades, and soon realized that native speakers also had trouble with scientific jargon and resorted to rote memorization as she did. She gained confidence in her abilities, lamenting that the only thing she really needed was more time.

When Mrs. Vaughn arrived in America, she found herself as helpless as a child. With the assistance of other women, she learned to drive and found a job. While working two jobs and raising two children, she also attended beauty school. It was a familiar trade, for she had once operated her own beauty parlor in Korea. With her new license, she went looking for a job:

> They all wanted to know if I had a *following*, you know, steady customers. But I just got my license, how could I have a *following*? Every place I went, they asked about a *following*. Finally, I found a job at one place.

Mrs. Vaughn soon developed a following, and she opened her own beauty shop in a section of her home. She continues to accept some of her original customers, even though she no longer runs a business. At the time of the interview, she was immersed in starting a church for military brides and their families, with bilingual services held in the basement of her sprawling, semirural home and conducted jointly by a Korean minister and an American one.

Beauty school was only the first of the schools that Mrs. Vaughn was to attend. When English courses for immigrants became available in the early 1980s, she began taking them at her local community college. She has taken numerous courses in English composition and conversation. After much effort, she received her G.E.D. Squeezing in her studies between work and family responsibilities, she took sometimes one course a year, sometimes two. She recalled working all day, and then hurriedly driving to evening courses while making do with a hamburger for dinner. By that time, she was raising two children alone. Her daughter, old enough to fix dinner and watch the younger child, made it possible for her to study. At the time of our interview, she was still taking courses, this time hoping to earn a college degree. Laughing, she said that given her pace of one or two courses a year, it would be a long time before she finished. But, she added, she loved to study. "I don't envy other people anything, except studying," she said. "I envy people who had the opportunity to study."

Mrs. Vaughn describes herself as alternately frightened and exhilarated by her studies. She is frightened that she will not be able to keep up with the class and that she is too old to study. She is exhilarated because she loves to learn, and because even at her age she has the opportunity to continue her education. When I asked her what she enjoyed most about studying, she replied:

That I can learn one more American word. *I understand words.* The new, unfamiliar words, the *vocabulary* that I didn't know at the start of the semester, I come across them as I read for class and I look them up in the dictionary. The next semester, I don't have to look them up. I know them. That's so thrilling. Ah, I've improved this much. *I earned this much knowledge.*

Mrs. Vaughn, who has taken psychology, history, and other courses at her local community college, cited American history as one of her favorites:

I like history, American history. In Korea, I never got to learn our history. The Japanese came and we studied Japan, so after studying Japanese *history*, then came the liberation and everything was chaotic. So it's so interesting to learn history here, it's so much fun.

"I'm Proud to Say I'm Korean"

Despite their initial disappointment with America, most of the women said that they preferred it to Korea. This declaration was often made out of the blue, in the middle of a discussion about something else or during a brief lull in the conversation. They emphasized their achievements—

families raised, skills learned, hard-won independence—and downplayed the hardships. They usually cited opportunity and individual
freedom as the reason for their preference. Said Mrs. Ferriman:

> In America, women can live their own lives while they . . . they can
> work toward their dreams. If they want to do something, they can do
> it no matter how old they are, they can continue to improve them-
> selves. They can continue to learn. There's no end to learning.

This professed preference for American life, however, was not accompanied by self-identification as American, nor was it necessarily accompanied by a belief that America was superior to Korea or that they had done
the right thing by marrying American men. Rather, their preference may
be better interpreted as self-validation of the lives they have lived. After
all, if they believe that their lives would have been better in Korea, that
is tantamount to saying that their lives in America have been failures. No
one I met was prepared to judge herself a failure. Even those who, like
Mrs. Ferriman, said they would never have married an American if they
had known what awaited them and that they always tell younger Korean
women to marry Korean men, looked over their lives with satisfaction.
Even those women who were in the midst of difficult times persisted in
believing that they would somehow overcome and brighter days would
be ahead. Whatever difficulties and hardships they faced or are facing,
they insisted on making the most of their lives.

Thus their conclusion that American life was preferable was not necessarily a judgment about America, but rather a judgment about themselves and the achievements they had wrought out of their situations. In
that light, Mrs. Ferriman's declaration that women can make something
of themselves in America is better interpreted to mean that she herself
has been able to make something of herself in America. Indeed, many
women were sharply critical of America, citing its materialism, individualism, laziness, and even hypocrisy. A common criticism was that
Americans were content with mediocre lives and have no interest in
working for improvement. Mrs. Ferriman, for instance, said she simply
did not understand why so many Americans, especially those she met in
her primarily working-class neighborhood, spent so much time playing
and doing nothing. Americans, she felt, were too wrapped up in fleeting,

individual pleasure. It bewildered her that while she could see so many opportunities available, Americans either saw nothing but obstacles or were too lazy to take advantage of opportunities. With this critique, the women position themselves as superior to the very Americans who often look down on them and affirm their own values of hard work, thirst for education, and ambition to improve their lives. Furthermore, the women's positive attitude is itself a form of resistance, for they are resisting despair, refusing defeat, and viewing their lives as meaningful and their futures as full of hope.

Along with this validation of the lives they have lived is a profound attachment to Korea and their Korean identity. Mrs. Pulaski, who expressed strong views about her preference for American life, said that she prefers her permanent resident status and does not wish to become an American citizen. Although she had considered acquiring citizenship so that she could more easily bring over her daughter from a previous marriage to a Korean, she decided against it, she said, because she had no interest in transferring her allegiance from Korea to America.

It's just, I'm Korean. I still have pride in being Korean. Because I love Korea. Why should I, why should a Korean become an American citizen? I have that kind of negative reaction, so I didn't. If I had wanted to, I would have already done it. But I still think that Korea is the best, isn't that right? Think about it. Why should I become an American citizen? Isn't that so?

This too can be read as resistance. She is insisting on her identity as a Korean while simultaneously laying claim to America as her home. It is her way of refusing to abandon Korea as the price of living in America. Citizenship for her is more than a legality that she can use for her own ends. It is a mark of special commitment and belonging. In her current dislocation as an immigrant, she has latched upon citizenship as a tie both tangible and symbolic to her Korean homeland and identity even as she continues to choose to reside in America.

I call the tie of legal citizenship tangible because it has concrete material effects on the way people can order their lives, the countries they can enter, where they can live, how they are identified by nation-states, the kind of identification papers they hold, and so forth. For example, Mrs.

Pulaski called on the material artifacts of citizenship and its psychological ramifications when she cited having a Korean passport as comforting. It would be strange, she said, to have an American passport and thus be identified as a foreigner when she enters her own homeland. At the same time, legal citizenship for her is symbolic because it is largely a background fixture, having little effect on everyday life and serving primarily as a badge of belonging to a particular ethnic community (Koreans) defined by a nation-state (South Korea), although not necessarily confined to that nation-state.

Negotiation and resistance can be seen in many women's discussions about their identities. Mrs. Mullen spoke at length about how being Korean is something that you are born with, something that you cannot change regardless of what you think or how you live. Even though her lifestyle may not have much that is identifiably Korean, she said, she is Korean because it is in her blood. *"You know, and I'm not shamed to say I'm Korean. I'm proud to say I'm Korean,"* she said. But she is not interested in returning to Korea to live, and said of America: *"Feels like, this is my home. Feels like I was born here, I live here so long, you know."* Although she said she finds incomprehensible the children of immigrants who claim to be American and not Korean, she also said, "Well, *everybody live here is American, you know,* maybe that's what they mean." She is Korean because she was born Korean, and she is American because she lives in America. She never mentions legal citizenship in her discussion of identity, indicating that, for her, it is not relevant. What is relevant are ties of blood, culture, and residence, ties that are constructed as material and concrete as opposed to the irrelevant legality of her unmentioned citizenship. These ties bring her membership in both Korea and America, and with this claim she identifies herself as belonging to more than one imagined community. She is refusing the exclusionary demands of both American and Korean societies and their attached nation-states to choose one over the other. Her negotiation of this complex terrain of membership and identity broadens, at least rhetorically, the definitions of both Korean and American and who can lay claim to those identities.

Other military brides describe themselves as wanderers, people neither here nor there but stuck in limbo. "We're not completely adjusted to American culture, and yet we are losing touch with Korean culture," said Mrs. Ferriman, who arrived in 1978. "In a word, we are like strangers, wanderers, just like wanderers, people who are drifting." For Mrs. Ferriman, language is a sign of her wanderer status. She complained that even though her English is far from fluent, her Korean is also becoming rusty. "Here in the middle, I'm not really an American, and yet I'm no longer fluent like a Korean," she said. "It's like we're floating in the middle somewhere." Here too, however, is a negotiation and a resistance, for Mrs. Ferriman refuses to cover up her wanderings and her feeling of being in limbo. Although she too says that she remains Korean, she expresses her sense of losing touch with things Korean. And while she also says that her home is now in America, she recognizes that here too she is not culturally fluent in things American. Even as women like Mrs. Ferriman focus on what they call their in-between position to express their sense of loss and the tenuousness of their attachments, they are claiming membership in multiple imagined communities, refusing to choose either Korea or America over the other.[21]

Surviving Resistance, Surviving Achievement

Although life in America wasn't like "sitting on a gold cushion,"[22] and their American husbands were not exactly the Prince Charmings they had dreamed of, military brides did more than survive. They engaged in a steady, quiet resistance to wrest some measure of power and control over their lives. While their resistance and their achievements are not always obvious, the women were able to maintain their dignity and sense of self throughout their American encounters.

CHAPTER 4

Cooking
American,
Eating
Korean

In the United States, where people of different cultures, races, and ethnicities have encountered each other since the beginning, food is a signifier of difference and identity.[1] It is a terrain where ethnicity is contested, denigrated, and affirmed. It is an arena of struggle between Americanization and adherence to native cultural ways, where the demands are often either-or, but the lives lived are more often constructed from pieces of both.[2]

The experiences of Korean military brides with food mirror their broader experiences as interculturally and interracially married immigrant women. As military brides learned to cook and eat American foods, they enacted a process of assimilation that was demanded of them by husbands, in-laws, and even children who had the weight of the dominant American culture behind them. The marginalization and stigmatization of Korean food within their households represent their cultural isolation within their own families. The incorporation of "palatable" Korean foods into American meals illustrated their own incorporation into their American families, their Korean culture and identity literally consumed as cultural accessories in a process that cultural critic bell hooks has called "consumer cannibalism." At the same time, their perseverance in cooking and eating Korean food and their insistence on maintaining a Korean identity testifies to the limits of the United States' ongoing project of Americanization.

Historian Donna Gabaccia's study of American foodways, *We Are What We Eat*, celebrates the incorporation of ethnic foods into mainstream American culture, drawing a picture of a harmonious and peaceful America full of what she calls multiethnics, people of different backgrounds who eat foods from different backgrounds. In her picture, conflict between native-born Americans and immigrants as expressed in "food fights"—particularly during the first half of the twentieth century—is a thing of the past. No longer do Americans turn up their noses at different foods and try to Americanize the eating habits of immigrants. Instead, they enthusiastically adopt new foods introduced by new immigrants. Eating a melange of ethnic foods has become the American thing to do. Marriage across cultural and ethnic boundaries is one way, she suggests, that multiethnic peoples and foods are produced.

The experiences of military brides, however, illustrate that "food fights" are not yet over; they are simply conducted more quietly and with less fanfare than in the past. Military brides' narratives reveal that a matrix of power relations surrounds the choice of what foods are cooked and eaten in the families that have resulted from interracial and intercultural marriages.

"Nothing to Eat"

The first part of the story is that of the deprivation that began with the physical absence of Korean food. Korean military brides who immigrated to the United States in the post–World War II decades of the 1950s and 1960s, a time when the proverbial land of plenty was basking in unprecedented economic wealth, told me that "here, there was nothing to eat." For these women, accustomed to the tastes and smells of Korean food, American food was not food at all. Like the overwhelming majority of Korean immigrants—indeed, like most immigrants from any country—they craved the foods of their homeland. Women who immigrated in later decades experienced few of the difficulties of their predecessors, for Korean food could be found relatively easily at stores and restaurants catering to the burgeoning Korean immigrant population. Many of them had already experienced American food in Korea, where hamburgers and pizza, along with McDonald's and KFC, became well known to urban dwellers beginning in the 1980s. Nevertheless, these women also spoke of missing Korean food, for not everything Korean could be found everywhere in America.

The very absence of Korean food in the midst of a bounty of American food is itself a powerful force for Americanization, for immigrants are faced with a choice between eating the food that is available or starving. The choice is obvious. The women ate American food. But their consumption of American food was not necessarily a sign of their Americanization. Even though they ate it, they did not necessarily like it. The women not only longed for Korean food, they also searched for it, invented ways to replicate it, and gave it an emotional loyalty they never developed for the American food they ate out of necessity.

Their longing for Korean food is a visceral expression of their longing for the homeland they left behind. The primary meaning of Korean food for most Korean immigrants, be they military brides or not, seems to be that of homeland and identity. In his study of Korean Americans, sociologist Pyong Gap Min notes that food and language become the mediums through which cultural identity is maintained and expressed. A study of second-generation Korean youth in North America found that kimchi, a quintessential Korean food, was one of two aspects of Korean culture that they wanted to preserve in their own lives.[3] This identification of food, and kimchi in particular, with homeland and identity can also be found among Koreans in South Korea. Kimchi, a spicy vegetable side dish that has been the focus of cultural embarrassment for its allegedly noxious smell and strong taste, was declared the national food during the 1988 Seoul Olympics. A newspaper report in the early 1990s showing that many elementary school children were not fond of kimchi provoked a public outcry and criticism of increasing westernization.[4]

For the military brides who arrived during the 1950s and 1960s, a time when immigration from Korea and other Asian countries was still legally restricted and Korean communities were small and mostly limited to Hawaii and California, the biggest shock was the food. Suddenly, every meal became a painful reminder of having left home. Not only did the ab-

sence of Korean food intensify their feelings of homesickness and loneliness, but it also caused physical problems: American food was so unpalatable that eating was difficult and hunger was a constant companion.
One woman, who arrived by boat in 1951 with her soldier husband,
said that the most difficult thing during her first years in the United
States was craving Korean food, but having to eat American food. Like
many other Koreans, she found American food to be heavy, greasy, and
bland. The smell and taste of butter, used in so many American foods,
was distasteful. "[A]t that time," said Mrs. Mullen, "I was very homesick, and the most difficult thing was food, eating, yes. It was difficult,
back then."

The craving for Korean food was so strong that even her dreams were
all about food:

Food, Korean food, very very . . . I think about it, I dream about it, in
my dreams there is no Korean food, or I am eating Korean food, or Korean food appears, this is what I dream about. When I first came, what
I survived on was, well, rice was, you know, but I survived on *American pickle*. And *spaghetti*, that's what I survived on. It was terrible, I
wanted so badly to eat [Korean] food, it was terrible. Oh, I suffered
very very much.

Searching for something that would provide the sharp, salty, and
spicy tastes of Korean food, Mrs. Mullen had settled for pickles and
spaghetti.[5] Pickles and spaghetti, however, weren't enough to sustain
her. Mrs. Mullen noted in a later conversation that she lost weight during those first years in America. This appears to be common among military brides of her generation. For some, the absence of Korean food
meant near starvation. Mrs. Crispin, who arrived in 1965, noted that
"[b]ack then, you know, there was lots of really good American food, but
when you first come here, you starve." No matter how good and plentiful the American food was, she emphasized, military brides starved for
lack of Korean food. Mrs. Crispin continued:

When I first came from Korea, I was one hundred thirty pounds. I was
a little heavy then. But I lost more and more weight, and finally I went
down to ninety pounds. When I went back to Korea after four years, I

was ninety-five pounds. Once I got sick, and I went down to eighty pounds. Then I went back up to ninety-five pounds [at which point she returned to Korea], then one hundred pounds, then one hundred ten. So I stayed there, it's been several decades.

Explaining the reasons for her weight loss, she said, "I came here and I couldn't even finish a hamburger. My insides felt all heavy and greasy and all I could think of was *kimchi*." Physically unable to eat sufficient quantities of American food to keep up her weight, and unable to find a steady supply of Korean food, Mrs. Crispin slowly starved during her first years in America and lost about a third of her original body weight. At a height of approximately 5 ft. 6 in., one hundred thirty pounds is not overweight and ninety pounds is anorexic. The weight she has maintained since then, one hundred ten pounds, is below the norm for her height. Mrs. Crispin attributed her low weight to the eating habits she developed during her first years in America, saying that she learned to get along with small quantities of food and that her appetite seems to have decreased.

Craving for Korean food was accompanied by homesickness and a loneliness that resulted from the absence of other Koreans in their lives. Both Mrs. Mullen and Mrs. Crispin spoke in the same breath about missing Korean food and missing Korean people. Mrs. Mullen said that "at that time, I was very homesick, and the most difficult thing was food, eating, whew! It was difficult, back then." Her discussion of food was punctuated by her discussion of people, as she noted that she had no relatives or friends in America and that there were no other Koreans. "*Yeah, I was very, don't have nobody,*" she said.

For Mrs. Crispin as well, missing Korea and missing Korean food were intertwined:

Back then, I was always thinking about Korea, in Korea this is delicious and that is delicious, just thinking about all the delicious things. So when we [she and other Koreans] sit and talk, the talk starts with food and ends with food. In Korea the pears are delicious and so are the apples, and so are the fried pancakes and so on. We talk about this the whole time and then go home, after just smacking our lips the whole time. We were lonesome for people, very lonesome, but back then eating was a big shock as well. The food just wasn't to our taste.

The opportunity to eat Korean food came with meeting other Korean people, again illustrating the connection between food and companionship. For Mrs. Mullen, that opportunity came through the first Korean woman she met in America, a woman from Seoul. The friend would sometimes go shopping in New York—a distance of some four hours by car—for Korean food. The two women would then cook and eat Korean food together.

Opportunities to eat Korean food for Mrs. Crispin also came with the first Korean woman she met in America. Noting that there were no Korean grocery stores in the area at the time, she talked about going to the American supermarket with her friend. There, the friend would go through the frozen food case, looking for a frozen fish similar to the Korean *dongtae* or pollock. If she found something similar, she would buy it and cook a Korean fish stew. "If it tasted like *dongtae* stew," said Mrs. Crispin, "then she would call me and tell me to come over. Even though she lived thirty minutes away, I would hurry and go, so that I could eat that stew."

The craving for Korean food was so intense, Mrs. Crispin said, that she would eat fish barbecued on a grill, sucking on the bones and searching for any hint of the taste of Korean barbecued fish. The lack of Korean food was compounded by the inability to cook Korean food. Like many other military brides I interviewed, both Mrs. Mullen and Mrs. Crispin had never learned to cook Korean food.[6] So even though some of the ingredients necessary to make Korean food, such as soy sauce, soybean curd, and Korean vegetables could be found at grocery stores in urban Chinatowns, many women were unable to duplicate the tastes of home.

In this context, Korean food was priceless, and those who had it treasured it. Mrs. Crispin related the story of a woman who had brought a jar of pickled peppers with her from Korea. The woman would eat an entire meal of just one large bowl of rice and a single pickled pepper. "She would touch the pepper once, suck her finger, and eat a mouthful of rice, that's how she ate an entire bowl of rice with just one pepper. Because otherwise the pickles would get eaten too fast," she said. Mrs. Crispin also noted that the status of vegetables and meat would be reversed if the meat was American and the vegetables were Korean.

At that time, if you had a piece of steak this big {she gestures with her hands} that was left over, you would just throw it out, but if you had even one piece of *kimchi* left, you couldn't bring yourself to throw it away. If *kimchi* is left over, you always save it. But if steak is left over, you throw it away. You don't even want to look at it again, so you throw it away. {laughs} And if some Korean vegetables are left over, no matter how small an amount, then you always save that too.

Red pepper paste and soybean paste, two crucial seasonings in Korean food, were virtually impossible to find during those early years. Unlike soy sauce, they were not available in Chinatown stores, for they are not part of any tradition of Chinese cooking. But the women were inventive and passed their inventions on to each other. Mrs. Crispin talked about learning to make imitation red pepper paste.

There was this *unni*[7] I know from Kentucky, she dried the heels from loaves of bread, and when she had accumulated enough, she would pour soy sauce over it. {laughs} When the bread became all soggy, she would sprinkle crushed red pepper and mix it all up. And then you call that red pepper paste and eat it! Even that, only those who knew how to make it could eat it. People like me, we depended on the generosity of others. We would ask, how did you make this? And ask them for a little.

The taste was not the same as the real stuff, of course. It could not be used for making stews, only as a condiment for rice. Mrs. Crispin once gave a new arrival a small container of imitation red pepper paste. This military bride, able to stomach neither the smell of Western red peppers nor the goo parading as a Korean seasoning, gave it away to another military bride. Mrs. Crispin reported with a smile that the woman, starved for Korean food, later asked the second woman to return the imitation red pepper paste. The second woman refused, and the first woman deeply regretted her previous action. Back then, Mrs. Crispin said, the real stuff was so scarce that even imitations were prized. It may not have tasted like the real thing, but it was better than the alternative of American food or, as was the case in U.S. bases in Europe, European food.

The women were inventive with other foods as well. The anchovies found in canned or bottled Italian foods, for example, substituted for the salted anchovies used to make *kimchi*. They would also go to stores in Chinatown in search of Asian foodstuffs. Mrs. Crispin recalled using canned mung bean sprouts to make a kind of soup, and buying cans of *kimchi* and packages of noodles at a Japanese grocery store that catered to Japanese business executives and their families. Sometimes she would make a clear beef soup using lots of garlic and red pepper.

Later arrivals found Korean food easier to find, for by the mid-1970s many American cities were home to sizable populations of Korean immigrants, and thus sported Korean groceries and restaurants. They also tended to be more familiar with American food, especially those who came in the late 1980s and 1990s, decades when Korea's urban landscape saw dramatic increases in restaurants selling American-style fast food. This may partly explain why they were better able to keep down a hamburger and live for a few days—or more—without Korean food. In general, the later the date of arrival, the less likely it was that food would be a major culture shock. Nevertheless, many of the later arrivals also spoke about food when they talked about missing home and being lonely. The simple fact that they were surrounded—both in their own homes and out in the larger society—by American food rather than Korean seems to have been part of the homesickness. One woman noted that no matter how prevalent Korean food has become in America, it can't compare with the prevalence of American food. In Korea, she pointed out, one can find Korean food anywhere and everywhere, and the variety is seemingly endless. But even in the so-called multicultural 1990s in America, one still has to know exactly where to look to find Korean food and the repertoire available in Korean restaurants is depressingly standardized and bland.

Even when Korean food was available in America, it apparently wasn't the same. Many of the military brides I interviewed stated that Korean food in America just doesn't taste as good as Korean food in Korea. Notice the way that Mrs. Crispin described Korea and Korean food: "Back then, I was always thinking about Korea, in Korea, this is delicious and that is delicious. . . . In Korea the pears are delicious and so are the apples, and

so are the fried pancakes and so on." It was Korea she was always thinking about, not Korean food. It wasn't Korean food that tastes good and
which they missed, it was food in Korea. Location was important.

This is the context in which military brides' statements that Korean
food in America doesn't taste as good as Korean food in Korea must be
understood. The issue here is displacement. Displaced from its home,
the food apparently loses a certain something. The women's craving for
Korean food is linked to a longing for a return home, to a time before
their displacement as strangers in a strange land.[8] While talking about
how they longed for Korean food, many women also talked about how
they often just wanted to go back home. In short, Korean food in America just isn't the same as Korean food in Korea. Both its presence and its
absence in America served to emphasize that America was not home, at
least not yet.

Eating American

Throughout the first half of the twentieth century, immigrant and ethnic
women were subject to native-born American women's attempts to
Americanize immigrant families by teaching the women how to cook and
eat American food. It was an urgent project, for Americans feared that
America would be "swallowed by foreigners" unless they were properly
Americanized. The fact that America at that time was more a conglomer-
ation of regional cultures than a unified national culture made America
seem vulnerable to foreign influence and thus endowed the project with
greater urgency. America had to hurry and Americanize the immigrants
before they "foreignized" America.

It was also a zero-sum project, for—in keeping with the prevailing
sentiment that immigrants must shed their old identities in order to become American—it was not enough to add American food to one's diet.
One also had to subtract or substantially alter the familiar foods of home.
It was also an endeavor that disguised its fundamental ethnocentricity
and nativism under the progressive banner of good health, science, and
economical housekeeping. Asian and southern European women were
told to feed their families more milk for proper nutrition. Italian women

were told not to cook meat, cheese, beans, and macaroni together because the combination allegedly hindered digestion. Mexican women
were told to use less tomato and pepper to make blander foods that were
purportedly easier to digest and kinder to the kidneys, and were urged
to stop the allegedly unsanitary practice of dipping with tortillas into the
same pot at the dinner table. And everyone was urged to eat plain, bland,
thrifty foods such as mashed potatoes and baked beans.[9]

In these admonitions to immigrant women by American women home
economists, nutritionists, and other professionals can be seen several
strong and interconnected ideas about food. One is the gendered con-
ceptualization of food preparation as the women's domain; another is the
endowment of food with cultural properties, such that what one eats and
how it is eaten become markers of group identity.[10] What one ate clearly
marked one as either a backward, ignorant immigrant or an educated,
modern American. Furthermore, the belief that educating immigrant
women would lead to educating and thus Americanizing their entire immigrant families rests on gendered assumptions about women as the
bearers of culture and thus the mediating force for Americanization. Although these Americanization-through-food projects fizzled as fears of
immigrant hordes receded during the 1940s and 1950s and disparate regions became increasingly bound within a "national culture" dissemi-
nated through the mass media and mass commerce, the underlying assumptions about food, gender, and Americanization have remained very
much in force.

Thus Korean military brides found themselves subject to pressures to
Americanize that were more overt than the absence of Korean food. These
pressures came not from social workers, home economists, and other institutional representatives who could be safely ignored within one's own
home and ethnic community, but primarily from husbands, children,
and mothers-in-law, people difficult, even dangerous, to ignore precisely
because they were intimate family members. There is remarkable consis-
tency in the women's narratives regardless of the time period in question.
A woman who came in the 1990s was just as likely as a woman who came
in the 1950s to face demands that she cook primarily, or even only, American food. The one difference is that the husbands and in-laws of women
who arrived in later decades seem to have been more open to incorpo-
rating selected items of Korean food into the household repertoire. This

seems connected to a general revival of interest in ethnic foods, however, and is not related to any desire to allow Korean women to maintain their Korean identity.[11]

Although they married Korean women, most husbands do not seem to have been interested in a Korean wife complete with all the cultural trappings of customs, food, and language. As discussed in chapter 3, they were looking for women with the traditional feminine values of submissiveness and deference to male authority, and believed that Asian women had such characteristics. They wanted wives who would serve them roast beef and potatoes, with English and a smile. In short, they wanted the traditional, all-American housewife of a bygone era and believed that Korean women—whom they viewed as docile and subservient—would be able to fulfill that role.[12]

The ostensible goal of Americanization, therefore, was to make sure that the foreign women would be able to properly fulfill their role as wives and mothers of Americans. Underlying this goal were fears that a foreign wife, unless properly Americanized, would "foreignize" her husband and children. One survey of Korean military brides found that the majority experienced conflict with their parents-in-law, and that the conflict stemmed from the in-laws' demands that the women "renounce" their Korean culture in favor of American culture.[13] In general, in-laws were not interested in bicultural families; they wanted American grandchildren.

Expressed in the language of teaching a new wife or new daughter-in-law how to please her husband and adjust to her new environment, the racial and cultural power dynamics of Americanization were effectively hidden in the gender dynamics of marriage. In this matrix of intersecting and overlapping power relations—between mainstream American culture and a "foreign," minority culture, between a neoimperialist United States and a neocolonial Korea, between American men and Korean women, between husband and wife, between primary breadwinner and dependent—Korean women were almost always at a disadvantage. Their acceptance of gender roles often led them into compliance, making overt expressions of Americanization on the part of husbands or in-laws unnecessary. But in acceding to these pressures, as did most of the women I encountered, they were not necessarily undergoing a willing or total Americanization. Rather, their compliance was part of the complex negotiation in which they alternately resisted and complied, a process discussed earlier.

As married women, they took for granted the expectation that it was their duty to cook for their husbands and that this meant cooking what husbands liked to eat, even if it was the very food that they themselves found foreign and unpalatable. Learning to cook American food, an experience that one woman described as universal for Korean military brides, was one that set them apart from their other immigrant compatriots in an important way. Most Korean immigrants were not interested in learning how to cook non-Korean foods, but instead focused on recreating Korean dishes in an American immigrant setting.[14] For military brides, however, learning to cook American food became one of their primary tasks as they learned how to become good American wives.

Numerous studies on food and mealtimes show that it is the women who are responsible for feeding the family, and that part of that responsibility includes preparing meals that the husband likes. The same dynamic seems to be at work in the families of Korean military brides, but with a significant cultural twist. The existing studies focus on families where the husband and wife come from the same general cultural background. Thus food preferences do not fall along a cultural divide, nor do they serve as markers of ethnic and racial difference. This is not so for the families of Korean military brides, where food preferences usually fall along cultural, racial, and ethnic lines. Since most American husbands prefer to eat American food, and some even dislike Korean food intensely, whatever Korean cooking ability the wives may possess is virtually useless. In accordance with the husbands' preferences, family meals are characterized by the presence of American food and the absence of Korean food. The wives must either eat American food with their husbands, or eat Korean food alone. Their biracial children also tend to prefer American food. Her son, Mrs. Peterson reported, doesn't like to eat rice, stating that he is an American boy and therefore must eat bread. This seven-year-old boy has already singled out food as a marker of identity, refusing to eat food that he considers foreign to his sense of self. The male prerogative of the husband coupled with the cultural dominance of America leave little room for Korean food at the dining tables of these intercultural and interracial families. Food is a marker of difference and of the accompanying power inequities of which every meal is a potential reminder.

Sociologist Marjorie DeVault has noted that feeding the family literally produces the family. It is at meals that the unity of the family is expressed and reinforced, that the individual members feel themselves to be part of a whole. Thus women's work of feeding the family is more than just nourishing bodies, it maintains a particular social unit, the family. But this family is also a cultural space. Therefore, to expand on this theory, the family produced, expressed, and reinforced in meal after meal has a particular cultural character. In feeding their families, wives and mothers are keepers of their families' particular cultures. This is a particularly important role for immigrant and minority women, who are designated the guardians of ethnic identity for the family and the maintainers and transmitters of homeland culture.[15] The cooking and serving of foods "from home" form an important part of this role. The role of food in reinforcing and expressing identity holds true not only for minority ethnic groups, but also for the white, European American majority.[16] It is the cultures of the husbands, be they mainstream white European American or minority ethnic American, that is expressed daily with every family meal. Thus, unlike other immigrant women, military brides become the transmitters not of their own familiar cultures, but of the foreign cultures of their husbands. This transmission, this production of family and expression of unity that takes place daily with every meal in interracial and intercultural marriages, is largely predicated on the suppression of the Korean identity and culture of the military brides.

It is a suppression that most military brides I interviewed seemed to regard as necessary for the sake of the family and the marriage. In partial acceptance of the definition of their families as American, they went about the task of learning to prepare American foods. Despite their own distaste for most American food, learning to cook it was so important that many women considered this task to be at the center of their adjustment to American life. This was also true of military brides who arrived in later years and had few problems eating American food. None of the women I interviewed had ever cooked American food before they married their American husbands, and they all said that they spent a great deal of time and effort learning how to cook to suit their husbands' tastes. Those who could not cook Korean food, or cooked it poorly by their own estimation, noted regretfully that they had had no chance to learn because they were preoccupied with cooking American food for their families. For these women, learning to cook American food had the result of blocking their acquisition of Korean cooking skills. An important expression of culture and self, food, thus changed dramatically for these women as a result of intermarriage and subsequent migration to the husbands' country.

At the same time, every woman I interviewed expressed pride in her ability to cook American food. Several women, such as Mrs. Goldin, said they cooked American food better than Americans, and many noted that their husbands complimented them on their cooking. This pride in meeting the expectations of their husbands and in acquiring new skills cannot be easily dismissed. It can be read as a partial, if problematic, resistance to the denial of Korean identity that their participation in the daily mealtime rituals of family production entails. They may be suppressing their Korean identity, but they are actively building a new life around their American husbands. By learning to cook American food and fulfilling the roles of mother and wife, they were also living up to the traditional ideal of Korean womanhood, which dictates self-sacrifice for the sake of the family.[17] Thus, learning to cook American food and the denial of ethnic self which that entails can be read as an ironic affirmation of their Korean womanhood, a merger of their struggle to be both good American wives and good Korean women.

In one case, the husband served as the cooking teacher. Mrs. Goldin, who arrived in America in 1972, told of being taught American cooking by her husband, who had once worked as a cook. Their first two years of marriage were spent at the U.S. military base in Okinawa, and her time was spent keeping house and learning to cook.

Mrs. Goldin, who had grown up in a convent orphanage in Seoul, knew nothing about cooking when she married. She described her husband as very picky and demanding about his food, saying that he never ate leftovers and refused to eat the same thing during the same week. As a result, she had to learn how to cook a wide variety of foods. Laughing, she said that even though the marriage ended after only a few years, she can still cook American food better than most Americans, but cannot cook Korean food at all.

Other women told of learning how to cook American food from their mothers-in-law, from cookbooks and television cooking shows, and from other military brides. U.S. military bases around the United States and around the world are home to Korean military brides, and several women who spoke with me noted that they had learned a great deal about cooking by living on-base where it is easy to socialize with other military brides. If a military bride was known as a good cook, others would ask her for advice. Military brides would exchange recipes that elicited favorable responses from their husbands.

Like most military brides, Mrs. Peterson, who arrived in the United States in 1986, learned American cooking from a variety of sources. Whenever recipes for American food appeared in Korean women's magazines, she would clip them out and save them. At the suggestion of her husband, she attended U.S.O. Bride School in Seoul before leaving for America. There she learned about American supermarkets, canned and frozen foods, making menus and shopping for a week's worth of meals, as well as a few recipes. During her first few months in the United States, when she lived with her husband's family, she learned how to cook her husband's favorite dishes from her mother-in-law.

Sometimes the women's attempts to cook unfamiliar food with unfamiliar tools resulted in humorous mistakes. Intending to boil cabbage as taught by her husband, Mrs. Goldin boiled lettuce instead. Unfamiliar with both vegetables (round cabbage and lettuce are not traditionally part of the Korean diet), she had confused the two. "He saw these lettuce leaves all wilted and floating in the water, and we just laughed and laughed," she said, laughing again at the memory.

When asked how she learned to cook American food, Mrs. Crispin began with the following story:

Cooking American food, well, how shall I say that I learned how to cook American food? Hmmm, cooking American food, once I, roast beef, I decided to make a roast beef. I was so hungry. So at that time I didn't know how much was enough for two, so I bought a hunk this big {gestures with her hands}. I bought it and put it in the oven and just turned it on high, thinking that if I put it on high, it would cook fast. So I did that and I'm waiting, and I smell something burning. I thought it was coming from outside, so I went outside, but it was coming from our house. I looked everywhere, but nothing in our house was burning. But when I opened the oven, the meat was burning. So I took it out and cut off the burned part. There was nothing else I could do, so I sliced the rest of the meat and cooked it in the frying pan, and warmed up a can of string beans, and that's how we ate.

Unfamiliar with ovens, which she had never seen before coming to America, and with cooking roast beef, Mrs. Crispin ended up burning the meat. With the aid of a cookbook she later learned how to prepare this kind of meat "with carrots and everything, and put it in the oven at the right temperature." She also learned how to make scrambled eggs and toast, bacon, lettuce, and tomato sandwiches, pork chops, salads, mashed potatoes, and other mainstream American fare for her white European American husband.

Mrs. Mullen's answer to my question about adjusting to American life was almost exclusively about learning to cook.

I watched people. *I want to learn all the time. I want to learn whatever I, I, I, I can still learn, you know, different kind of cookies and . . .* how to make them, how to make all kinds of things *I'm very interested, learning, I like the challenge. I like to learn, anything I do. I watch people cooking, I watch what they do, how they do, that's how I learn. . . . I watch, ask questions. I still ask a question, something new dish. You know, Italian dish, like a, ah, different kind of dish. What you were put it in, you know. What else, I watch TV cooking thing, I always watch, and listen and pay attention. Cookbook, cookbook you kind find a too many gadget. I just like simple style. . . . I don't like too much gadget.*

For Mrs. Mullen, learning to cook was an enjoyable challenge, and something that she pursued continuously. She expressed pride in her ability to cook, noting that her husband enjoyed the meals that she prepared. Like many other military brides, she also commented that American food was easy to prepare compared to Korean food. They noted that canned, frozen, and packaged foods often reduced cooking to heating up the contents. Once one had figured out the basic configuration of what can be called a standard American meal, described by several women as a salad served first, followed by meat, potatoes, and a vegetable served together, the rest was easy. In a pinch, particularly at lunchtime, one could just throw together a sandwich or open up a few cans. The kitchens of these military brides were filled with food products common to middle-class Americans across the nation, from A-1 steak sauce and Heinz ketchup to Oscar Mayer bologna, Kraft American Cheese, and Quaker Instant Oatmeal. This was true regardless of the specific ethnic background of their husbands. Their comments and their kitchens demonstrate that while America may not have a national cuisine, it certainly has national food habits that are readily discernible by newcomers. As more than one scholar has observed, these foodways are closely linked to commercialized, processed, and prepared foods whose brands are household names and can be found everywhere from the supermarket to the neighborhood corner grocery.[18]

In addition to salads, bacon, lettuce, and tomato sandwiches, and steak, many women also learned to cook dishes reflecting their husbands' particular cultural backgrounds. Mrs. Weinberg, who came in 1969 with her Jewish American husband, learned to cook blintzes, potato latkes, and chicken soup, among other dishes. With pride, and some self-conscious laughter for complimenting herself, Mrs. Weinberg said that she had become quite a good cook. Mrs. Goldin, who said she can cook American food better than many Americans, learned to cook soul food for her African American husband. Mrs. Bugelli, who arrived in 1959, learned to cook Italian food, including all kinds of Italian cakes and cookies, for her Italian American husband and his two sons. Packing me a bag of her latest batch of cookies, she apologized that they were not up to her usual standards. To me, however, they seemed professionally made. Sometimes the women were not immediately aware that the food they were learning to cook was considered ethnic. One woman, while preparing a meal of barbecued pork ribs, greens boiled with ham, corn bread and biscuits, potato salad, and spice cake for her family's Fourth of July dinner, said that it was several years before she realized it was African American food that she was learning to cook. "To me, the food in America was just all American food. But later I found out that the women who married white men never learned how to cook things like greens with ham," she said.

Despite the presence of ethnic foods, however, standard or mainstream American food seemed to predominate. The woman preparing the

Fourth of July dinner made a particularly astute comment: "I can make most of the foods that the [Korean] wives of white men make, but they can't make the foods I make." Asked whether American food or Jewish food was eaten more often in her home, Mrs. Weinberg replied that Jewish food was eaten occasionally, especially at Passover, but that most meals were "just American." This resonates with research on ethnic identity among white Americans which argues that ethnicities such as Italian American, Irish American, and the like are expressed occasionally as a kind of choice, particularly in areas of cultural consumption, of which food is certainly a part. Sociologist Richard Alba's study of white Americans shows that while eating the foods of one's own ethnic background (Italian, Polish, Irish, German, and so on) is the most common ethnic-related activity (reported by 47 percent of respondents), such foods are eaten less than once a month by the majority of these respondents.[19] Although food appears to be the primary vehicle for ethnic expression among white Americans, expressing a mainstream American identity rather than the identity of one's immigrant ancestors appears to be by far the most common choice.

Kimchi and Meatballs

As described above, the families of military brides also eat primarily standard American foods. Korean food is marginalized, even stigmatized, while the American food—and the ethnic food—of the husband dominates. Although the women expended a great deal of effort in learning how to cook foods to fit their American husbands' tastes, few husbands seem to have made the effort to learn to like Korean food, much less to cook it. Korean food is rarely part of a family meal. In some families, the husband disliked Korean food so intensely that it was virtually forbidden. In contrast, in none of the families I met was the food of the husband banned or stigmatized. Indeed, none of the women I interviewed had ever encountered or heard about such a case. The women who said their husbands and children ate Korean food generally cited the same foods—Korean-style barbecued beef, glass noodles with vegetables and beef, and stuffed dumplings—and invariably added that these were

Korean foods commonly enjoyed by non-Koreans. Foods with distinctive Korean tastes such as *kimchi,* soybean paste stew, or seaweed soup were rarely accepted by husbands, children, or in-laws. The eating of Korean food, in addition, did not seem to be accompanied by the acceptance of other Korean cultural practices. Many of the same husbands who resisted celebrating Korean holidays or teaching their children Korean customs, for example, ate a few select items of Korean food. In the families of Korean military brides, these foods became part of meals that remained distinctly American.

Based on observations of her own family's eating habits and preferences, sociologist Mary Douglas has aptly observed that meals have structures.[20] While the meals she analyzes are British, her general observation can be applied to both Korean and American meals, as both cultures have fairly clear ideas about what constitutes a proper meal. Korean meals are structured around a bowl of rice and several side dishes.[21] There are no courses and everything is served at once. The side dishes usually include a bowl of soup or a pot of stew, and always include *kimchi.* Only rice and soup are served in individual portions; other side dishes are served each in its own dish placed at the center of the table. Diners use their own chopsticks or spoons to take mouthfuls of the side dishes. Many of the side dishes, including different varieties of *kimchi,* are prepared in advance and eaten slowly over a period of several days or even several months. Some side dishes actually require advance preparation, since several days or weeks are needed to produce the desired flavor. Eating the same side dishes meal after meal is common.

The structure of American meals, on the other hand, more closely approximates Douglas's formula of 1a + 2b, that is, a main dish accompanied by two supporters.[22] Families that put together a full dinner usually have a main course (1a) and a first course and dessert (2b). Soup or salad is often served as the first course. The main course usually consists of meat or fish (1a) accompanied by two side dishes (2a) served on the same plate. If rice is served, not only is it unlikely to be Korean-style rice, but it appears as a side dish, not the meal's center. Everything is individually served, and diners do not dip their eating utensils into the same bowls or plates of food. Eating the same thing twice in a row is usually considered to be eating leftovers. Dessert, a common ending to middle-class American meals, has no equivalent in Korean meals. Only recently have middle-class Koreans begun to finish their meals with servings of fruit. Even then, the fruit is not discernibly a dessert, but rather an after-dinner snack, for it is often eaten some time after the meal is over.

The following two examples illustrate the ways in which Korean foods become incorporated into American meals.

In one case, the wife asked her husband to serve himself while she changed their son's clothes, telling him what was available and where. After wondering aloud whether he wanted a salad, he decided against it because it was too much of a bother. He then served himself a plate of Korean barbecued beef, Korean-style white rice, frozen mixed vegetables steamed with butter, and a dinner biscuit, along with a glass of Coke. He ate this with a fork and knife. This was not long after the wife had served me and several of her friends, also military brides, a very Korean meal of rice, soybean paste soup, Korean barbecued beef, seasoned Korean vegetables, and roasted barley tea, all served in their separate dishes. We had eaten with chopsticks and spoons, taking mouthfuls from the common bowls of side dishes.

In another case, Mrs. Vaughn, her husband, several of Mrs. Vaughn's military bride friends, and I ate a meal together. Mrs. Vaughn asked her husband if he wanted her to boil some noodles to go with the meatballs. He replied that he would just eat it with rice. She then served him a plate of meatballs with tomato sauce, Korean-style white rice, and steamed vegetables. For the rest of us, she served bowls of rice, bowls of seaweed soup, and various kinds of Korean side dishes. We ate with chopsticks and spoons, all of us dipping into the same bowls of side dishes. Her husband ate with a fork, touching only the food on his own plate.

These meals are remarkable for their conformity to the structures described above. The structure of the meals I ate with the wives, as well as their content, were distinctly Korean, while the structure of the husbands' meals, despite some Korean content, was distinctly American. In one meal, Korean-style barbecued beef became the meat portion of an American main course, with rice serving as one of two side dishes. In the other, rice was again the side dish. The presence of Korean foods did not make the meals Korean. Instead, Korean foods were incorporated into American meals.

Korean foods are incorporated into other American food rituals as well. Mrs. Orellana, who arrived in 1991, expressed surprise that her husband, their preschool son, and her parents-in-law enjoyed eating seasoned *keem*, thin sheets of dried laver. *Keem* is a common side dish at Korean meals, where it is eaten wrapped around a spoonful of rice. She then noted that while they also like rice, they never ate *keem* with rice and refused to eat *kimbap*, rice and vegetables wrapped in unseasoned *keem* to form a kind of log which is then sliced into rounds. Instead, to her surprise, they ate the seasoned *keem* like a snack while talking or watching TV. Crisp, salty squares of *keem* were not seen as a side dish or an accompaniment for rice, but as a snack akin to potato chips. Thus they were eaten like potato chips. Again, a Korean food is accepted by the American family, but on their own terms. Their basic perceptions of food and of meals seem to have remained unchanged.

This is not to say, however, that the families do not identify the foods as Korean. They do. They are aware that they are eating Korean *keem* and not American potato chips, Korean barbecued beef and rice, not American steak and potatoes. These Korean foods are incorporated into a larger American structure of meals and food habits so that rather than the foods "Koreanizing" American meals, the incorporation "Americanizes" the foods even as they are labeled "Korean." It is one of the steps toward Americanization that various other ethnic foods—pizza, corn chips, tacos, hot dogs, and bagels come to mind—have taken in the course of American history.[23] The new foods serve to enrich, not transform, American culture, and eating them does not necessarily turn Americans into multiethnics.

The interest in Korean food seems linked to a general surge of interest in ethnic foods that began in the 1960s and soared in the 1980s. Mrs. Orellana's mother-in-law, for example, took an interest in foods from different cultures and bought a Korean cookbook in preparation for meeting her new daughter-in-law in 1991. Another woman, who arrived in 1989, said her sister-in-law commented that having a Korean in the family made life more interesting because it allowed them to be close to a different culture. Although friendly interest is preferable to hostility, this does not necessarily place the Korean cultures of the women on par with the American cultures of the husbands and in-laws. The husbands and in-laws can choose whether or not to learn about Korean culture and eat Korean food, that is, they can choose whether or not to make their lives more interesting, but the women do not have similar freedom of choice regarding American culture. Nor does their acquisition of American culture serve to strip it of context and transform it into a consumer item for pleasure and cultural enrichment. When the husbands, children, and in-laws of military brides consume selected items of Korean food, this is not necessarily evidence of biculturality or multiethnicity. Especially in households that otherwise devalue and stigmatize the Korean culture of the wife and mother, it is just as likely to be a shallow gesture that appropriates bits and pieces of Korean culture for a variety that adds "spice" to American life.

In most households I observed, a few items of Korean food are present, but the husbands and children generally eat American food. Mrs. Orellana and Mrs. Vaughn, for example, both said that they cook primarily American food for their husbands. Mrs. Orellana noted that while her husband occasionally even eats *doenjang* stew, whose broth is made from soybean paste and is generally disliked by non-Koreans, he prefers to eat American food. Since she wants to eat as a family, she also eats American food. To satisfy her desire for Korean food, she said, she eats a Korean meal for breakfast after he has left for work.

This pattern of eating American food with their husbands and Korean food when alone was common among military brides I met. Some women, especially those who arrived before the 1970s and gradually became accustomed to living with only sporadic encounters with Korean food, simply ended up eating primarily American food with their families. Cooking Korean food just for one, especially for those who did not know how to cook before they immigrated, was simply too burdensome to do daily. Like Mrs. Orellana, they saw the family meal as an affirmation of family togetherness. The price of clinging to Korean food, they believed, would be the rupturing of family bonds. Maintaining the family and fulfilling the gendered role of producer of the family required the adoption of American food at the expense of Korean food. In short, it required the suppression of part of one's cultural identity.

Those who insisted on eating Korean food daily often found themselves cooking two sets of meals, serving one and then eating the other alone. Rather than a family affair eaten together that symbolizes and reaffirms the unity of the family—albeit one that is predicated on the suppression of the culture and ethnicity of the wife and mother—meals became individual affairs eaten separately that symbolized the internal cultural dissonance within the family. While describing how she learned to cook American food and noting that her husband enjoyed her cooking, Mrs. Peterson started to say that therefore there had been no trouble over food in her marriage. Mid-sentence, she corrected herself and talked at length about food differences between herself and her husband:

> So problems with food, problems with food, there aren't, there are. Because Dennis's father eats American food and I eat Korean food. I absolutely hate American food. If I have to, I eat it, but I'd rather eat Korean food, I don't eat American food. When he was in Korea, he had no choice but to eat Korean food, but after we came to America, he didn't touch Korean food. In Korea, I made Korean food for him. There's not much American food, and there's no place to buy it, so he ate Korean food. But after coming here [America], he doesn't eat any. Not a bit. He eats only American food. But once in a while I guess Korean food comes to mind. Korean barbecued beef, Korean noodles, the things he ate once in a while when I cooked them while we lived together, but now I don't because we're separated. Sometimes he asks, how do you make this or that. If you go to a Korean restaurant, will they have it, sometimes he asks. Once in a while he wants to eat it, because he ate it in the past. But he doesn't eat other kinds of Korean foods. Give him rice, and he doesn't think of that as a meal. It's like a snack. Rice leaves him hungry, he says. So he doesn't like it, because when he eats rice, he's still hungry. Give him rice, rice and meat, and he says, ooooh, how can I eat this. This won't do, give me bread. . . . You have to give him bread. He says rice leaves him hungry. So while living with Dennis's father, there wasn't much affection that built up. A couple should sit together and eat meals together, but we didn't do much of that. The reason is that I have to eat Korean food, and Dennis's father has to eat Western food. So I have to cook twice. First I cook Dennis's father's dinner and serve him. I serve him first. Dennis's father sits alone and eats. I go back into the kitchen and cook Korean food and eat. So we didn't eat together much.

Unable to accept each other's foods, this couple ended up eating separately. Mrs. Peterson counted this as one of the causes of their separation, saying that eating separate meals resulted in a lack of marital affection, the sort that builds up through day after day of household routines. She chided herself for clinging to Korean food, saying that perhaps if she had eaten meals with her husband things might have turned out differently. It never occurred to her that her husband shared in the responsibility for their separation, since he clung to American food.

Nevertheless, she said later, at least he didn't mind her cooking and eating Korean food. He rarely complained about the smell of Korean food, she said, except once in a while when she cooked *doenjang* stew or *kimchi* stew. This was a common refrain among women who cooked Korean food at home: even if he doesn't eat it, at least he doesn't complain much about the smell when I do. The feeling seemed to be that they were among the lucky ones.

Many Korean immigrants, not just military brides, are keenly aware that non-Koreans, especially Westerners, find Korean food smelly. A good number, perhaps the majority, accordingly change their behavior to accommodate these sensibilities. A Korean immigrant in Chicago devotes to this topic an entire chapter of her book on her experiences as a bilingual teacher of immigrant Korean children.[24] The chapter, entitled "Garlic Smell," begins with her decision to forgo Korean food for lunch, no matter how much she craves it. The decision is made after she goes to a Korean restaurant for lunch and then hears from a fellow teacher that she smells of garlic, even though she had brushed her teeth after the meal. Discussing several different incidents, she writes that American teachers, wondering what their Korean students eat for breakfast, often complain that they smell of garlic. A little sensitivity on the part of parents, she writes, would prevent such complaints. She then says that she has little choice but to caution the children. In short, she accepts American complaints and decides that the only choice is to make every effort to get rid of the smell, even if it means giving up Korean food.

For this immigrant Korean woman, her responsiveness to American sensitivities doesn't necessitate giving up Korean food entirely. Dinners at home with her Korean husband, as she notes, always consist of Korean food. In addition, her responsiveness—although shaped in a context where Korean culture is subordinate to American culture—is a voluntary reaction to American comments and complaints. But most military brides don't have the luxury of a voluntary reaction, nor is their home a Korean haven away from complaining Americans. If their American husbands dislike Korean food and its smell, then military brides cannot have Korean food in their homes.

Korean women who live with their husbands' parents are usually even more restricted. Mrs. Peterson spoke of having no access to Korean food for the several months that she lived with her husband's family before joining him at his new army post. Mrs. Crispin spoke of having little more than soy sauce to season her food while living with her parents-in-law, noting that she dared not bring more because they would object to the smell. Some women endure bitter complaints by husbands who detest the smell of Korean food and persist in keeping Korean food in the house. One woman, who arrived in the mid-1960s, told of years of playing hide-and-seek with her husband. She would hide the Korean food; he would seek it out and throw it away. Sometimes he would burst into a rage, she said, but usually he would just shake his head as if to say, when will she ever stop.

Those who were unable to keep Korean food at home spoke of attending Korean functions where food was served, simply to eat some Korean food as well as to see some Korean faces, or of calling up other military brides and getting themselves invited over for a Korean lunch. Some women told me that one of the most enjoyable aspects of going to Korean churches was the food. Gatherings of military brides, such as the monthly meetings of military bride organizations, invariably include Korean food. Even their fund-raising dinners—aimed at a mixed audience of Koreans and Americans—usually feature Korean food. Every military bride who spoke with me about participating in such organizations noted that the chance to eat Korean food was a major attraction. A military bride interviewed by sociologist Kim Sil Dong described life without Korean food at home as follows:

> My husband hates that I keep the smelly Kimchee [kimchi] in refrigerator. As you know, Koreans have to have Kimchee on dinner table. But, since my husband threw out all my Kimchee I usually call HJ during the lunch hour and have her invite me over to her home. She picks me up when I call her. . . . I eat all sort of Korean foods in her house like a pig. She feels sorry for me but there is nothing she can do about it except that she prepares Korean food for me once in a while. . . . I attend every single Korean party where Korean meals are provided.[25]

Other women were able to keep Korean food in the home, but only on sufferance. Mrs. Weinberg, for example, had a separate refrigerator for Korean food because her husband complained about the smell, especially of *kimchi*. For that same reason, she never ate Korean food with him and rarely cooked Korean food in the house. Instead, friends would occasionally bring her soups, stews, and side dishes. When her mother came to visit from Korea, she was only allowed to cook those dishes whose smells are not considered strong or pungent by her husband. When I interviewed Mrs. Weinberg, she was living in a town house while waiting for their new home to be finished. We had eaten a meal of Korean food, with cabbage soup brought over by her friend, another military bride, and side dishes made by Mrs. Weinberg's mother, who had just returned to Korea after a visit to her daughter. As Mrs. Weinberg cleared the table, she put the Korean food into airtight containers and wrapped them in several layers of plastic bags before putting them in a remote corner of the refrigerator. Wrinkling her nose and laughing, she commented that it was no use, since her husband would detect the smell anyway.

Even when they have become accustomed to a life of American food, military brides do not forget the taste of Korean food. The longing may no longer be as intense, but it seems to remain. Mrs. Mullen, who said she rarely ate Korean food, said that she liked turkey stuffing, seafood, steak *"once in a blue moon,"* and lived mostly on vegetables, rice, and noodles. When she and her husband went out, however, she always ordered seafood:

> *I, I like, you know, so you can make, I make seafood home, but it's not like you get from restaurant.* It doesn't come out the same. Of course, if you make it the Korean way, it's much tastier. Uh, in your home, I don't know if your mother and father eat Korean style or not, if they eat Korean food, but you know, Korean food is salty and spicy, lots of seasonings, right? So it's tastier. Fish is tastier if you do it the Korean way. . . . But the American way, it's *very flat.*

Even as she talked about the American foods she ate regularly, even as she noted that she rarely ate Korean food, Mrs. Mullen spoke of Korean food as tastier and American food as *"very flat."* Her eating habits may have become so Americanized that Korean food occupied little space in her life, but her opinions of food still resonated with the Korean tastes she grew up with. This emotional loyalty to the tastes of her childhood can be read as an affirmation of her identity as a Korean woman.

More Than Just Food

Although they maintain their families through the cooking and serving of meals that suppresses their Korean culture and identity, and although they live under constant awareness of the marginalization of their cultures, military brides do retain their identities as Korean women. They negotiate through and around the suppression and marginalization, finding ways to express their Korean selves and to eat the foods they crave. Even if, like Mrs. Mullen, they rarely eat these foods, their views of the tastiness of Korean food versus American food tend to favor Korean food. They speak as if it were natural that they should concede the family territory to American food but reserve a slice of personal space for Korean food, for themselves. Eating Korean food is a way of expressing Korean identity, of partaking of ethnic community, of being connected to kin, hometown, and fellow immigrants. The women spoke of a strong need for the comforts of the familiar, for affirmation of self, and for emotional sustenance. Eating Korean food and retaining their loyalties to it appear to be a way of meeting these needs and keeping body and soul together.

While we ate the small tart-sweet oranges characteristic of Korea after our taped interview had ended, Mrs. Peterson wondered aloud why these oranges tasted so much better to her than the large American oranges. "I feel empty when I eat American food," she said. "It's only Korean food that satisfies me. Even with fruit, Korean fruit tastes so much better. When I was living with my in-laws and couldn't eat Korean food, I was going crazy. So I think it must be more than just food, you know?"

The women at New York's Rainbow Center, a women's collective of and for Korean military brides, know that food is more than just food. They have experienced its healing powers. Many of the women who come to the Rainbow Center come after suffering years of abuse. As a result, some have emotional and mental problems. When center women know that a new woman is due to arrive, they make sure that the house is redolent with the fragrance of Korean food. The new arrivals are treated to meal after meal of Korean food: *doenjang* stew, *kimchi* stew, *kimchi*, and lots of rice. The dominant language at the center is Korean, the atmosphere is familial, and the kitchen is filled with Korean food and Korean eating utensils. In this deliberately Korean atmosphere, said the center's founder and director, the Rev. Geumhyun Yeo, the women slowly come back to life. During some twenty years of working with military wives, she said, she came to realize that many of the emotional and mental problems that troubled military brides are linked to their deprivation of Korean food and Korean companionship. Surrounding them with these things is therefore an essential part of the Rainbow Center's program of resuscitating abused military brides, she said.[26]

While preparing our dinner after our formal oral history session, Mrs. Crispin talked about the different ways of cooking seaweed soup, which was on our menu for the evening. Asking me how my mother cooked it, she said that she usually first sauteed the seaweed and dried anchovies in sesame oil, then added hot water and simmered it until done. My aunt, I replied, usually used bits of beef instead of dried anchovies, while my vegetarian mother used neither but added only a different variety of seaweed that is used primarily to make broth. Women from the coastal regions of Korea used fresh clams and other shellfish, Mrs. Crispin noted, recalling her childhood years spent in those regions. She then sighed a little and said, "It's more than just fun to talk about this, don't you think?" Noting that she had lived in the United States for so long that it seemed like home, she said that times like this, cooking and eating Korean food with another Korean woman, even a stranger like myself, gave her an indescribable feeling. Searching for words to express herself, she said, "Maybe something like drinking water after being thirsty for a really long time."

CHAPTER 5

Prodigal
Daughters,
Filial
Daughters

The story of the prodigal son always
brings tears to her eyes. That's us, she would tell me over coffee at Mc-
Donald's, we who married American soldiers and left our families behind, we are prodigal daughters. Although she never sat for a formal interview, she told me bits of her life story during several meetings, always
over coffee drenched in cream and sugar at the same McDonald's. Her re-
curring message to me was that the lesson she had learned during some
three decades of American life is that military brides were prodigal
daughters, but that unlike the biblical son, the women are rejected when
they become filial daughters and try to return home. Both family and
ethnic kin spurn the women out of shame. This, she said, is the military
bride's *han*, an unquenchable grief arising from injustice and tragedy.

Another military bride, Mrs. Crispin, calls military brides orphans.
The women are cut off from kith and kin because of a shameful marriage,
reduced to the family skeleton in the closet. But unlike a real orphan,
military brides are rejected by the living, and the pain, the *han*, is that
much worse.

Whether the metaphor is that of the orphan or of the unwelcome
prodigal daughter, military brides tend to agree that family is a painful,

emotional issue. Many uttered the identical sentiment: It's the *han* of us internationally married women.

Koreans talk about *han* a great deal, but this particular *han* is peculiar to military brides and other Korean women who marry foreigners.[1] As married women, they may no longer be considered full-fledged members of their natal families, in accordance with patriarchal customs that transfer a woman's familial identification from that of her birth family to that of her husband's family. As women who married foreigners, not only are they veiled with the camptown shadow, but they are also seen as having married out of the Korean people and into the foreign people of their husbands. For most internationally married women, their subsequent migration to the country of their husbands, usually America, serves to accentuate this perception of having left the national, familial fold. Korean military brides, then, are often seen as no longer really Korean by virtue of their marriage to foreigners and their migration. For these reasons, many military brides are subjected to contempt, ostracism, and betrayal by other Koreans as well as their own families.

Most military brides, however, still identify themselves as Korean. As daughters and sisters, they consider themselves to be part of their birth families, and they use the metaphor of family to insist that they are still part of the Korean people. As one woman put it during an informal conversation, "I was born Korean. How can my marriage change that?" This kind of insistence on their Korean identity can be read as a challenge that opens up and complicates the meanings of Korean identity and the questions of who can claim membership among the Korean people, and indeed, who the Korean people are.

Separations and Reunions

Some military brides were able to maintain positive ties with their families but most found that their marriages caused serious damage to these relationships. Upon their marriage, some women were even disowned by angry and horrified parents, usually fathers. Mrs. Ramos and her sister, both of whom married American soldiers and came to the United States in the 1980s, were disowned by their families. Only later, when the

women became parents themselves, did contact with their families re-
sume. But, said Mrs. Ramos, the relationship is strained. Her family sees
her and her sister as outcasts and the source of family humiliation. Other
military brides maintain relations with their families for years, sending
them money, sponsoring their immigration, and helping them settle
nearby. While some continue to have close relationships with these relatives, others find themselves subtly given the cold shoulder or even blatantly shunned once they outlive their usefulness.

   While family relationships were varied, relations with broader Korean
communities overwhelmingly tended to be difficult. Virtually all the
military brides I spoke with had had some negative experience with
other Koreans due to the prejudice and stereotypes that surrounded military brides. Although some had close relationships with other Koreans,
many more said that they felt distant from, and even wary of, the Korean
community.

   Those who came in the 1950s and 1960s usually found they were the
lone Korean, if not the lone Asian, in a sea of Americans. Letters from
family in Korea were often the only contact they had with other Koreans
for several years. When that link was broken, the women often experienced great loneliness. Mrs. Dennison, who arrived in the United States
in 1958, said that she lost contact with her family several years later
when she moved east from Kentucky. Letters she sent were returned as
undeliverable. Although she was painfully lonely, raising several children alone kept her too busy to dwell on it. Nearly twenty years later
she received a phone call from a barely familiar voice. It was her younger
sister, calling from Korea. Her family had traced her through the U.S.
military.

   She was most concerned about her parents, for they had been terribly
upset when she married and left for America. In 1958 in Seoul, her
mother and siblings came out to wave good-bye as she stepped into the
American car sent by her husband to take her to the airport. But her father, choked with tears, remained inside the house. It would be the last
time she was to see her parents. Over the years, she hungered for news of
them, but she had the feeling that they were already deceased. Whenever she closed her eyes, her mother, dressed in a long white skirt and
sweater, appeared before her. She felt that this was a sign from her
mother's spirit informing her of their death. When she was once again in

touch with her siblings, they did not talk about their parents, and she was afraid to ask. Instead she asked them to send wedding pictures.

If you look at wedding pictures, you can tell. So, in the wedding picture of the sibling right below me, our mother is there, but not our father. So I knew that our father had already passed away then. And in the wedding picture of the third sibling below me, both of our parents are missing. So I called them and asked if our mother and father had passed away . . . and they said that they hadn't told me about it because they were afraid I would be upset. They didn't live long. Our father died in 1964 and our mother died in 1969. When I went back to Korea, it was twenty-two years after I had left, and it turned out to be *Chusok* then. So we went to their graves, and I asked them why there was only one burial mound, and they said that they had buried them together.[2]

During that trip to Korea, she also heard from her siblings that both parents had died calling out her name.

Whenever my mother received some spending money from my older brothers, she would save it. When she had saved enough, she would visit a fortune-teller. Was her daughter alive or dead? That's what she would ask the fortune-teller. Every place she went, they all said that I was alive. When she died, she died of cancer, but when she died, you know, she disciplined me a great deal when I was growing up, I was spanked by her a lot, oh, she spanked me a great deal. But when she died, she called out my name, she could hardly speak, so it was more like the sound of the wind, calling out my name as she died. And our father, when he died he too died calling out my name.

Mrs. Dennison sighs, and a long silence ensues. For a split second, as if prompted by a reporter instinct looking for the juicy quote, I want to ask if she feels that she has been a bad daughter for causing her parents pain, but I can see her own pain etched on her face. I keep quiet, and we turn to other topics.

Mrs. Dennison's experience is unusual among military brides of her generation because she visited Korea after coming to the United States.

Most do not. Some—like Mrs. Bugelli and Mrs. Mullen—have no families left to visit; some don't go because their family ties were irrevocably
severed upon marriage; some because their finances do not permit it; and
some—remembering long sea voyages—because Korea seems too far
away to visit.

Some military brides find it difficult to maintain contact with old
friends, even though they remain close to their families. When Mrs.
Weinberg married her American husband and moved to the United
States in 1969, she stopped contacting her close-knit circle of childhood
friends. When asked why, she replied, *"Because I was married with an
American guy, I guess, I don't know.* {laughs} The image in Korea isn't
very good, you know."

Mrs. Weinberg was worried that her friends would see her differently,
that her friends' husbands would not accept her and forbid their wives
from associating with her, and that in general her new status as a military bride would expose her to rejection. Although she returned to Korea
every two or three years to visit her family, she never once met any of
her friends. During a trip to Korea about seven or eight years after she
married, the aunt of one of her friends called her. She chastised Mrs.
Weinberg for being a disloyal friend slipping in and out of Korea like a
shadow. A few days later, Mrs. Weinberg received a call from a childhood friend, inviting her to a gathering. The reunion was emotional and
tearful.

> It was so good to see them, I guess. It was really . . . emotionally, both
> sides were very, everyone cried and there was a big fuss. We had all
> been terribly close. But then, they said that I was a bad . . . that it was
> just my own thoughts, how could I have come to Korea so often and
> never contacted any of them. *Even [to] this day they still call my mother.*

From then on, Mrs. Weinberg said, she has been in close touch with
this circle of friends. No one can be as close, she asserted, as the people
with whom you grew up.

Mrs. Morgan also cut her ties to many of her friends, but she seems to
have been motivated by more than the fear of rejection based solely on
her outmarriage.

When I came to America and experienced the reality of life here, I was very, very disappointed. So, well, only a couple [of] friends knew that I had married. I didn't contact anyone to tell them that I was living in America.

Mrs. Morgan, who arrived in 1983, had expected to marry well and when she married an American she had expected to live the American dream of prosperity. When she found the paycheck-to-paycheck existence of an enlisted man's family instead, her disappointment and her pride kept her from seeking out her childhood friends.

Both women were very conscious of having chosen a different path than their peers, and in their own particular ways, they feared rejection for so doing. Their perceptions of the role of class and material prosperity, however, as well as the realities of their individual situations, had a major impact on the ways in which they dealt with their friends back in Korea. Mrs. Morgan felt strongly that she needed to be prosperous to validate her choice before other Koreans, even her childhood friends. On the other hand, Mrs. Weinberg's class status—an upper-middle-class housewife who never worked outside the home after her marriage to a military-officer-turned-successful-businessman—is visible in her well-coiffed hair and tasteful makeup, expensive clothes, jewelry, and the luxury car in her driveway. It is likely that she assumed this position the moment she married her husband. He came from a prominent family, and their first home in the United States was in a posh, newly built apartment building in a well-to-do section of his hometown. It is unlikely that she could have afforded to visit Korea every few years throughout the 1970s unless she was financially well-off. Thus when she was reunited with her childhood friends, her prosperity, as well as her stable marriage, was a positive that offset the negative of marriage to a foreigner. She may well have avoided a reunion if her marriage had not been stable or if she had been poor. Her stable marriage and upper-class status allowed her to command a measure of respect and show her friends that her outmarriage had not been a mistake. Indeed, her friends may well have envied her apparent fulfillment of the American dream, especially during the 1970s and 1980s when the "American fever" was burning its way throughout South Korea.

Gender and Intermarriage

For military brides, class, marital stability, and the race of the husband are important elements in relations with Korean immigrants in the United States. Although the importance of class and marital stability are variations on traditional concerns, the importance of race has a great deal to do with the influence of American racial hierarchies. Koreans came into contact with this hierarchy first through the U.S. military, which still had segregated troops during the Korean War, and later through American cultural images portrayed on television shows and in movies, and their immigration experiences in the United States. The status of blacks at the bottom of American society, discriminated against and disproportionately poor, was easily visible. Koreans who dreamed of going to America were dreaming of upward mobility, and so they dreamed of living like whites, not like blacks. Fueled by a desire for upward mobility and ignorant of the American legacies of slavery, conquest, and exploitation, the racial prejudices of Koreans mimicked the racial hierarchy they found in American society.[3]

Thus Korean women whose husbands are African American or Latino tend to suffer greater and more blatant ostracism from other Koreans. The general view is that women married to blacks or Latinos married into the dregs of a foreign society and that such women must therefore also have come from the dregs of Korean society. They are more likely to be treated as former camptown women than women whose husbands are white. Several Korean immigrants, upon learning of my research, confidently told me that I would find a few refined women among the wives of whites, but that the wives of blacks were all from the camptowns.

Class prejudice and notions of what constitutes success for women also worked their way into the distinctions made between military brides. Military brides with stable families and prosperous, professional husbands are less likely to be shunned as blatantly as those who are divorced or lower income or whose husbands are working class. Lives that meet Korean criteria for female success—stable family, well-educated children, a husband with a steady job or career—can offset the choice to marry a foreigner and earn military brides a grudging degree of respect such as, "Well, at least she knows how to be a good wife and mother." A life that exceeds these criteria—prosperity greater than that of the average Korean, a husband with a highly respected professional career—can even help to validate that choice.

But only to a point. Both military brides and clergy who have ministered to them told me that while military brides with some social status were treated decently to their faces, behind their backs they were subject to the same insults, contempt, and pity as those without such status. Military brides, no matter their achievements, are seen as somehow outside the realm of Korean society, women who are abnormal, suspect, even polluted, in their difference. The assumed camptown past haunts even those who have never been near a camptown.

Koreans seem to think that military brides are tainted, or polluted, by their intimate association with foreigners. Korean terms for sexual relations, mixing bodies, and for producing children, mixing blood, connote the intimacy and the physicality of these acts. To mix bodies and mix blood with non-Koreans, at least when done by women, is seen as dirty. Men who marry foreigners, however, are not subject to this prejudice.[4] This may in part be due to the sexual double standard. Women are seen as being invaded, taken, or possessed when they engage in sexual relations, while men are seen as conquering, taking, or possessing when they do the same. This is imbedded in the Korean vocabulary describing sexual relations: men pluck women (*dda-muhk-da*), possess women (*gaji-da*), occupy women (*chajiha-da*), while women give their bodies to men (*momeul joo-da*) and receive men (*bahd-da*). Regardless of who the partner may be, a woman who engages in sexual relations is seen as having had the integrity of her body violated. The only exception is under marriage, when the violation is seen as something a wife must accept. A man who engages in sexual relations, however, is seen as simply demonstrating his healthy male vitality.[5] When extended to relations with foreigners, then, women become doubly contaminated, because the violation to their bodies is committed by men who are not Korean. In this case, not even marriage, it seems, can cleanse women of this pollution.

Patriarchal definitions of marriage are also a factor. In a study of Chinese immigrants in Thailand, anthropologist Jiemin Bao illustrates that Thai women who marry Chinese men are seen as Chinese, while Chinese women who marry Thai men are seen as having become Thai. These interpretations carry over into lifestyles, so that the Thai women often live with their Chinese in-laws, learn Chinese customs, and raise their children as Chinese. Chinese women, on the other hand, learn Thai customs and raise their children as Thai. In both cases, the men retain their ethnic identities while the women exchange theirs for that of their husbands.[6] Similarly, the prevailing Korean interpretation of marriage—that women marry out into the family of their husbands—is extended to interpretations of intermarriage. Thus, although a number of prominent Korean men—including such historical figures as Syngman Rhee and Philip Jaisohn—have married foreign women, there has been little criticism of their marriages and few intimations of inferiority, pollution, or dirt.[7] Instead, it has often been assumed that the women will learn how to become Korean. The children bear the father's name and are considered Korean. In the case of Rhee, the first president of South Korea, his wife publicly embraced the notion that she had become Korean by marrying a Korean man, wearing traditional Korean dress, and making a point of learning Korean culture. Similarly, an American woman who married a Korean man wrote an account of her life in the early 1950s entitled *I Married a Korean*, describing how she forsook country, kin, and friends to enter Korean society and learn how to become a good Korean wife and mother.[8]

On the other hand, women who marry non-Koreans are all categorized as "internationally married women," a term for which no male equivalent exists. They are seen as having taken on the foreignness of their husbands. Their children are considered foreign. This is the case even if the children grow up in Korea and are completely fluent in Korean language and culture. Several well-known pop singers in Korea during the 1960s and 1970s, for example, were born of Korean mothers and American soldiers. Although they sang in Korean and had Korean names, part of their popularity derived from the exotica associated with their perceived foreignness. In other words, it was a thrill for Koreans to see "foreigners" who seemed so "Korean." This fascination with mixed-blood Koreans seems to have resurfaced in the 1990s, for they can again be seen among backup dancers for pop stars and in small roles in television dramas. As the mothers of these "foreign" children, the foreignness of outmarried Korean women is reinforced.

Furthermore, the term "internationally married women" is so thoroughly drenched in the camptown shadow that it immediately calls forth a myriad stereotypes about former prostitutes married to American soldiers. Thus even women who married not American soldiers but American lawyers, international businessmen, Ivy League professors, influential politicians, and other successful, prosperous, and professional men find themselves subject to intimations of inferiority and suspect morals. In addition, there are no separate terms in the Korean language for women who marry American soldiers, for second-generation Korean American women who marry the white American boys next door, for Korean women who marry their fellow graduate students while studying abroad, or for professional women who marry their colleagues. The particular experiences and situations of these diverse women are collapsed into one monolithic category on the grounds that their husbands are not Korean. Said Mrs. Crispin:

> *Doesn't matter* whether she [your daughter] married in Korea or in America, whether your daughter is a *doctor* or not. Everyone who marries a foreigner is an internationally married woman. They pick up on just that one thing. So even here, if a daughter marries an American, the parents don't even send out wedding invitations. They just do it quietly.

The stigma of "international marriage" also has a great deal to do with the notion that Korean women belong to the Korean nation—to Korean men, in particular—and represent the Korean people in ways that Korean men do not. From the masculine point of view of the Korean nation, foreign men are taking away its women and thus slighting the sovereignty of Korea and the masculinity of Korean men. When the women are viewed as representatives of Korea, their "violation" by foreign men symbolizes the violation of the Korean people as a whole. For Korean immigrants, the marriages of their daughters to Americans also symbolize loss of Korean identity and subsequent Americanization, which many Korean immigrants view negatively.

Because of the stigma on internationally married woman, it is rare to find a military bride whose interaction with other Koreans extends beyond attending the same church. Even then, the internationally married women, mostly military brides, are usually clustered apart from the other congregants. Numerous ministers of Korean churches in the United States told me that relations between military brides and other congregants are superficially polite and deliberately distant. Said one minister: "Koreans look down on these women, so they don't want to associate with them. There's the feeling that these women are polluted, that they are dirty. You know, they married foreigners."

The First Link

In spite of this treatment, military brides have been crucial in the formation of Korean immigrant communities. By inviting their family members to the United States under the family reunification provision of U.S. immigration law, it is estimated that military brides are responsible (directly and indirectly) for bringing 40 to 50 percent of all Korean immigrants since 1965.[9] Using records from the U.S. Embassy in Seoul, the South Korean news monthly *Mal* reported in 1988 that a statistical average of fifteen relatives follow every military bride to the United States.[10] Military brides often formed the first link in chain migrations that include numerous extended family members.

As wives of U.S. citizens, military brides were able to immigrate during a time when immigration from Korea and most of Asia was legally blocked. Thus they make up the largest group of adult Korean immigrants between 1945 and 1965, when immigration laws were liberalized after some five decades of strict, anti-Asian immigration restrictions.[11] Social welfare scholar Daniel B. Lee notes that between 1962 and 1968, for example, Korean women who immigrated as wives of U.S. citizens accounted for 39.4 percent, the largest single immigration category, of all Korean immigration to the United States. Lee estimates that between 1950 and 1989, some 90,000 Korean women immigrated to America as wives of U.S. soldiers.[12] They followed their husbands to every corner of the United States, from rural Kansas to urban Philadelphia, to places where they were the only Korean, if not the only Asian. A Korean immigrant presence in rural America is often the presence of military brides and their families. In most cases, a U.S. military base is nearby. This is true in Colorado, for example, where until recently the Korean community was primarily composed of military brides who had followed their husbands to Fort Collins. Nearby Denver now has a small but growing community of Korean immigrants. When the women invited their family members—usually parents and siblings—to immigrate to the United States, the relatives often settled nearby. The women help their relatives adjust to American society, find jobs, work their way through U.S. bureaucracy, put their children in schools, and find places to live. Often, the women provide these services for other immigrants as well.

The military brides I met and interviewed were most likely among the first Koreans to settle in the areas in which they lived. Many of the women I met had come with their husbands as early as the 1950s and nearly all of them were connected in some way to one of two nearby military bases that were about an hour's drive from the closest city. The Korean immigrant community, based in the city itself, did not begin to form until the late 1970s.[13] Anecdotal evidence shows that here, as elsewhere, military brides played important roles in the formation of this immigrant community. Nearly every military bride I met had sponsored at least one relative, and most relatives settled nearby.

Mrs. Vaughn, for example, began sponsoring her relatives about ten years after she immigrated in 1960. First she sponsored her two nieces and a nephew so that they could attend school in the United States. The following year she sponsored their mother, her older sister. In later years the elder niece returned to Korea to marry, bringing her husband to America. Her husband then sponsored four of his siblings for immigration, most of whom in turn returned to Korea to marry and brought their spouses to the United States. These spouses then sponsored their siblings for immigration and these siblings in turn sponsored their spouses. Mrs. Vaughn's nephew also returned to Korea to marry and brought his wife to America. She in turn sponsored two of her siblings and her mother for immigration. In this way, Mrs. Vaughn has been the crucial first link that has allowed at least twenty-five Koreans to immigrate to the United States during the 1970s and 1980s. Nearly all of them settled in nearby areas. Some twenty years later, they own small businesses, attend Korean immigrant churches, and participate in various Korean community organizations such as merchant associations. Their children are part of the 1.5 and second generations increasingly visible in American schools, at American workplaces, and within Korean American communities.[14]

Other examples abound. Mrs. Crispin sponsored her mother, several siblings, and their families; most settled nearby and some later moved to other cities. Her nieces and nephews grew up in the same city, and one graduated from the local Ivy League university. Mrs. Dennison sponsored one of her older brothers and his family. Because she lacked contacts within the Korean community and thus could not help him find adequate employment, he moved to California where an older cousin secured him employment. Mrs. Brennan sponsored most of her siblings and their families, who settled nearby. Several moved elsewhere, but most remain in the area. Mrs. Goldin sponsored three of her siblings, all of whom live nearby. The majority of the immigrants sponsored in this fashion run their own family businesses, such as fast-food restaurants, neighborhood groceries, dry cleaners, gift shops, wig and beauty supply shops, fruit and vegetable stands, delis, clothing stores, and shoe stores. Many scraped together the startup capital in ways now well-documented by scholars of Korean American small businesses: rotating credit associations, money saved during years of working in another Korean-owned business, and loans from family members or friends.[15]

Military brides not only sponsored these immigrants, but they also assisted them at crucial points in their efforts to gain a foothold in their new environment. Military brides provided transportation; translation services; information about American bureaucracies that facilitated obtaining green cards, citizenship, business licenses, driver licenses, and the like; assistance in finding apartments or other places to live; introduction to local Korean institutions such as churches, grocery stores, community organizations; assistance in finding employment or business opportunities; and sometimes the money necessary to open one's own business. The assistance often began long before the relatives were sponsored for immigration, and extended far beyond immediate family members to the general Korean immigrant community.

A year and a half after Mrs. Goldin came to the United States in 1972, she ran away from and divorced her abusive husband. With few job skills and an infant to support, she ended up turning to her in-laws. Through them and other Americans, she was able to find housing and a job working at a factory. She recalled with hurt and sorrow that while Americans helped her, not a single Korean lent a hand. Nevertheless, Mrs. Goldin strove to make contact with the growing Korean immigrant community and made herself available to those who needed assistance. Ministers came to rely on her to provide translation for church members who

needed to face English-speaking American officials and for a thousand
other tasks. She also helped many Korean women get jobs at her factory
and trained them as well. At one point, she said, there were more than
twenty Korean women all working in the same division of the factory
who had been trained by her. But they excluded her from their circle:

> Whenever something happened or there was an event, they would just
> talk among themselves. Because I had married a black person, they
> would call me a nigger yankee whore and would have nothing to do
> with me. They would call on me when they needed someone to trans-
> late. I translated for them as I worked. And at that time I was having
> such trouble looking for an apartment {because no one wanted to rent
> to a single mother with a child, especially an Asian woman with a half-
> black, half-Asian child} and Americans helped me. They gave me cans
> of food and old clothes, but not a single Korean helped me at all. They
> just looked the other way.

Mrs. Goldin also helped several families during their first years in the
United States. Each of them turned their backs on her when her assistance was no longer needed. One family in particular seems to stand out
in her memory, for she mentioned them several times. She met them
when the wife began working in the factory. The family of five was
barely getting by after having been cheated out of their life savings by
an unscrupulous minister within months of their arrival in America.
Both the husband and wife had left stable careers because the wife was
convinced that life in America would be better. But unable to pass rigor-
ous licensing exams due to his limited English, the husband could not
practice medicine, and the wife's credentials as a college professor were
worthless in America. Their dream of starting a profitable business was
dashed when they lost their savings. Through her network of American
contacts, Mrs. Goldin supplied them with shoes and clothing for their
three young children, used furniture for their apartment, and other necessities. She became close to the children, who called her auntie. When
the wife was laid off from the factory job, Mrs. Goldin took time out from
her own job to help them begin a business selling fruits and vegetables
as street vendors. The business did well, and the family began to pros-
per. One day, Mrs. Goldin said, they moved to a different section of town

without telling her and cut off all ties with her. "The mother was ashamed of knowing someone like me," she said.

Mrs. Goldin was clear about the cause of her ostracism and was well aware that she was used by other Koreans. "Koreans don't like me because I married a black man," she said. "They call on me when they need me to translate, but they don't invite me to their homes for dinner. They avoid talking to me."

Sometimes if they were not pleased with the help they received, she said, they would curse her:

> I've known this woman for about twenty years and during that time I've helped her a lot. But once she wasn't pleased with the way things turned out, and she decided that it was my fault. And so right to my face, she called me a nigger yankee whore bitch. That's what she called me, a nigger yankee whore bitch. So you can imagine the kind of things people call me behind my back.

When asked why she continued to help Koreans when they treated her so badly, she answered:

> Because I was lonely, lonely. And also, because when I was growing up in the convent, I was taught to sacrifice, to help others, to always do good works. . . . And I was lonely. I wanted to talk to other Koreans, so that's why I helped them. But I always got hurt. I always got hurt.

As the eldest of five children, Mrs. Goldin never forgot her siblings and her parents. She said that she felt guilty because she had been well fed at the convent while they had often gone hungry when growing up. She sent money to them regularly, even when she herself was barely getting along. Twice when they needed large sums, she raised the money by entering into contract marriages with Korean men seeking permanent residency. Later, in the years when she prospered from running several businesses, she visited Korea to buy land, putting it in her brother's name because as a U.S. citizen she was not allowed to purchase Korean land in her own name. She helped them buy apartment homes and set them up in a factory business. Three of her siblings and their families immigrated under her sponsorship. She gave them her newspaper distribution business, which earned a steady income, and helped them find housing. They lived with her for a time in the upstairs apartments of her two-story home. But they too, she said, have treated her badly.

The brother remaining in Korea, she said, claims the land as his own and acts as if he had never received help from his sister. She had hoped to retire to Korea on that land, she said. The siblings in America accused her of using them, Mrs. Goldin said, because she gave them the newspaper distribution business. They contact her only when they need help. Mrs. Goldin recounted a recent incident, saying that she felt betrayed and was ready to give up.

There was a storm and the electricity went out when the trees near the house fell over. So I called my siblings and the younger sister, the one you saw earlier at the restaurant, answered the phone. So I told her that there was a big storm and what had happened, and I asked her to bring me some *ice water*, because there was nothing in the house at all and I wanted to at least have some ice. She said that she's sick and so she can't come. So I told her then to send our sister-in-law over, our brother's wife, and she said she would. I waited and waited, but no one came. No one even called to see how I was doing, whether I was dead or alive. No one brought me the water and ice I [had] asked for. They don't live far from me, but no one came by, not a single person. So at that time, I thought about a lot of things. Even siblings can't be counted on. I don't need them. I don't need anything, that's what I realized.

But a year later, she was still in contact with her siblings, and she was still helping them maneuver their businesses through American bureaucracies, interact with their children's schools and teachers, and otherwise manage immigrant life. "I still have to help them, they are my siblings," she said.

Mrs. Crispin also eventually realized that her siblings, who arrived in the early 1970s, contacted her only when they needed help. When her nieces and nephews became sick, she would take them to the doctor. In the summer, she took them to swimming lessons and on other outings. She would take two at a time at her home, offering them something akin to summer camp for a week or two. She tried to provide them a little bit of the fun that their parents, busy with work and unfamiliar with America, were not able to give. But now the nieces and nephews are all grown up, she said, the families are settled, and no one needs her any more. She has no contact with her family any more, she said, except occasionally with her mother.

So if you look at the life situation of military brides, they are like orphans, orphans. So now, I *give up. I just give up.* If I think about my family, it just makes me sad, so I just think of myself as an orphan without a family. That's how you have to live. . . . If they can gain something from you, then there is contact. Otherwise, nothing. . . . They are worse than strangers. Others, they call me and ask, "How are you doing?" When there's an event at the church, they call and tell me to come. But these brothers and sisters, no. Do they say, "Today is Chusok and you're alone, so come over"? No, there's nothing like that. "It's *Thanksgiving,* come over for some *turkey."* No, they don't do that. Before, I would invite them to *Thanksgiving, Christmas,* but now I am alone, what am I going to cook when I am alone? The ones with the large family should have holiday dinners and invite people like me who are alone. But *they not call me.* I don't want to call and say why don't you call me, why don't you write, why don't you send a *Christmas card.* No. There's no point. *I don't want to bother them.*

As for her youngest sister, Mrs. Crispin said, she hadn't had any contact with her for twenty years:

From my point of view, if I had a sister who lived alone, I would at least send a card, but you know, *why I bother her* when she doesn't do that? And now that she has her own family, she's probably busy. But someday she will realize . . . *That's all I wish for,* for her to realize. But then it will be *too late.*

Mrs. Crispin attributed difficult relations between military brides and their families to differences in acculturation. Misunderstandings often arose, she said, because the siblings did not understand the Americanized lifestyles of their sisters. She emphasized, however, that the fundamental issue was shame at having an internationally married sister.

Most of the women I met, whether settled in stable marriages or divorced, had difficult relationships with their families and cited instances of ostracism. But some women had good relations with their families. Without exception, they had stable families of their own. Often, but not always, their husbands were open to Korean culture and lifestyles. In several cases, the mother lived with the daughter and American son-in-law either permanently or for several months of the year. Some military brides shared with their siblings the responsibility of caring for aged parents, usually by sending money for living expenses and medical care.

At the level of family relations, then, gendered concepts of women marrying out of their families do not necessarily prevent close relationships with the women's natal families. In fulfilling these filial duties, military brides are emphasizing their identity as sisters and daughters and as Koreans. Women who are the eldest seem to have the greatest sense of responsibility, perhaps because in Korean society the eldest daughter is often placed in a quasi-maternal position vis-à-vis the other children. Although her siblings did not seem to appreciate her efforts, Mrs. Goldin, for example, stressed her sense of responsibility as the eldest. Mrs. Brennan also stressed her position as the eldest child and said with pride that she has always put her family first. As a young woman in Korea she left the family farm to work in Seoul, sending most of her earnings back home to her family. As a married woman in America, she continued to send money home. Her efforts on behalf of her family appear to have won her the lasting respect of her siblings. She recounted a recent incident in which she dressed down her brother, a middle-aged man in his fifties who lives in Korea, for not inviting their mother for a long visit. A few weeks later, she said, airplane tickets arrived for their mother, who had been living in America with another adult child. Mrs. Brennan said with pride that as the eldest, she is "still the queen" because her father had always supported her as the leader of the siblings and because she had always done her best to take care of them. "Even when I had nothing, I would send them something," she said.

During her first years in America, for example, she would deposit in the bank money that she earned taking care of other people's children. Her deposits were small—ten, fifteen, or twenty dollars—but regular. When the account had grown to thirteen hundred dollars, her husband was startled. Like Mrs. Brennan, he also came from a large and poor farming family and he had never seen such a large amount of money. Mrs. Brennan told him that she was going to send it all to her family in Korea. It was the sum total of their savings. He agreed, and the money was sent to Korea with the stipulation that it be used to buy a tractor. Mrs. Brennan made these kinds of remittances to her family as often as she could in the belief that she was helping not only her family, but also her country. By sending her hard-earned money to Korea, she was expressing her loyalty to both family and country and thereby affirming her identity as a Korean and as a daughter and sister. Said Mrs. Brennan:

> I'm uneducated, and living as an unlearned person, well, it's not like I earn lots of money and can be a big help to Korea. But I decided to send even small amounts to Korea. This kind of calculation came out, even from this ignorant brain: If I send one hundred dollars to Korea, where does this money go? It goes to Korea, right? So if in Korea they use this one hundred dollars they can make lots of products, sell them to foreign countries, and earn more money. That's what I figured out. So, even if it's only a penny, let's send it to Korea, that's what I decided. Sometimes I would empty out all my pockets and send it all, even though it wasn't much, it was what was in my reach, the best I could do. So when I send money, I am joyful, joyful, because not only is it a help to my family, it's also a help to my country.

Mrs. Brennan never went beyond the sixth grade, but she understood economics well enough to make a sophisticated link between personal economic behavior and national economic growth. She understood the importance of foreign exchange and that money is made with money, that is, the necessity for capital. With this understanding, she acted in the way that she believed would best help both her family and her homeland.

Eventually, Mrs. Brennan sponsored her family for immigration, first her mother and then several siblings. With the cooperation of her husband, she continues to help them. At the time of the interview, her husband had gone south to work at her brother's fast-food restaurant. This brother's wife had recently died after a long illness, and he needed help running the business. Mrs. Brennan credited this kind of involvement and support from her husband for helping maintain close relations with her family.

Outsiders

Regardless of whether relations with family and friends are good or bad, however, relations with other Koreans tend to be strained. Virtually every military bride I spoke with said that there was a feeling of distance, as if there was a wall separating them from other Koreans, and many spoke at length and with some emotion about their negative experiences. Many women noted that differences in lifestyle set them apart. Military brides feel that they cannot talk about their family lives, for instance, because other Koreans would not understand what it is like to live with an American husband. In addition, women felt that anything they said about their families might be taken as evidence for one or another stereotype about military brides. Others said that expressions of curiosity by Koreans made them feel like freaks. Many said that other Koreans often stopped their conversations when they approached, as if they were discussing secrets. One woman commented that sometimes she felt as if they treated her like a spy for the Americans. Military brides said that they often felt uncomfortable listening to complaints from Koreans about American culture, about the difficulty of living in America, and about racism, for it seemed to be a backhanded way of criticizing them for their marriages to Americans. Nearly all said that even when other Koreans are friendly, it was superficial. Other Koreans would associate with them at church or similar public spaces, but would never invite them to private gatherings, family events such as weddings, or to other social occasions that might lead to the development of a friendship.

Language is also problematic. For instance, most military brides do not use informal and disrespectful terms for Americans and non-Koreans, while many other Koreans sometimes do. Several military brides said that they were uncomfortable listening to Americans referred to by such names. In these situations, their use of the more polite terms would cause subtle ruptures in the flow of conversation, for it indicated a difference in perspective and opinion. Some military brides, especially the younger ones, find that other Koreans use casual forms of speech when talking to them, an indication of disrespect when used among adults who are neither close friends nor relatives. In most cases, it is a grave breach of etiquette, especially for men, to use such casual forms when speaking to married women, even if the woman is significantly younger. Their use by Koreans, both men and women, when speaking to younger military brides is thus a serious sign of disrespect and an indication of the low social status of military brides among other Koreans.

Some military brides who came decades ago find that they have forgotten a great deal of Korean. Self-conscious because they feel that their Korean is not refined and educated, they often avoid lengthy conversations. Mrs. Bugelli said that when she began attending meetings at a local military bride organization, many of the other women gently teased her for her clumsy Korean. After living in America for nearly forty years with virtually no contact with other Koreans, she had forgotten much of her mother tongue. When a military bride she met at these meetings persuaded her to attend Korean church, Mrs. Bugelli found it more comfortable to limit her interactions with the other Koreans to simple greetings. While military brides understood her situation, she said, other Koreans would not.

The efforts of some Koreans to hide their connections to military brides in their own families also makes social relations between military brides and other Koreans difficult. These immigrants are often more difficult to get along with, several military brides said. Said Mrs. Vaughn:

> If a sister has married an American, then that person is sometimes friendlier, but other people, *shame they think*, so they say that they came as students, they say they graduated from college. *Mostly they say that*, that they graduated from college, the ones who came like that, even though they can't even write the ABCs, they say they graduated from college. They say that life was good in Korea and they came here for nothing. Then I tell them to go. Why are you here, go back to your country, that's what I say. We married Americans and came here, so this is our country and we live here, but if you prefer Korea, then go back. Why do you criticize someone else's country? Just go. That's what I tell them.

Even as she described her vigorous retorts to other Koreans, Mrs. Vaughn said that she prefers to avoid their company. Language is one factor. A combination of a Japanese colonial education and years of life in America have prevented her from acquiring educated Korean speech.

It's been a long time since I came to America, and my Korean is poor, so I don't associate much with men, with intellectuals. Just say hello, and then spend my time with the women and that's it.

Like Mrs. Goldin, Mrs. Crispin went to great lengths to keep in touch with other Koreans. She always made herself available to help at church bazaars, to visit those who were ill, and so forth. Much of her activity was through churches. She recalled that she always made time to help out whenever she was called. After more than twenty years, however, she realized that none of her service provided her with a respected and stable position in the Korean immigrant community. By the time we met in the mid-1990s, she had curtailed much of her activity. There were so many times, she said, when it was clear that people failed to give her proper respect because she was a military bride. She recounted one such recent incident.

About five of us were going somewhere in a car. And one person says in a loud voice, "Oh, those internationally married women, they're a big issue." As long as they don't *bother* her, why is it a problem? I was upset, so I didn't get out of the car. That person didn't even know why. But another person figured it out and called me later that evening. She told me not to be upset. And I said of course I'm upset, I'm an internationally married woman and when I hear that kind of thing, naturally it upsets me. Then she said that her daughter married an American, she has an American son-in-law, but she's not upset. And so I replied, that's your daughter, not you. You'd feel differently if you yourself were the one who married an American and then heard those words. Then she told me that the person who made that comment didn't mean to, that it just slipped out, and that her daughter [had] also married an American.

Mrs. Crispin said that she does not understand why Koreans have such strong prejudices against women who marry foreigners, especially when their own daughters are marrying Americans they meet at school and at work.

Many military brides said that sometimes they don't like going to Korean grocery stores with their children because of the stares from other customers. They prefer to go alone and avoid these encounters. Mrs. Sommer, however, said she refused to let people's prejudices affect the way she leads her life. She takes her two elementary school daughters to Korean grocery stores and restaurants. For a time, she also took them to Korean school on Saturdays. Once, she said, a friend told her not to lose heart just because she had married a foreigner. She replied: "Lose heart? Why should I lose heart? Those people don't take care of me. They don't feed me, they don't teach me how to live. I'm in charge of my own life, so I don't pay any attention to them."

Yet this response seems to be partly bravado, for her next words indicated that the reactions of other Koreans do affect her.

> When I take the children out, sometimes people stare. The children look different, you know. So then I make the first move. I say, "The children are *tweegee*,[16] half Korean and half American." Then they say, "Oooh, no wonder." . . . I make the first move, so that they are left with nothing to say. There's no point in trying to ignore it or hide it. It doesn't work. But some Koreans, some Koreans stare and stare.

Mrs. Sommer criticized Koreans for treating military brides like curiosities or freaks and for putting a distance between themselves and military brides. She described Koreans' reactions when they find out that she married a foreigner:

> When they see our wedding pictures, they say, "Oh, your husband's a soldier," and already their tone of voice changes. Their tone of voice changes, it's like they're thinking, so, you're this and this and this. Their tone of voice is all different and what they say changes too. Another friend of mine, her husband said it's all in my head. I'm not stupid like a baby. I'm human and I'm over thirty, and it's not all in my head. That's what I told him. They say my daughters are pretty, and they see that they look a little different and they're confused. Then when they see my husband's picture, they say, "Ooh, he's American. Ooh, he's a soldier." The ends of their words get all stretched out, it gets all different. They say he's handsome and they ask what his parents do. When I tell them that they're college professors, they say, "Ooh, you got yourself a good husband." And they look me up and

down. I'm not imagining this because I'm self-conscious. It's so obvious in the way they look at me and the way they say, "Ooh, you got yourself a good husband." So I just reply, "Yup, I sure did." Koreans have to stop behaving like that, they really do.

Mrs. Brennan also sharply criticized Koreans for their treatment of military brides. When the owner of the local Korean video store told her that she was in a Korean television documentary about military brides, saying that it wasn't very good, Mrs. Brennan immediately sensed that the documentary presented negative images of military brides. Angry that military brides were singled out, she asked the storeowner, a Korean immigrant with a Korean husband, which of them was better off.

Are you as free as I am? No, she says. Are you as happy as I am? She says nothing, nothing at all. Why? Why do people think this way about internationally married women? Why? Frankly, even though I married a foreigner, I received more love from my mother-in-law than from any Korean mother-in-law. I didn't do anything much, but she's still alive today and she still loves me more than any Korean mother-in-law. What Korean mother-in-law wouldn't even let her daughter-in-law wash the dishes? That's naturally the daughter-in-law's task. And my husband, after twenty years of living together, he can tell when I'm angry just from the sound of my voice. And then he's careful not to further aggravate me, in case I explode. Would a Korean husband do that? Be afraid that his wife would get angry and explode, be afraid of this and so be careful not to aggravate her, how many Korean husbands would do this? What percent? Why do people look down on internationally married women? Why do people compare us and treat us differently like this?

Mrs. Brennan continued:

What I really want to say is this: If you marry a foreigner, you live with your husband. If you marry a fellow Korean, you live with your husband. So why do people emphasize that you married a foreigner? Don't women who marry foreigners eat *kimchi*? Do only those who marry fellow Koreans eat *kimchi*? No. We are all Koreans, the same people, all of us. The women who married foreigners, we are all the same Koreans. Don't look down on us.

Mrs. Brennan said that she was never told that the reporters were working on a documentary when she was interviewed, but was only asked to talk about a woman who fellow Koreans suspected had been killed by her American husband. She criticized the producers and the reporters, whom she called intellectuals, for making a documentary that focused only on the worst cases and for treating the women as objects rather than as human beings. Commenting on how such tragedies sensationalize people's lives, she said:

> I wish they would stop these foolish acts of lying down and spitting,[17] those intellectuals. That word keeps coming out, those intellectuals. I wish they would stop these foolish acts of lying down and spitting. If I meet those reporters again, I definitely have something to tell them. . . . Those people [featured in the documentary] are human beings too. They are not less than you. . . . Why did you see them as less than you, as if they were human garbage, and put them out there like that? They are human beings, those people, they have human dignity.

The documentary that provoked Mrs. Brennan's ire, a special two-part broadcast of a popular Korean newsmagazine program called *Producer's Diary*, discussed the fifty-year history of military brides.[18] Advertising itself as the first Korean broadcast to reveal the experiences of Korean women who married American soldiers, it promised to show both the "brightness" and the "darkness" of their lives. Part One, entitled "Abandoned American Dream," focused on military brides who were abused, divorced, addicted to drugs, living with abusive husbands, had mental or emotional problems, or had died or disappeared under suspicious circumstances. The two male reporters unrelentingly emphasized the lurid, the sensational, and the tragic for the full hour of the program. The women are figured as pathetic victims who chased the American Dream only to be abandoned and ruined. The footage presents the women as objects, inviting viewers to examine what is presented as grotesque phenomena on their bodies, evidence of their broken dreams and their ruined status. During an interview with one military bride, the camera zooms in for a close-up of her broken and missing teeth—damage done by her husband during repeated beatings—while the reporters talk about how difficult it is to look at such a miserable sight.

In other footage, the camera takes lengthy close-up shots of needle tracks and burn scars on a woman's arms and legs, while the reporters inform viewers that the woman is a drug addict and a prostitute who has been abandoned by her husband. The two reporters comment that such a fate is tragic. Aided by the camera, they repeatedly persist in casting the women as victims who have fallen to less-than-human status and invite viewers to look at the ruins. They miss opportunities to present the women as fellow human beings and to allow the women to tell fuller, more nuanced stories. Interviews with military brides at the Rainbow Center, a New York shelter run by a female Korean minister and a collective of military brides, focus only on the difficulties of their married lives and the ways in which they were victimized by their husbands. The women's resistance in leaving abusive husbands, their persistence as they struggle to heal themselves, their courage in constructing new lives, and their act of collective strength in working together to help fellow military brides is never mentioned, much less adequately addressed.

Part Two, entitled "The Korean Women of Killeen, Texas," purported to focus on one geographic community of military brides. Instead it focuses on the family lives of military brides in several areas, including Killeen and New Jersey. The picture presented here is again a bleak one. The reporters interview women whose husbands and in-laws are abusive, who have poor relationships with their children, whose parents and siblings have disowned them, and otherwise have difficult family lives. Although the reporters claim that no one had really known what happened to military brides until they produced this documentary, the documentary serves to reinforce pervasive stereotypes about the tragic, depraved lives of these women.

The documentary also displays a double standard by simultaneously chastising military brides for being too Korean and for allowing their children to become Americanized. Noting that the abused women seem to be adhering to Korean traditions that teach women to endure suffering and honor husbands, the reporters speculate that this behavior may have aggravated the abuse they suffered from their husbands. Invoking the old adage, when in Rome do as the Romans do, they remark that the women shouldn't cling to Korean ways but should instead become more American. What the American way of dealing with an abusive husband is, however, or how it would prevent abuse is not discussed. By suggesting that the women could have avoided abuse if they had behaved differently, the reporters are not-so-subtly turning the responsibility for the abuse onto the abused. In another passage, the reporters comment regretfully that the children of most military brides are completely Americanized and remark that the mothers should have paid more attention to this matter. Then they present as good examples a Korean-language school for the children, run by a church in Killeen, and a military bride who says that she teaches her children Korean. Her family is presented as a model military bride family, with the implication that the woman's efforts are responsible for this success. The overall effect is to divide military brides into successes and failures—with abject failures presented as the overwhelming majority—and to turn the responsibility for success or failure onto the women themselves.

The documentary also frequently suggests that women who married American soldiers aspired to a better life and hoped for the American Dream. This gives the impression that the women who married American soldiers were deluded fools while the remainder of the Korean populace knew better. Nowhere do they mention that South Korea as a whole has been captivated by the American Dream for more than five decades. The reporters also note with an air of regret that Korean immigrants in America ostracize military brides, and end the documentary with a plea for Korean immigrants to extend warm, helping hands to their less fortunate fellow Koreans, the military brides. Because they fail to mention that Koreans in Korea also ostracize military brides, they give the impression that, unlike Koreans in Korea, immigrant Koreans care little about the fate of fellow Koreans in a foreign land. This resonates with opinion in South Korea that Korean immigrants are grasping, greedy people who value money more than human life, an image that was reinforced by Korean media coverage of the killing of Latasha Harlins by Soon Ja Du.[19] The effect is to position military brides and other immigrant Koreans as different from and inferior to Koreans in Korea.

Military brides are also unfairly represented in the Korean-language press in the United States. Articles tend to emphasize their suffering and their hardships, attributing this to their marriages with Americans, or depicting them as unfortunates in need of assistance. Immigrant Koreans, in contrast, are positioned as the norm and as potential benefactors. A series of articles in the Philadelphia edition of the *Dong-A Ilbo*, for example, profiled a military bride with a terminal illness whose husband was searching for her family in Korea. Due to her illness, she and her husband were destitute and dependent on the assistance of others. The newspaper began collecting funds from readers and provided regular updates on the couple. Articles chronicled their trip to Korea to meet the woman's family, who had been found, their return home, and their life.[20] Another article featured a woman hospitalized with a terminal illness, emphasizing that she had been completely abandoned and had no one to even visit her. Accompanying the article were photos of an emaciated woman in a hospital gown, displaying—under the guise of sympathy—a military bride's body as grotesquerie for viewers and readers to look at in much the same manner as the Korean television documentary.[21]

Stereotypes about military brides and their presumably miserable lives are so prevalent and strong that any article about a destitute Korean woman is assumed to be the story of a military bride. A *Dong-A Ilbo* article about a homeless Korean woman is a prime example.[22] Her situation was publicized by a Korean shop owner and trustee of the Philadelphia Korean Association who was appalled that she was apparently selling sex in exchange for crack cocaine. The reporter never talked to the woman herself, relying solely on the male shop owner for information. The owner was quoted as saying that while ultimate responsibility for her situation lay with the woman, he didn't like to see a "woman of his own kind" being treated like a prostitute by foreign men. Here one can read a clear expression of Korean male pride linked to the behavior and fate of Korean women. The article ended with an appeal for help. Although this article did not say that the woman was a military bride, the local Korean community took it for granted that she had been abandoned by an American husband. They simply could not imagine a different scenario.

Military brides can also be claimed as fellow Koreans when their stories can be told to match classic scripts about respectable women's lives and when there is some reflected glory to be gained. The Atlanta edition of the *Korea Times*, for example, carried a story about a University of Georgia football player, a rising star in college football, whose mother was Korean.[23] Headlined "The Son of a Korean," the article cast his mother's life as one full of tears and solitary suffering endured for the sake of her son. She was thus made to fit a traditional Korean character, the long-suffering Korean mother who endures hardships for the sake of her children. Following the classic story line, the article concluded that her suffering had been rewarded because she had raised a successful son who, displaying traditional Korean filial loyalty, vowed to take care of his mother. Her son was also subtly claimed as Korean by virtue of his filial piety and his Korean mother, even though the biracial children of military brides are generally considered Americans.

Many military brides noted that other Koreans tended to treat them sometimes as Americans and sometimes as Koreans, depending on what best suited their interests. Mrs. Crispin recounted an incident with the Korean immigration office while she was in Korea and her husband was in Vietnam. After accompanying a friend to the immigration office, she discovered that she was supposed to register as a foreigner within six months if she wanted to stay in the country for a longer period. When she told the immigration official that she had already been there for eight months and had not known about the registration requirement, the official confiscated her passport.

> They told me that I had entered someone else's country and vio-
> lated the laws and that this was a serious offense and that foreigners
> couldn't go around violating laws. So here they're treating me like an
> American. But on the other hand, they tell me that I'm Korean, and
> how could I possibly not know the laws of my own country and be-
> have so badly among my own people. So it's just a big headache.

Other military brides echoed Mrs. Crispin's sentiments. When associating with other Koreans, they said, these seemingly arbitrary flip-flops made relations difficult. As one bride put it, "When they need you, they treat you like a fellow Korean, but when they're done with you, they treat you like a foreigner." Koreans' positioning of military brides as Americans in one context and as Koreans in another, rather than being a way to cope with shifting fields of power, is a way to exert power. By defining military brides so that the women are always at a disadvantage, other Koreans are asserting their power over people they consider inferior. Similarly, by distancing themselves from military brides when association would be a humiliation and claiming military brides as one of their own when such association confers benefits, Koreans manipulate identity to their advantage.

There are limits to the malleability of identity, however. Even as Koreans treat military brides as outside the realm of Korean society and as foreigners, they view them as fundamentally connected to Koreans, as a skeleton in the closet that they would rather not discuss. Thus the overwhelming majority of Koreans who learned of my research topic winced as if I had wounded them, and then said something like, "Wouldn't it be better not to root about in the shadows? Why not write about something we can be proud of?" Some Koreans, particularly second-generation Korean Americans, recounted stories of their experiences with military brides. Most simply remarked, "Oh, you're studying those women who always sit together at church, the ones that no one else talks to." One Korean American woman, a college student, recalled that one of her aunts had married an American soldier. This aunt had sponsored their immigration to the United States, and most members of the extended family had come to America through her. But this aunt was rarely invited to family gatherings. Furthermore, the student said, the adults in the family made it clear to the children that having a military bride in the family was to be kept a secret. While racism is certainly part of the dynamic of this kind of shunning, it is also a way for Korean immigrants to become American, much the same way that shunning camptown women allows Korea to be a sovereign nation in partnership with the United States. At the same time, it also allows Korean immigrants to affirm a Koreanness that seems threatened in the context of lives lived in America.

Cultural critic Lisa Lowe argues that Asian immigrants are forced to negate their own histories—of war, of oppression under imperialist and neoimperialist powers, of racial discrimination—in order to become American. Post-1965 Asian immigrants, she argues, go against the American sense of national identity precisely because of that history. Becoming American, then, requires negating that history and adopting the U.S. national narrative that disavows American imperialism.[24] For Korean immigrants, negating their history of subjugation under the United States begins even before they step on American soil, for the ostracism of camptown women discussed in chapter 1 is nothing less than that negation.

This negation continues with their shunning of military brides. By shunning her, the Korean immigrant simultaneously denies the history of subjugation, thus adopting the U.S. national narrative, and denies that he or she is like her in any way, thus affirming his or her Koreanness.

In the Korean (immigrant) imaginary, the military bride is figured as a lost soul, someone who has turned her back on her culture and her people in favor of an American and an American life. The military bride is thus seen as somehow not really Korean, as one who has crossed a border separating Koreans from non-Koreans. That her children are not full-blooded Koreans only serves to underscore this otherness. She is also figured as a pathetic wretch, a victim of domestic abuse, betrayal, and abandonment by an American husband, someone who may "return" to prostitution, or an easy sexual conquest. Her status as victim—mostly at the hands of American men—serves to warn Korean women that crossing that border over into non-Korean territory leads only to disaster. Her image as an easy sexual conquest serves to separate her from other Korean women, who are positioned as virtuous women. A common rumor circulating among Korean immigrants in the Philadelphia area has it that a group of military brides would gather once a week or once a month and go "hunting" for Korean men. Korean men seemed to believe that military brides were "hungry" for their companionship and therefore sought them out in this manner. Many men recounted this rumor to me as fact. Korean women tended to believe that military brides were morally suspect and would pose a threat to the stability of their marriages. Some women repeated this rumor to me as proof that it wasn't a good idea for a decent Korean woman to make friends with a military bride. Said one middle-aged woman, "They'll get close to you and steal your husband. They're crass and dirty, those women."

But these characterizations of military brides are not only gross stereotypes, they also serve to deflect attention away from the status of Korean immigrants themselves in relation to Koreans in Korea. Korean immigrants, like the military bride, have crossed a border by crossing the Pacific Ocean to live in a foreign land, raise their children as citizens of that land, and die in that land. To Koreans who have remained in Korea, the *jae mi gyopo* (a term for people of Korean descent in America) is a dual figure, someone to be envied for having achieved access to the American utopia, but also someone who has forsaken the homeland. Portrayals of Korean Americans in the Korean popular media, in television dramas such as "L.A. Arirang" and "1.5" illustrate this duality. In addition, media accounts of Korean-black conflict and the 1992 Los Angeles civil unrest have portrayed immigrant Koreans as crass and greedy money-grubbers who have encountered little more than suffering and tribulation in their pursuit of the American Dream. The overall image is one of failure and an uncertain future in a foreign land. Thus for Korean immigrants who may be insecure about their identity, ambivalent about their own history of immigration, and uncertain whether coming to America was the right thing to do, shunning military brides is one way to simultaneously affirm an identity as Koreans and claim the American Dream. In other words, Korean immigrants portray themselves as success stories, people who have established stable, satisfying lives in America while maintaining their Koreanness, unlike military brides, whom they cast as failures, people who failed both to achieve the American Dream and to maintain their Koreanness.

The ostracism of military brides is so severe that it carries over even into Korean churches, where they are shunned by their fellow congregants. As the remarks by second-generation Korean Americans indicate, it is common to see military brides sitting alone during church services. Church members sometimes accept one or two, particularly if the women are middle- or upper-class and appear well-educated, as members of church organizations such as the church women's group. But in general, other Koreans do not allow military brides to participate in church activities. The Rev. Geumhyun Yeo recounted the following incident from her church: The military brides gathered together and decided that they wanted to participate in the life of their church. After much discussion, the women decided that they wanted to help prepare the food for the annual Thanksgiving dinner. Their proposal, however, was rejected by the church women's group which was composed of Korean women married to Korean men. These women believed that military brides were dirty, unclean, unsanitary, and just not fit to prepare food. The message to the so-called "internationally married women" was clear: "You are not really one of us. We will tolerate your presence, but only as long as we can ignore you."

Self-Definition

Military brides do not always accept this ostracism, however. Faced with blatant rejection, the military brides at Rev. Yeo's church did not quietly return to the shadows assigned to them. They went ahead and prepared the food. In a direct response to stereotypes of dirt and uncleanliness, they wore pure white aprons and chef's hats to serve up a Thanksgiving meal of turkey with all the trimmings. (Since the Korean women were preparing Korean food, the military brides wanted to prepare something different.) It was a hit with the children at the church, and the food prepared by the military brides ran out while the food prepared by the other Korean women was left over.

For these women and other military brides, their marriage to Americans has not stripped them of their sense of Korean identity. Although at times military brides may position themselves as Americans—as Mrs. Vaughn does when she tells Koreans complaining about life in America to return to Korea—they usually position themselves as Koreans. In doing so, they refuse to accept the notion that they are no longer really Korean due to their outmarriage. Sometimes, in a move common to other immigrant Koreans, they position themselves as more Korean and as more patriotic than those who have never left Korea. Said Mrs. Brennan, "You have to go overseas to become a patriot. When you're on your own land, you don't know." Discussing her buying habits, she continued:

> Why should I buy Japanese things? I want to help them sell even one piece of Korean product, so whenever possible, I want to buy [things] made in Korea. Why? Because I'm made in Korea. I have to help my country, I can't ask others to do it for me, isn't that right?

Mrs. Crispin also presented military brides as more Korean than other Koreans, saying that military brides displayed more traditional Korean traits in their lifestyles:

> When I look at how Korean families live and how military brides live, they are so thrifty, these military brides. And they do twice the work, for their children, for their husbands, for their relatives, they do all this faithfully. But if you look at the Korean families, they take care of

only their own [nuclear] family. "We don't have to get involved with others," that's how they are. But despite all this, the ones who are never treated well are always the military brides. So I always say, the ones who are really good housewives and everything are the military brides, yet they are the ones who don't get any recognition.

To be recognized by fellow Koreans as respectable Korean women is a common desire among military brides. It is also a common self-definition asserted in the face of dissenters. This is captured in the title of Chon S. Edwards's autobiography, *I Am Also a Daughter of Korea*.[25] "Daughter of Korea" denotes the ideal Korean woman, and her assertion that she too is a daughter of Korea—"I am also" rather than simply "I am"—indicates both her awareness that others do not agree and her resistance to that disagreement. Another military bride put it succinctly:

They treat me badly, so I avoid them. It's more comfortable to associate with other women like me. But no matter what they say, they can't change who I am. I'm a good person, a good Korean, and I work hard to be a good wife and a good mother. When they curse me and treat me badly, they are only spitting in their own faces.

In their assertions of self-identity, military brides consistently display a gendered sense of self, as daughter, sister, wife, and mother that occupies as important a space as their sense of self as Koreans. Indeed, the two are not easily separable, for their sense of what makes a good daughter, sister, wife, and mother is bound up with their sense of being Korean. With these self-assertions, they resist the equally gendered identities of fallen woman and outmarried Korean that are imposed upon them by Korean-American communities.

CHAPTER 6

Sisters Do It for Themselves

Building Community

When Mrs. Bugelli first arrived in the United States in 1957, her father-in-law clipped an article in the local newspaper about another Korean woman who had married an American. He arranged for the two women to meet. Mrs. Bugelli recalled that she was so happy to see another Korean that she could barely contain herself. It is impossible, she said, to describe her joy at meeting another Korean after being alone in a sea of foreign faces. But because both women were busy with work and family, they were unable to meet regularly. Eventually they lost contact. Mrs. Bugelli was to have little contact with other Koreans until she was drawn into a regional military brides' organization in the 1990s.

Mrs. Crispin, who arrived in 1965, recalled that an American asked for her phone number at an open house she attended during her first months in the United States. The American knew of another Korean military bride in the area and promised to get them in touch. One day, Mrs. Crispin's telephone rang. When she answered, "Hello?" a woman responded in Korean. It was the first time Mrs. Crispin had heard Korean since her arrival in America several months earlier. The two women became friends, working at the same factory, cooking and eating Korean food together, maintaining contact as they followed their husbands across oceans and to different states. This new friend had arrived in 1957 by boat, eight years before Mrs. Crispin. The two women remained close until, faced with her husband's adultery, Mrs. Crispin's friend committed suicide in the mid-1970s. Feeling the need for military brides to formally organize themselves, Mrs. Crispin was to become a founding member of a military bride organization in 1979.

These are just two examples of Korean military brides connecting with each other during those early years when fellow Koreans were hard to find. Some, like Mrs. Bugelli, found that the pressures of making a living and caring for a family left no time for socializing. Others, like Mrs. Crispin, built lasting friendships that led to the desire to create organizations of military brides. Whatever her situation, however, every military bride I met spoke of trying to meet Koreans. Many said that while they wanted to meet Koreans in general, they were most interested in meeting military brides like themselves. Some remembered that other Koreans, particularly students who often came from wealthy families and assumed that military brides were uneducated and lower class, maintained their distance. Only with fellow military brides, they said, could they develop close friendships.

In those early years during the 1950s and 1960s when Koreans were few and far between, sympathetic husbands and in-laws often helped them connect. As was the case with Mrs. Bugelli, articles in local newspapers about hometown boys bringing back Korean wives, when spotted by an in-law, sometimes became the link that connected them to their first Korean acquaintances. Sometimes word of mouth through fellow church members or colleagues at work provided in-laws with information about other Korean military brides and the means to introduce them. Some military brides, however, recalled that their husbands and in-laws frowned on their meeting with other Koreans, effectively preventing such meetings. For these women, it was often years before they would be able to connect with fellow Koreans. Other women recalled coincidentally meeting other military brides at workplaces such as factories.

Sometimes women would contrive ways to accidentally meet other Koreans whom they encountered in public spaces. Mrs. Crispin recalled that whenever she and her husband spotted an Asian, especially an Asian woman, her husband (using a Korean term of endearment reserved for married couples) would call out to her, Yuhbo! If the person looked up or paid attention, said Mrs. Crispin, then that was a sign that she was Korean. At the Chinese grocery store where Mrs. Crispin bought food items similar to those used in Korean cooking, she would sometimes spot a woman whom she felt was Korean. Then she would accidentally bump grocery carts, excuse herself in Korean, and strike up a conversation if the woman turned out to also be Korean.

This same method was used by Mrs. Ramos, who arrived more than two decades later, in 1987. Mrs. Ramos explained that even though most people at the Korean grocery store were Korean, you couldn't simply approach them and begin talking. There had to be an excuse. So she would look for young women like herself, bump carts, or perhaps absent-mindedly walk backward into them while examining a potential purchase, and then begin a conversation. As a young military bride widowed just months after her arrival in the United States, Mrs. Ramos was desperate to make friends. Mrs. Ramos said that she was able to make two friends this way, and that she is still in touch with one of them, who like herself is a military bride.

When the women were stationed with their husbands at a major military base, connecting with one another was easier, especially by the late 1960s. Several women recalled meeting many Korean military brides while stationed with their husbands in Germany or Okinawa during the 1970s or 1980s. Mrs. Peterson, who spent the late 1980s in Germany, remembered regularly getting together with other Korean women and their soldier husbands for barbecues, and meeting other Korean women to go shopping, have coffee and a long talk, take their children outside to play, and for lunches of Korean food. There were Korean women everywhere, so it was really easy to meet each other, she said, noting that she remains in touch with several of the women.

Because most of the women followed their military husbands from base to base, they met and made friends in numerous geographical locations. These friends would also move from place to place. As a result, many women had a web of friends and acquaintances spread across the United States. Nearly everyone I met, for example, spoke of friends in other states, adding explanatory remarks such as, "We met in Germany." They often exchanged information about the areas where they lived and about the situation of Korean military brides. Women who were plugged into these networks had access to a wide variety of information, from how to make imitation red pepper paste to how to find a job. These networks sometimes coalesced into formal organizations, sometimes remained informal groupings of friends, and sometimes were based in churches. Membership in these networks often overlapped, so that churches, organizations, and informal groupings were linked through personal ties and mutual members.

In forming these networks, Korean military brides were adapting familiar social forms to their unfamiliar situations as intermarried Korean immigrant women. Networks of female friends and women-only organizations have played significant roles in Korean women's lives throughout the twentieth century. Usually formed by women attending the same schools or living in the same neighborhoods, these friendship networks have provided women with companionship, information, and a peer group against which to measure themselves and their lives. Women in South Korea have also organized themselves to address various issues in their lives.[1] Factory women have played a major role in the labor movement, and middle-class housewives have organized consumer associations, parent associations, and neighborhood associations. Although these housewife organizations ostensibly concern themselves with traditional female domestic concerns such as children's education and the proper way to keep house, they have also used the rhetoric of domesticity to expand the boundaries of acceptable activities for respectable women. In addition, these seemingly conservative organizations—often derided as groups where "idle housewives" meet to socialize—can become forums for women to critically question their condition and the forces shaping their lives, and thereby become a site for subversive action.[2]

Likewise, the socializing of Korean military brides seeking familiar companionship in a strange new world created spaces where the women could define themselves and their worlds, provide critical assistance to each other, and affirm self as they affirmed one other. Through their socializing, then, they created community and sisterhood out of their common status as Korean military brides. At the heart of this community were several kinds of social organizations: the Korean immigrant church, specifically those churches located near military bases which catered primarily to military brides; independent, regional organizations of

Korean military brides; on-base military bride organizations; and informal networks of friends and acquaintances that stretched across state
lines and even across oceans and continents. By the 1970s and 1980s, military brides newly arrived in the United States or just moving to a new
area were able to tap into these organizations and find assistance as they
settled in, companionship, and the opportunity to belong to a community of their own. Unlike those women who arrived in the 1950s and
1960s, they were not dependent on sympathetic in-laws or husbands to
meet each other, and they were not "alone in a sea of foreign faces."

Some women were able to plug into these community networks even
before they arrived in the United States. Mrs. Orellana, for example,
participated in an on-base association of Korean military brides after
she married in Korea. There she began to become acquainted with the
world of Korean military brides, hearing stories about life at other U.S.
military bases such as those in Germany and Japan, advice on what to
do and not to do in America, and tips for adjusting to life as a U.S. military dependent.

Once she arrived in the United States in 1991, Mrs. Orellana was able
to rely on these networks each time she followed her husband to a new
post in a different state. Her minister, whose church in most cases was
near the base and whose congregants were primarily Korean military
brides, would usually be able to refer her to a Korean church in the area
she was moving to. Military brides with whom she became friends
would sometimes also be able to put her in touch with their friends in the
area. In this way, Mrs. Orellana moved to each new location equipped
with personal introductions to a new set of contacts.

The community created by Korean military brides should not be ex-
aggerated. There is no national organization that formally links the numerous regional organizations. Links between organizations are often
tenuous and dependent on personal connections. The women have not
yet been able to create institutions of their own that fully meet their common needs. Most organizations are social clubs rather than associations
devoted to community service for military brides. Dependent on volun-
teers, they are often limited in the scope of activities they can pursue.
And military brides do not control all the organizations that sustain
them. Although the women as congregants can exert a great deal of control over their churches, for example, the churches are nevertheless

under the formal control of denominational organizations. The ministers are Korean men who often have little knowledge or understanding of military brides before they are assigned to a military bride church.[3] The nomadic life of military families results in an ever-revolving congregation for most such churches, which only serves to weaken the women's influence over them. In addition, it is impossible for these organizations and networks to reach all Korean military brides. I met numerous women who were isolated from any organization and lived rather solitary lives. Nevertheless, Korean military brides as a whole have built a network of ties—personal and organizational—that allow them to connect with one another and often provide valuable, practical assistance. Perhaps more importantly, they have imagined themselves into a coherent community with common interests, a community in which they can express and receive affirmations of self and of sisterhood.

For Us Women Only

The hotel nightclub is suddenly filled with Korean women, boisterous, laughing, dancing together, snatches of shouted Korean hanging in the air against the music. They are on vacation, these women, and they are reveling in the freedom from husbands, children, and daily household chores, their communal play a respite from the often alienating lives they lead as wives of Americans. The others, mostly white Americans, stare in surprise. Mrs. Vaughn laughs with delight as she describes their reactions:

> This is what is so *fun* about it. We go into a hotel. *They are really wondering*. How come so many Asian women are coming here alone? There are more than one or two things that are surprising. And then of course these people think that Korean women are just sooooo quiet. But we like to *enjoy* and we are very lively, so these people just don't know what to do. We like to dance, too, so when the music comes on we all go out to dance and it's just filled with Asians, with women, dancing. Because all of us women dance together, wherever we go people are surprised, they are really startled. Some Americans ask us why

we are only women. They think we came from a foreign country, they don't realize that we live in America. When we say that we left our husbands at home, they ask us how we can do that. They are so surprised, Americans, because they don't do that. They always travel together. So they are so startled. They ask us how come the husbands don't say anything. A lot of things surprise them.

Since 1978, a regional organization of Korean military brides has been going on vacation and startling Americans every year. They have been to Cancun, to the Bahamas, and to many tourist destinations in the United States. At the time of the interview in 1996, they were planning a cruise. Although such "women-only" trips may be unfamiliar, even strange, to most Americans, they are contemporary extensions of intimate female friendships common in Korean society. Some middle-class women in Korea, for example, go on trips with their women friends during college and again after their children are grown and married. For the women in this organization, the trips are a chance for personal enjoyment and a way to affirm their bonds of friendship as Korean women married to Americans. Some women, like Mrs. Vaughn, also took pleasure in Americans' surprise, a pleasure linked to breaking American stereotypes that label them as quiet, docile, and subservient to husbandly authority. Her comment that American couples always travel together can thus be read as a subtle way of asserting the freedom of Korean military brides in comparison to supposedly liberated American women. It is a way of saying that Americans think that Korean women are bound to their husbands, but in fact it's American women who do not have freedom. As the women express themselves in loud, boisterous behavior, as they dance and shout to each other in Korean, they proclaim their shared autonomy and identity.

The annual vacation was not always a women-only event. Husbands were included in the first vacation. Consequently, Mrs. Vaughn explained, that first trip was no fun. Husbands have since been excluded from what has become the highlight of the group's annual activities. Mrs. Vaughn, a cofounder of the organization, explained why traveling with the husbands turned a vacation into work:

You have to worry about food, you have to go around with them all the time. We women just want to have fun together talking and enjoying, but if the husbands come along, it's no fun. . . . You have to look after everything for them. What are you doing? What do you want to eat? What shall we eat? If we go by ourselves then we can just cook Korean food for ourselves, but if we take the men along then we have to prepare American food for them and it's just a nuisance.

She also noted that when the women are by themselves they can talk in Korean, but that if the husbands come along, then they have to use English. It just isn't the same, she said, explaining that the whole atmosphere, the entire feel of the vacation is altered. The vacation is meant to be a break from daily life, but if the husbands come along, the burdens of daily life intrude. Mrs. Vaughn's comments indicate that those burdens are cultural ones as well, the burden of adapting oneself to American culture in order to perform one's role as the wife of an American. Without the husbands, the women are free to enjoy themselves, to eat Korean food and speak Korean and laugh and play. There is no need for them to mold themselves to the role of wife or to the demands of American culture. Without necessarily denying or negating their lives as military brides, they can temporarily forget its burdens.

In seeking out other Korean women, particularly others also married to American men, military brides are often seeking a respite from their daily lives as well as companionship that they cannot find with foreigners, even those as intimate as their husbands. The annual vacation is perhaps the most overt expression of this need, but it is also expressed through other activities in numerous formal organizations and informal networks of military brides. Most areas with military brides have at least one formal military bride organization. They are generally called Korean American Wives Association or International Wives Association and are open to all so-called "internationally married women," that is, Korean women married to non-Korean men. In practice, however, the vast majority of members are military brides, for other internationally married women tend to shun military brides in an effort to avoid the stereotypes associated with them.

In the area in which I did most of my research, there are three regional Korean military bride organizations with a combined membership of several hundred. These organizations were founded by the women themselves with little or no prodding from others such as husbands, social workers, or ministers. In all three cases, the women felt the need for a group and set about organizing one. The two military bases in the region also have their own Korean military bride organizations, as do many U.S. military bases around the nation and the world. Although the on-base associations are loosely sponsored by the military as one of numerous military-dependent organizations, such as other military wives' associations that are expected to provide volunteer service, the regional associations are independent of any external sponsorship. The base associations are often an arena where women compete on the basis of the husbands' rank and promotions, such that a social hierarchy emerges among the women that mimics the military hierarchy of their husbands. Service in such on-base associations can sometimes influence a husband's promotion, and association presidents are invariably the wives of officers.

The regional associations, however, offer a more relaxed atmosphere of fellowship. This is largely because most members of the regional association are a step or two removed from the military, their husbands now living civilian lives. Women who had participated in both on-base and regional associations saw the on-base associations as just an "activity," but viewed the regional associations as tightly knit communities. The latter offer members the chance to be part of a community and have a sense of belonging, which many military brides have been denied by both mainstream Korean and American communities. Some organizations also offer opportunities to work for causes that military brides feel are close to their interests, such as Amerasians in Korea or fellow military brides who have fallen upon hard times.

A Group of One's Own

As military brides found themselves shunned by the growing Korean immigrant community and by their own relatives, and also found that no matter how wholeheartedly they embraced American ways, Americans still saw them as "Oriental girls," they came to feel the need to develop their own community, explained Mrs. Crispin, a founding member of a regional Korean military bride organization.

It's hard to associate with Americans, they call us *Oriental, Oriental girl* and this and that, but if we try to get involved in Korean communities, then they label us as internationally married women and say this and that about us, so there's no place for us to go. So that's why this *group* started.

The organization, which I will call the ABC Korean American Wives Association, held its first meeting in 1979 and drew its members from a wide area that included an army base, an airforce base, and a major metropolitan area with a sizable Korean immigrant population. Cofounders and initial members included not only women who had married American soldiers, but also Korean women who had married other foreigners, such as the daughter of Korean novelist Yi Kwang Soo, who had married a South Asian and taught at an American university, and Chon S. Edwards, who had married an American in the early 1950s and became an exemplary example of the internationally married woman as civilian ambassador.

According to Mrs. Kingston, another founding member, several women had talked among themselves for three or four years about the need for an organization for internationally married Korean women. Finally, they decided to do it. After contacting several other women, they held an organizational meeting in 1979. About eight women attended that first meeting. Once the organization was founded, she said, so many women became members that people wondered where they had all come from. The organization grew to several dozen members. Several dozen more women, although not members, were acquainted with the organization. People were surprised, she said, that there were so many military brides.

The organization began to have some internal problems, however, and the president proposed dissolving the association. The issue seems to have centered around the association president. Women who were members at that time recalled that some members found the president domineering and not sufficiently respectful of others. Some felt that the president, who came from a prominent family and was married to a civilian professional, may have looked down on those members who came from less-educated backgrounds and were married to enlisted soldiers. Mrs.

Kingston explained that while the president was a very smart woman, she lacked social skills and the ability to get along with the diverse group of women represented among military brides:

> Some people came because they did not like [the sexism in Korea], some women had run away from home and become *prostitute* and met an American *yankee* and came that way, . . . some people met at the *PX* or the *commissary*, oh, there are all kinds of people. But the smart ones are smart, so the *members*, they thought, what kind of a president is this? And they started to drop out.

When members began to leave, according to Mrs. Kingston, the president told the remaining members that the organization should be dissolved. Mrs. Kingston explained why she felt that she had to step in and keep the organization together:

> Those internationally married women, that's what other people are going to say. Those internationally married women were all yankee whores, they've never been educated. A bunch of ignorant and crass women got together, what else can you expect from them? Of course they break up. That's how Korean society sees us, that's their perspective. *They do, of course they do.* So in the end, I became the president and we enjoyed quite a boom.

Mrs. Kingston's awareness of stereotypes and prejudice against military brides prompted her to work to keep the organization together. She did not want to provide "evidence" that would bolster the prejudices against them. Other women agreed that they could not let the organization die, and joined her in winning back former members and sponsoring a wide variety of activities. They organized fund-raisers for Korean orphans and Amerasians, held social gatherings for military brides, and spoke out in the local Korean media about the successful lives of military brides in an effort to combat negative stereotypes. They also helped military brides who had suffered from domestic violence, whose husbands had abandoned them, or who needed jobs. As the organization grew, it spun off a second organization, which I will call the XYZ Korean American Wives Association. The two organizations divided their geographical territory, so that the original ABC Association drew its members from outlying suburban and semirural areas, while the splinter organization drew its members from the major metropolitan area. Both organizations remain active, sometimes sponsoring joint activities. Several women note that only the dedication and unity of the women have kept the two organizations running these many years.

From this episode threatening dissolution early in the organization's history emerge themes of respect and solidarity. Often denied respect by other Koreans as well as Americans, the woman demand it from each other and show little tolerance of those fellow internationally married women who are unable to respect them. Having joined an organization where they expected to enjoy companionship and mutual respect with other women like themselves, they were dismayed to find a president who failed to properly respect the members and displayed biases similar to those readily encountered among mainstream Korean immigrants. Such biases had no place in the community that the women had envisioned for themselves.

That episode also reveals that while all Korean women who marry non-Korean men are categorized as "internationally married women," the women themselves make finer distinctions. A fundamental distinction is that between women married to soldiers, the military brides, and women married to civilian foreigners. Women in the latter category often strive to set themselves apart from military brides and the camptown shadow associated with the label "internationally married women." Often perceiving themselves to be superior, some women simply avoid the company of military brides, while others try to assume leadership roles over women they view as uneducated and in need of uplift. This is in part also a class division based on the husbands' status, for the civilian husbands are often well-educated professionals, such as scholars in Asian studies and related disciplines, diplomats, or businessmen engaged in international trade, while the military husbands are generally enlisted men. In part, it was this division between military brides and other internationally married women that threatened to destroy the organization. Rather than being resolved through a coming together across differences, however, the divisions were sidestepped as the military brides took control of the organization and the other internationally married women stepped down into peripheral roles or dropped out altogether. The solidarity that emerged is more a solidarity of military brides than one of internationally married women.

A Cause of One's Own

Around the same time that the ABC Association was founded, Mrs. Vaughn and another group of military brides were also forming a regional organization that I will call International Daughters of Korea. This group of women also felt the need for military brides to gather together. Although the women had numerous friends and contacts who were military brides, they were often too busy to stay in touch. The early years of working, raising children, and adjusting to American life had left them with little time for developing friendships or organizing formal activities. When one of the women passed away, her death became the impetus for forming an organization. Their grief was suffused with a deep regret that they had not been able to make the time to develop intimate ties with the deceased woman. A formal organization, the women felt, would provide an excuse for regular fellowship and a forum where bonds could be forged. Said Mrs. Vaughn:

> It was so sad. We had not been able to see each other that much, we just worked all the time. We came to America and just worked and then we had to part like that, so we said, let's form a group. . . . That was in 1978, we said let's form a group. Only Korean women married to Americans, it had to be that way. *We are same, so we talk everything.* There's nothing to be ashamed of.

Mrs. Vaughn and other founding members felt that the organization needed a concrete purpose, so that the women could work together toward a common goal rather than simply socializing. They settled on orphans in Korea, particularly Amerasian children, as their cause. The organization's major event is the annual fund-raising dinner, which has grown each year. The proceeds are donated to Korean orphanages or organizations such as the Pearl S. Buck Foundation that provide services to Amerasians in Korea. Held in December, the dinner features Korean food cooked by the women, a raffle, music, and other entertainment. The women sell several hundred tickets each year through churches, friends, and other contacts. Raffle prizes—round-trip tickets to Korea, television sets, kitchenware—are donated by local Korean associations, churches, and even Korean corporations. Because nearly everything—the food, labor, prizes, and equipment—is donated, the dinner costs virtually nothing. Most years, the only expense is the cost of renting an event hall. Sometimes that too is donated by a local church or association able to let the military brides' organization use its space for free. Some years, the dinner raises as much as $3,000.

Other annual events include the yearly vacation described above and a holiday party for the women and their families. Embedded within these activities is the women's sense of community and affiliation with others. The vacation is just for them, the party includes family and friends, while the fund-raiser is a chance to promote a positive image of military brides to outsiders and acquaintances, both Koreans and Americans, and to obtain support for their cause. The activities place the women at the center of widening circles of family, friends, and acquaintances—in short, at the center of a world of their own.

The communities formed by military brides serve other practical functions as well. They exchange information about jobs, often providing each other with references for job openings. When a military bride changes jobs, she often fills her place with a fellow military bride, thus keeping jobs "all in the family." They take in newcomers and teach them how to survive in America. They baby-sit each other's children and cook each other food. Groups of women at the church I attended, for example, looked out for each other in numerous ways. It was common for women rushing to work after church to ask another woman to take their children home. Sometimes that meant simply giving the children a ride, at other times it meant taking the children home and feeding them dinner. One older woman baby-sat the children of a younger woman as she migrated to different states in search of work. Each year, several women gather together to go blueberry picking, that is, to work as migrant labor in the blueberry fields. They also gather to clean oceanfront condominiums during the tourist season. These seasonal job opportunities were generally acquired through one or two women with contacts and information, who then spread the word to other women.

When a young woman arrived in 1995 with her Air Force husband straight from a U.S. Air Force Base in Korea, the women at the church organized to get her settled in. They showed her how to get her driver's license, where to buy Korean foods and other items unavailable at the PX and commissary, gave her advice on various on-base facilities that might come in useful, and quickly drew her into the weekly round of church activities. A similar welcome was shown those who moved from other areas of the United States. But it was clear that this particular woman was receiving special care, for she was not only a newcomer to the area, but a newcomer to the country.

She was the beneficiary of a community that had been created where there had once been none. Women who arrived in the 1950s and 1960s noted that they had not seen themselves as part of a community. They could not, for it did not exist. Some stated that women arriving currently were lucky, for they had a ready-made community. In contrast, women who arrived in later decades, especially the 1980s and 1990s, spoke a great deal about military bride community. For them, the community was something that already existed and to which they gained entrée through their marriage to an American.

Initially brought together by their shared ethnicity, gender, and status as military brides, the women consciously developed those ties as they constructed community among themselves. The women's choice of activities reflects their efforts to define themselves and their community. Aware that many military brides have difficult lives in the United States, they sought to help their less fortunate fellows. As mothers of biracial children, they took on the cause of Amerasians in Korea. They chose this cause even though they risked strengthening the camptown shadow that loomed over their lives. Some had already embraced such issues in their personal lives. Mrs. Crispin, for example, adopted a young boy whose mother was Korean and father an American soldier. Lack of financial support had prevented Mrs. Vaughn from opening an orphanage, something she had wanted to do for several years before she immigrated to the United States. Later, her focus shifted from orphans to Amerasians. Like several other women, she said that she felt a bond to Amerasians and that they reminded her of her own children.

In choosing activities that they linked to their own lives as military brides, the women acknowledged their difference from both mainstream

Korean immigrants and Americans, while simultaneously asserting that that difference does not make them inferior. They were also proposing and reinforcing a vision of community that binds people together not on the basis of personal acquaintance, but on that of their links as wives of Americans. They were creating what historian Benedict Anderson has called, in the context of nations and nationalisms, "imagined communities." These communities, however, were not sustained by printed material but by word of mouth as the military brides traveled from one region to another. In this way military brides became aware of each other and each other's organizations. They came to feel that even if they did not directly know each other, they were somehow connected. The ability of military brides during the 1980s and 1990s to tap into Korean military bride networks, as Mrs. Orellana did, and move smoothly from one regional community into another is one tangible manifestation of this overarching "imagined community."

Although Anderson argued that the printed word played the crucial role in constructing the "imagined communities" of nationalism, face-to-face encounters linking people together in the quotidian everyday also play a critical role.[4] Military brides' sense of community was created and sustained by these direct encounters. Their "imagined community" was created through a web of personal relationships that served as conduits for information about each other's lives and situations. Learning about each other from each other, their sense of community transcended direct, personal contact to include people they had never met and were unlikely to ever meet. Their face-to-face encounters facilitated the development of their belief in shared community based on a shared status as Korean military brides. Through direct, personal contact, military brides imagined themselves into community that went beyond personal contact.

Nevertheless, personal contact remained a central mode for conceptualizing relationships among military brides and expressing their sense of community. Even though they knew full well that they would never be able to meet all the other Korean military brides, the women frequently insisted that military brides all know each other or will come to know each other sooner or later. This is a belief expressed by women who came in later years, not by those who arrived in the 1950s and only rarely by those who arrived in the 1960s. This assumption appears to have been prevalent before formal organizations were founded, attesting to the strength of informal friendship networks and their importance in the creation of community. Asked how the founding women came to know one another, for example, Mrs. Kingston was briefly puzzled, and then replied, "If you become a military bride, you get to know the others, you *know?* From connection to connection, you get to know them all." In contrast, Mrs. Mullen and Mrs. Bugelli, who arrived in the 1950s, expressed some surprise that other Korean military brides were able to contact them. Mrs. Bugelli, for example, wondered aloud how women at the regional association came to know of her.

We Are Korean Women Together

The community that military brides have constructed is distinctly, even deliberately, Korean. This is a response largely to the forced Americanization and consequent cultural deprivations that many women undergo, but it is also a response to other Koreans who see them as impure and "not really Korean." The women express their ties through food, language, and the affirmation of what they see as Korean patterns of thought. It is no accident that these are also the areas in which many women have been forced to adopt or submit to American ways.

The monthly regional association meetings and the weekly church services would not be complete without Korean food. In their preparation and consumption of the food, the military brides are expressing their sense of Korean female domesticity and affirming their connection to Korean womanhood.

In most associations, the hostess for the month prepares most of the food, while other members also bring additional dishes. The meetings are an occasion for the women to show off Korean cooking skills that are usually unappreciated by their family. At one meeting I attended, the table literally groaned under huge platters of Korean barbecued beef, short-rib stew, spicy calamari, stuffed dumplings, spicy stewed chicken, fried zucchini, and various vegetable dishes called *namul*. On the counter was a huge steaming pot of *kimchi* stew and another of rice. The women ate before the official business meeting, loading their plates high. Some women ate again after the meeting, as they relaxed and socialized. One woman laughed as she reached for seconds, remarking that she had to eat a month's worth in one day. These were women whose husbands did not allow Korean food in the house.

The women also talked about the food. One savored a spinach dish, and reminisced that as a child she had hated it. Now, she said, it tasted so good. One woman asked another how she had made the stuffing for the dumplings, exclaiming that it must have taken a lot of time to stuff them all. The other woman replied that it had, indeed, taken a long time. Her husband, she said, had commented that she was crazy to spend so much time making the food. Instead of talking about how she made them, however, she began to talk about her childhood memories of stuffing dumplings with her mother. Like many other Korean mothers, her mother would tell her that if she made pretty dumplings, she would marry a wonderful man and have a beautiful daughter. Eager for that promised future, she would carefully stuff the dumplings into half-moons, dimpling the edges just so. Other women nearby nodded in recognition, for they too had similar memories. Wondering aloud if Korean mothers still tell their daughters the same stories, one woman asked me if my mother had induced me to make pretty dumplings with such promises. When I said yes, she nodded in satisfaction, saying, "Yes, yes, it's an old tradition, perhaps it will never die out." Another woman's words broke the mutual reverie: "But look at us now! We ended up with American husbands who can't appreciate our cooking!"

At the military bride church I attended, Sunday service was followed by lunch, always Korean food. Rotating groups of women prepared the meals each week, laboring for hours every Sunday morning to cook for up to a hundred people. The meals were simple, usually rice, *kimchi*, and a soup or stew. Sometimes it was noodles and *kimchi*. Sometimes donuts left over from the fellowship following the earlier English-language service, held for husbands and children, would also be sitting on the counter with the Korean food. I never saw a woman touch the donuts. Instead, they were usually eaten, rather surreptitiously, by young children or teenagers. For some of the women, cooking and eating Korean food was an activity limited to church. One woman, who often rushed to work after church, said that church was the only time she was able to eat Korean food.

The church women also gathered regularly to make large amounts of *kimchi*, a domestic ritual traditionally performed by the women in a family. Once, upon finding some soured *kimchi* as they cleaned out the church refrigerators, several women fried up a batch of *kimchi* pancakes, sending out plates of them to the minister and church elders holding a meeting, to the children playing outside, and to the women tallying the week's offering. As the women fried the pancakes, they also ate them sizzling from the griddle, commenting that they were most delicious eaten in this way, with hot bubbles of fat dancing on the crisp, golden edges of the pancakes. They reminisced about girlhoods watching older women cook, commenting that the large pancakes, some twelve inches in diameter, were only possible on the old-fashioned griddles, impossible to find in America. Turning to me, one woman said, "Oh, she's too young to remember! Besides, you grew up here, right? You've never seen those griddles, have you?" Before I could answer, another woman, who had visited Korea in recent years, remarked that she had seen those old-fashioned griddles used at marketplaces in Seoul by women frying and selling the pancakes to passersby.

In these two conversations about stuffed dumplings and *kimchi* pancakes, the women were narrating not just memories, but their sense of self as Korean women. They were also expressing themselves as storytellers and historians, whose personal stories were embedded in and inextricable from the broader history of Korean women, indeed, of the Korean people.

Ideals of domesticity and communities of women were recurrent themes in their histories. It was among women and from women—mothers, grandmothers, aunts, neighborhood women—that they first learned to dream of a future life as a wife and mother, and learned to see domestic skills such as cooking as important steps toward the fulfillment of those dreams. By questioning me, a younger woman, in some cases young enough to be a daughter or even a granddaughter, they placed themselves in a community of Korean women that spans generations and continents and is bound by similar ideals, memories, and experiences. The dumpling question, especially, sought affirmation that the ideals represented by their memories and experiences—the domesticity of women, the importance of cooking and thus of the women who provide the food, the goal of a good husband and children—remain ideals for younger women like myself. The griddle question, however, served a rather different purpose. By subtly excluding me from the commonality of their experiences based on generational difference and on my having grown up in America rather than Korea, they were asserting that they were "truly Korean" in contrast to me, Korean by blood but presumably more American by upbringing. In the history they narrated with their memories, the women emphasized their identity as Korean women rather than as military brides.

The comment that they had ended up with American husbands unable to appreciate good Korean cooking reminded everyone of the difference between their childhood dreams and their present lived reality, the dissonance between their identity as Korean women and their status as military brides. It also reminded them that in the eyes of mainstream Koreans, they were seen as military brides first. The comment was not welcomed by everyone at that monthly meeting. It elicited nervous laughter from some, but no other direct response. Although the women openly discussed cultural conflicts within their families among themselves, this particular comment was seen as a breach of etiquette. Instead of emphasizing their Koreanness, it emphasized their deviation from the ideals of Korean womanhood, as well as their deviation from dominant narrations of Korean history, and implied that with American husbands, acting out their ideals was at best difficult, at worst impossible. In pointing out that American husbands do not appreciate their wives' Korean cooking, the comment by extension also emphasized that the women's culture and thus the women themselves were not fully appreciated within their families. In effect, it emphasized the women's displacement. The problem with the comment was not so much that it brought up these issues, but that it emphasized the wrong note.

The women's discussions of cultural conflicts within their families, rather than emphasizing their deviation from Koreanness, instead emphasize their adherence to Korean ideals and mores. The ideal of Korean womanhood that the women evoke most often is that of the suffering woman who endlessly sacrifices for the sake of her family and specifically for her children. The stories the women told each other at that meeting, for example, generally revolved around giving in to American ways for the sake of family peace or on maternal love for wayward children. Among themselves, they could share their experiences of cultural alienation from their husbands and children and find both an affirmation of the mores rejected in their families and an understanding based on similar experiences.

One woman at the monthly meeting, for example, talked at length about her teenage daughters. She did not approve of the way they dressed, their makeup, their long telephone conversations, and their desire to date. Whenever she reprimanded them, she complained, they would say that this is America. Then they would tell her, she said, stumbling over an unfamiliar piece of youth slang, "something like 'get it with,' or maybe 'get along.' They're telling me that I don't understand." But the ones who don't understand, she said, are her daughters. They should pay more attention to what their mother says, she said. Invoking a common Korean image that portrays women as both sufferers and as bearers of life, she said, "I brought them into this world with the pain of labor tearing my belly, they should listen to what I say." This prompted nods of assent from the women gathered in the living room and a discussion of the pain that children so casually inflict on their mothers. Several women said that their children always simply repeat, "This is America," like a broken record. Only when they themselves become parents, the women concluded, will the children understand the sacrifices that their mothers have made for them.

What is striking about this conversation is its familiarity. I have heard Korean women in Seoul make similar comments about their children using the very same image of labor and childbirth, the very same connection between their pain in giving them life and the children's obligation to respect their mothers. I have heard immigrant Korean women in the United States invoke the same image with the exact same words. The conclusion in those conversations has also been identical: the children will understand only when they too become parents. It is no surprise that the military brides, being roughly of the same generation as these other women, would engage in similar conversations about their children. But the strand of cultural conflict that the military brides acknowledge but downplay renders this conversation slightly different. By using an image of suffering motherhood and ungrateful children, the military brides subsumed their children's casual dismissal of them based on cultural difference into a discourse on generational difference. Invoking an image that is so common as to be iconic among Korean women of their age, they downplayed the cultural conflict and their own alienation within their families and emphasized instead their status as long-suffering Korean mothers.

Providing the social space in which such discussions can be held and such assertions of self made and affirmed is one important role of these regional associations. Mrs. Vaughn stated that she and the other founding members felt that the women needed a space of their own where they could talk to others who had the same experiences and would immediately understand and empathize. Although ostensibly about cultural conflict and thus about the difficulties of being a military bride, the discussions are actually focused on the Koreanness of the women. In these conversations, the women express and receive affirmation of their identities as Korean women.

The dominance of the Korean language in the associations and at Korean churches also plays an important role in nurturing and affirming the women's sense of Korean identity. This is especially the case for older women, many of whom grew up during the Japanese colonial regime and thus never had a chance to be formally educated in the Korean language. One older woman told me that her Korean skills were poor. Growing up in the 1930s and 1940s, she had gone to Japanese schools. Then she migrated to the United States and had to learn English. It was only as an adult that she learned the Korean alphabet, and only as she attended immigrant Korean churches in the United States that she learned to read and write Korean. When I told her I too had never been formally educated in the Korean language, but had learned to read and write virtually on my own, just like her, she nodded. "So you know," she said. "You know how important language is."

The next Sunday, she presented me with a leather-bound, Korean-language Bible in which she had inscribed our names in firm, confident Korean letters. She had learned to read Korean with this Bible as she attended church, she said. At first she had a hard time keeping up during the call-and-response portion of the service when the minister and the congregation alternately read aloud a passage from the Bible. But as she read her favorite Bible passages over and over and as her reading skills improved, she said, she felt confident enough to read aloud on her own during Bible study sessions. With this confidence, she said, came a great sense of pride in herself as a Korean woman, a daughter of Korea, and a daughter of God.

Mrs. Bugelli recalled that when she first went to a military bride association's monthly meeting, she was stunned to find herself immersed in a Korean-language environment. "So many Korean women, all chattering away," she said. After decades of little contact with other Koreans, it felt strange to her. Sometimes she couldn't quite catch what the other women were saying, and although in her mind the Korean words flowed smoothly, they stumbled over each other when they reached her tongue. But as she continued to join the women in their monthly meetings and then left her American church for a Korean church, she said, her tongue remembered how to speak Korean, and the words began to flow in a way she found comfortingly familiar. She smiled, saying that it was an indescribable delight to find that her Korean came back to her. "So now I can speak to you like this," she said. "Before, I couldn't speak well at all."

Struggling to make ends meet and dealing with a divorce during her first years in the United States, Mrs. Bugelli had no time to socialize. By the time she remarried and began to enjoy more stability, she had lost contact with the few other Korean women she had met. By then, she had established friendships with Americans and begun attending an American church. It was only in the early 1990s when another military bride sought her out that she began to associate with Koreans. By that time she was more comfortable with English than with Korean. Nevertheless, it never occurred to her to speak English with the other military brides. English, she said, has a different feel, and it doesn't feel right to speak it with other Koreans. Pointing out that her English is also limited, she said it makes more sense to speak stilted Korean with other Koreans than to speak stilted English. Besides, she said, "I never felt completely comfortable in English. It always felt like something was missing. I could never find exactly the right word to say what I felt." Although sometimes she feels the same way in Korean, she said, she feels that there is a closer match between her thoughts and Korean.

During one conversation, Mrs. Vaughn laughingly complained that Korean was not a good language for carrying out business. "Maybe because I don't know the right kind of Korean phrases," she said, "but sometimes it's just easier in English." When I asked Mrs. Vaughn if the women had ever considered using English during their monthly meetings, she looked surprised. "Oh, no," she said, "We must use Korean. Only in Korean can we really express our feelings, our thoughts. No matter how good our English is, even if we have lost some of our Korean, our real inside selves can only be expressed in Korean." If English is needed for clarity during the meetings, she said, they can just insert the necessary English word into their Korean discussions.

These women are articulating a complex relationship with language. Although fully fluent and literate in neither Korean nor English, they are emotionally more vested in Korean, for that, as Mrs. Vaughn says, is the language of their innermost beings. It is also the language of their identities. Thus while the acquisition of reading skills in Korean bring pride in herself as a Korean woman, the older church woman saw her acquisition of English skills in a completely different light. She did that, she said, because she had to. The satisfaction was that of gaining a skill, not an affirmation of her being. For Mrs. Bugelli, only Korean will do when speaking with other Koreans. Even if she peppers her Korean with English phrases, what is important to her is that the default, dominant language—the language that structures her thoughts and speech as well as her relationship with the listener—is her mother tongue. A similar view is reflected by Mrs. Vaughn, who sees Korean as the language that expresses "real inside selves" and English as a language sometimes necessary for carrying out business. One is personal, tied up with one's identity and being, while the other is impersonal, tied up with practical matters and work. While discussing the importance of the women's associations, Mrs. Crispin said that it all boiled down to one thing: "We are Korean women together, we can talk about everything and we understand each other." Although expressed as "Korean women together," this solidarity is limited to Korean military brides. The associations were founded to give military brides a forum of their own. As Mrs. Vaughn said, if other Koreans were to join, the military brides would not be able to talk freely, but instead would have to watch themselves for fear of reinforcing the stereotypes mainstream Koreans have of them. Besides, said several women, other Koreans do not have the same interests as military brides.

The Limits of Sisterhood

Military bride solidarity, however, does not include all military brides. Sisterhood has its limits. Within the military bride community, those limits are usually defined by race and class. Regional associations, for example, counted few wives of African American soldiers among their members. In addition, most of their members were able to maintain stable, relatively secure lives. Indeed, there seemed to be little cross-class mingling. Mrs. Goldin noted that even though she knew the founding members of the ABC Association, she was not invited to join the fledgling organization. The reason, she concluded, was because she "had married a black man." Among the women I met, most women who had married white men associated with other women who had married white men, while most women who had married black men associated with other women who had married black men. The exceptions generally fell into two categories: (1) when the women were of similar class status, both in terms of their backgrounds and their current lives; (2) when one woman or group of women (usually married to white men and/or of a higher class status) was reaching out to help another woman (usually married to a black man and/or of a lower class status).

These racial boundaries among the women are most likely to mirror racial divides among the men. In her study of camptown women, Katherine Moon writes of the ways that American soldiers demanded that the women observe racial boundaries between black and white. It was generally a demand that white soldiers made by refusing to frequent the same clubs as black soldiers.[5] Similarly, military brides told me that racial boundaries were the strictest among women living on military bases, where the women were exposed to the racial hierarchy among the men and within the dominant American military culture. One woman said that her white husband frowned on her associating with a certain Mrs. Yonkers because her husband was black. Apparently oblivious to his own biracial children's vulnerability to the epithet, he would occasionally call her children "mongrels" and tell his wife not to let their children play with them.

The sisterhood that organization members, who generally led relatively secure and stable lives, offered to the wives of black men and to military brides of lower-class status was that of charity. Organization members were anxious to help women less fortunate than themselves. Although in some areas, such as the Tacoma-Seattle area studied by Sil Dong Kim in the 1970s, regional organizations were able to hook up with local social service agencies to assist military brides facing domestic violence, divorce, abandonment, unemployment, illness, and other problems, the organizations in the area in which I conducted my research were not. This severely limited their ability to help women. The assistance was temporary and given on an ad hoc basis, and the organizations were unable to develop a systematic response to or analysis of the problems that their fellow military brides faced. Recalling the case of one woman who had been abused by her opium-addicted husband, became blind, and was left destitute with two children, Mrs. Kingston said:

It was so sad. *What to do? Life. There is life. Something come sad.* The organization tried very hard to help those kinds of people. But there's a limit, you can't just give and give forever.

Unable to put together a program that would effectively help the women turn their lives around, the organization women were able to offer only temporary aid. They visited military brides in the hospital, helped place them in shelters for the destitute, brought them home-cooked Korean meals, and offered amateur counseling, encouragement, and moral support.

Mrs. Kingston discussed the motivation of the members:

We wanted, us military brides, to unite together. So we did and we did lots of good work [helping other military brides during difficult times]. We helped a lot of women.

Ultimately, however, it became increasingly difficult for the members to continue to offer that assistance. In an effort to develop a more systematic program of aid, Mrs. Crispin had tried several times during the mid-1990s to link the XYZ Association with the local Korean women's center. The center operated a hotline for women facing domestic abuse and offered activities for military brides such as English language classes. But, said Mrs. Crispin, the XYZ Association women were resistant. Apparently, she said, they were afraid that they would be dominated by outsiders.

One area where military brides have formed a collective with the assistance of an "outsider," a female Korean minister, is New York. Located in Flushing, the heart of New York's Korean immigrant community, the Rainbow Center offers Korean military brides shelter, a chance to heal, and an opportunity to reach out to other Korean women. This community of military brides focuses on assisting women build self-sufficient lives and on helping their families cope with cultural differences. Founded in 1993 by the Rev. Geumhyun Yeo (also known by her married name of Rev. Henna Hahn) with several other women, the center runs a variety of social services for military brides. Military brides themselves are crucial to the center's operations. They are the ones who welcome newcomers and surround them with the sights, sounds, and tastes of Korean culture, acting on the belief that many of the emotional disturbances exhibited by the women seeking shelter are due to cultural deprivation. They gather regularly to make *kimchi* and their own soybean paste, traditional domestic rituals they have deliberately chosen to honor as psychically and culturally healing acts. They also run a thrift shop, thereby earning funds for the center as they learn business skills.

A Positive Image

The gaze of outsiders—both other Koreans and Americans—has been a continuous force in the lives of the women, for one of their goals has been to show the world what military brides could do and thereby combat the prejudice they felt so keenly. Awareness of this gaze, for example, motivated Mrs. Kingston to take a leadership role at a crucial moment in her organization's history. It also motivates the women to portray themselves positively to both Koreans and Americans. During the early years of the ABC Association, for example, one of the women's goals was to let the Korean community know that military brides were intelligent, well-educated, and living interesting, productive, and fulfilling lives. Said Mrs. Kingston:

We showed them the reality of military brides, in a grand way, we showed them that there were these fine women. *They think, but* . . . they think that we are all Korean women who did, you know, and then married foreigners, that we are all uneducated. But we showed them that we military brides are really something.

Similarly, Mrs. Vaughn displayed newspaper articles in both Korean and American newspapers reporting on the activities of her organization and said that the organization has helped to show people the strength of military brides and to break stereotypes about them.

Military brides also often assume a civilian ambassador role, presenting Korean culture for the consumption of mainstream American society. Although events sponsored by Korean immigrant associations—street festivals, Korea Day parades, and the like—play this function as well, the role of military brides may be far greater. While Korean immigrant associations usually operate in metropolitan, multiracial, multiethnic contexts such as New York, Los Angeles, and Chicago, military brides often operate in primarily white American communities. As schools and community associations across the country began to hold multicultural festivals, those in rural areas, small towns, and outlying suburbs seemed to have turned to military brides to represent Korea, for many women spoke of participating in these events.

Since 1990, the local school has called upon the women at the church I attended to participate in its annual multicultural festival. Wearing traditional Korean clothes, the women prepare and sell Korean foods such as stuffed dumplings, barbecued beef, glass noodles with meat and vegetables, and rice and seaweed rolls. They also display their prized valuables—lacquered jewelry boxes, embroidered screens, ceramic vases, jade jewelry, and the like—to show Americans Korean cultural goods. Eager to show Americans that Korean culture—and thus by extension Korean people—is worthy of appreciation, they are often oblivious to the ways in which multicultural thinking can set them apart as aliens even as it advances "culture" for the appreciation of Americans.[6]

America's multicultural discourse, a reformulation of cultural pluralism that began in earnest in the 1980s, offers Korean military brides and other minorities the promise of inclusion, respect, and equality, even as their daily lives betray the hollowness of that promise. The cultures displayed in multicultural festivals—those of the Third World, of African Americans, Asian, Caribbean, and Latin American immigrants, and sometimes Native Americans—are usually subordinate to mainstream American and Western culture. At a multicultural festival, it is Chinese opera, not Italian opera or American rock 'n' roll, that is sung; Hawaiian hula, not ballet or modern dance, that is performed; Korean jade jewelry, not diamond jewelry, that is displayed; and Japanese rice cakes, not apple pie and chocolate cake, that are sampled. Their display, as Lisa Lowe has observed, does not attest to the cultural richness and heritage of the cultures, for these cultures are flattened and equalized as simply "other" through their displacement in festivals that "forget" the ongoing history of domination of the peoples whose cultures are displayed. Indeed, the festival is staged not for them, but for those who belong to the dominant culture. Multicultural festivals appropriate the cultures of racial and ethnic minorities to signify the liberal ideal of a "nation of immigrants" in which all cultures, and by implication, all peoples, have equal access and are equally represented.

Thus the language of multiculturalism is used to prove America's superiority and exceptionalism vis-à-vis subordinate cultures. It is a historical continuation of the melting pot metaphor which once held prominence, and as such it is fundamentally assimilationist. Dramatized in a turn-of-the-century play, the melting pot metaphor depicted America as a furnace ingesting people of different cultures, melting them down, and producing a new and superior breed of man, the American.[7] Like cultural pluralism before it, multiculturalism imagines these cultures as the "ethnic" cultures of America, properly subsumed and disciplined within a social and cultural system that allows superficial difference for pleasure in the variety, but harshly rejects substantive difference as "un-American." An occasional "ethnic" meal, for example, is permitted, even lauded as evidence of appreciation for one's heritage or as tolerance of one another's differences, while English is insistently promoted as the only proper language for America. The diversity that multiculturalism celebrates is a thin cover-up for America's hegemonic homogeneity.

Hazel Carby has observed that multiculturalism not only fails to recognize racism, but it also fails to account for the possibility of resistance.[8] For the military brides, multicultural festivals are an opportunity, however limited, to show Americans the beauty of Korean culture, and thus an opportunity to receive positive validation from Americans (rather than fellow military brides) as they affirm their Korean identity. For those women who live in families where the children dismiss their maternal reprimands with an offhand, "This is America, Mom," and husbands refuse to eat Korean food, it is a rare opportunity to feel accepted among Americans as Korean women. These can be moments that nurture confidence and self-esteem. Said one woman:

> They are so interested. They ask all kinds of questions, about my clothes, about the food. One man told me that before, he only thought of war when he thought of Korea. Now, he said, he can think of beautiful silk dresses and fine art work.

This made her feel that she was spreading a positive image not only about military brides, but also about Korea itself. One woman, who arrived in the mid-1970s, noted in a private conversation that her husband often made derogatory comments that painted Korea as a godforsaken, backward country that couldn't even defend itself but depended on Americans. Like other women whose husbands made disparaging comments about Korea, she felt that his words were intended to put her down and noted that he often said such things when he was angry with her. When her husband accompanied her to one of these multicultural festivals, he was surprised to see that the Korean display was popular. It affected his behavior, she said, albeit temporarily, saying that he commented favorably on the display several times over the next few weeks and uttered fewer insults about Korea. Seeing this, she said, also made her realize that while she could not change his attitudes, the positive reactions of other Americans to Korean culture could.

Although the festivals are aimed at affirming an ethnic, and hence American, identity stripped of substantive difference, the women themselves used those festivals as opportunities for resistance, to affirm identities rooted in that very difference. The woman whose husband disparaged Korea, for example, stated that she wished Americans could see that the beauty of Korean culture is connected to the suffering of the Korean people. Clearly, she sensed that multicultural festivals through their display are displacing cultures, delinking them from history and community. She herself relinked them, placing Korean culture within her understanding of Korean history as suffering. Thus she articulated two critical observations that directly attack the underpinnings of multiculturalism.

Military brides' insistence on expressing their culture and seeking ways in which to do so subverts multiculturalism's insistence that cultural identity be superficial. For Korean military brides, cultural identity is critically important. Women who attended the monthly meetings of regional associations sometimes did so despite the opposition of their husbands. Mrs. Weinberg, who accommodated her husband's wishes in most cases, "giving up" many expressions of her culture for the sake of family harmony, also insisted that husbands have no right to forbid their wives to attend these meetings, even if they run past midnight.

Even as military brides strive to portray a positive Korean identity for an American audience, they often display for other Koreans their personal links to America. This can be read as a response to stereotypes of military brides that paint them as oppressed and victimized by abusive American husbands, as well as a bid for the status that many Koreans associate with access to mainstream America. This display is often subtle and emphasizes the advantages gained by marriage to Americans. It can be seen in a military bride's casual remark that her American brother-in-law secured her family a terrific deal on their new car, or in the remark of a fund-raising dinner's organizer that she was able to get the event hall for free because her father-in-law was a member of the veteran's association. Sometimes military brides openly expressed their belief in the practical advantages of marrying an American. Mrs. Crispin, for example, explained that she encouraged her younger sister to go ahead and marry an American because she believed that as long as one was going to live in America, it made sense to marry an American. That way, one could gain the benefits of having an "insider" in the family, one who knew how to get around in American society. Mrs. Peterson expressed a similar belief. Even as she talked about the difficulties of her married life, she stated that it was more practical to marry an American if one was to live in America.

Military brides also exploit the image of the American male as Prince Charming, contrasting it with the image of the Korean male as chauvinist pig, to position themselves as liberated vis-à-vis Korean women married to Korean men. Again, the goal is to counter stereotypes about abused and victimized military brides. Thus when Mrs. Brennan felt the cold shadow of the camptown in her encounter with the owner of the Korean video store, she responded by asking the other woman who was more liberated and free: she with the American husband who catered to her moods, or she with the Korean husband who by definition did not. The video store owner had little choice but to answer that Mrs. Brennan enjoyed more freedom, for she too subscribed to the same images of Korean and American men as do many Koreans. Although military brides acknowledge among themselves that reality does not conform to these images, they also readily use them in encounters with other Koreans to validate their decision to marry American men.

Communities of Resistance

The dominant Korean self-identity fails to recognize diversity among Koreans. According to anthropologist Kyeyoung Park, for example, 1.5 generation Korean Americans have their own distinct sense of identity, one that incorporates and transforms elements of their Korean and American upbringings.[9] Korean adoptees and many second-generation Korean Americans may not seem recognizably "Korean" to South Koreans or to the immigrant generation, but they too claim membership in Korean and Korean American societies. Mixed-race people who are part Korean are increasingly claiming their Korean heritage and insisting that "full-blooded" Koreans recognize their claims to inclusion. This diversity—marginalized, suppressed, and ignored—belies the dominant Korean discourse of homogeneity.

At the same time, the insistence of these "deviant" Korean Americans on claiming and expressing racial and cultural difference in the face of efforts at erasure, suppression, and appropriation can also be read as a challenge to the homogenizing discourse of American multiculturalism. As one adult Korean adoptee wrote: "[W]e're being told that our cultural displacement had a purpose—multiculturalism. By growing up in white families, we can be examples, Luuk. We can show others that racial harmony is possible. We just can't show our burdened backs."[10]

The imagined community of military brides is likewise a challenge to both Korean and American definitions of self, and thereby a challenge to both Korean and American nationalism. Military bride community is primarily based on an acknowledged sense of sisterhood that flows from shared identities as Korean women with intimate ties to America, as "internationally married women," and more specifically as Korean women who married American soldiers. Although mainstream Koreans and Korean Americans often see them as "less Korean" due to their links with American society, the military brides themselves do not. They reject the notion that they are no longer "really" Korean due to their outmarriage and immigration to the United States, and have created their own forms of Korean identity. This identity—gender specific and particular to their situation—challenges the validity of a monolithic Korean identity and opens up spaces for difference within Korean communities.

At the same time, their insistence on substantive difference—in terms of language, modes of thought, history—challenges the valorization of the "ethnic" in American multiculturalism, for they are in effect refusing to become ethnicized. In a society that sees becoming ethnic as a prerequisite to immigrants becoming American, this refusal is a direct challenge to American nationalism. Their communities stand as eloquent rebuttals to mainstream Americans who would like to see them assimilated within American families, as refutations of the multiculturalism that would render their culture a mere accessory to the ongoing creation of American exceptionalism, and as refusals to relinquish their Korean identity even when the demand might come from their husbands. But even as they maintain and construct their Korean identities, they are also insisting on their right to do so in America and to be Americans. The women have no plans to leave America, and many consider this country as their home.

Military brides are struggling to move beyond resistance—against both American and Korean prejudices—toward transformation. Whether consciously or not, they are pressing for a transformation of both Korean and American identities, away from the narrow and exclusive and toward the broad and inclusive. To both Americans and Koreans, they are posing the same question that bell hooks asked in another context: "Why do we have to wipe out the Otherness in order to experience a notion of *Oneness*?"[11]

In imagining themselves into community, military brides have created a space of their own. This creation emphasizes that while they may be multiply connected to multiple communities, they are not split among these communities, but rooted in their own community. Recall the annual events—vacation, holiday party, and fund-raiser—that placed military brides at the center of an ever-widening circle that included both Koreans and Americans. Recall how they lay claim to both Korea and America, refusing to give up one for the other.

Military brides have shown the possibility of knitting together communities at the interstices of nations. They seek a transformation in the way people are grouped and bound into communities. As such, the real and imagined community of military brides challenges both the definition of a people as belonging to a single nation and nationalism's insistence on internal homogeneity.

BIOGRAPHIES OF WOMEN
INTERVIEWED

MRS. BRENNAN, interviewed in November 1996, at her home. Born in 1941, she married in 1973 and arrived in the United States in 1975.

She is the eldest of five children and the only daughter from a farming family. She sponsored two of her brothers to the United States: one runs a grocery store and another runs a fast-food restaurant. The other two brothers farm in Korea. Her husband comes from a farming family of ten children. Both she and her husband attend the military bride church, and they have a daughter who is married with two children and a son in the military.

I knew her and spoke with her for more than two years before the formal interview.

See chapters 3, 4, 5, and 6.

MRS. CRISPIN, interviewed in September 1995, at her suburban home, where she has lived for more than twenty years.

Born circa 1945, she arrived in the United States in 1965 after marrying her husband, then an enlisted man. She has one adopted son, the child of a Korean woman and a U.S. soldier, whom she adopted during a visit back to Korea. During their nearly thirty years of marriage, her husband became an officer and steadily rose through the ranks. They divorced in 1991 and she lives on her alimony, half his military pension, which she calls compensation for living the army life with him.

She sponsored her entire family for immigration as soon as possible, and her mother, older brother, and two younger sisters arrived in the early 1970s. She was involved in starting a military bride organization, and has worked with all three organizations in her area.

See chapters 3, 4, 5, and 6.

MRS. DENNISON, interviewed in April 1995, at a beauty supply store owned by another military bride.

Born in the mid-1930s, she married in 1957 and arrived in the United States in 1958.

They have one son and three daughters, all grown. In the early 1960s, she separated from her husband because he became violent, but they did not formally divorce so that she and the children would have access to medical care and other benefits. She worked numerous minimum-wage jobs to support her children. They divorced in 1976 after the children were grown and she remarried soon thereafter. In March 1996, her daughter organized a *hwang-gap* celebration in honor of her sixtieth birthday. The entire congregation of the military bride church, of which Mrs. Dennison is a member, attended.

See chapters 3, 5, and 6.

MRS. EDSON/SOMMER, interviewed in January 1995 at her home. Born in the late 1950s, she arrived in the United States in 1980 after entering into a contract marriage with a U.S. soldier. They lived together for two years in Texas until she received her permanent residency and then divorced. She met her second husband, also a U.S. soldier, some time later while working as a waitress on-base. At the time of the interview, they had been married for ten years and had two school-age daughters. She came from a poor family in Korea and had been tricked into prostitution. At the time of the interview, she was working as the manager of a bar catering to Korean men. These bars employ young Korean women who receive a commission for every drink their male customers buy. At the women's discretion, relationships with male customers can extend into prostitution. Most cities with significant Korean immigrant populations have such establishments.

See chapters 2 and 5.

MRS. FERRIMAN, interviewed in May 1995 at her home, a trailer house in a working-class neighborhood.

Born in 1957, she arrived in the United States in 1978 with her husband, an enlisted man in the Army. A deaconess of the military bride church, she has two daughters in high school and one daughter who was just a toddler. Her husband is often unemployed and drifts from job to job. She worked full-time at a factory and attended school to become a nurse. Her dream is to become a medical missionary after her children are grown. She is highly respected at the church for her hard work, cheerful attitude, and ardent faith.

See chapters 2, 3, 4, and 5.

Mrs. GOLDIN, interviewed in December 1993 and July 1995, at her home.
Born in 1946, she arrived in the United States in 1972.

Mrs. Goldin was the first military bride to grant me a formal interview, and we became quite close. Some of the interviews were conducted while I spent the night at her home. She revealed her camptown background gradually. Her husband is African American, and they lived in Okinawa immediately after their marriage. There they had a son and the family moved to Texas in 1972. She took their son and ran away from her husband while in Texas, no longer able to tolerate his beatings. Although other military brides I met spoke about violent husbands, she was the most candid about the abuse she endured. She worked in a variety of jobs and eventually was able to go into business. She has engaged in numerous business ventures, mostly small stores, but her financial stability is tenuous. Her son ran away in search of his father when he was fourteen, and she has heard from him only intermittently since then. She wrote her life story in Korean in a short handwritten manuscript, in the hope that someone in Korea would be interested in turning it into a novel or movie.

See chapters 2, 3, 4, 5, and 6.

Mrs. GRANT/BUGELLI, interviewed in January 1996, at her suburban home.

Born in 1932, she arrived in the United States in 1957 with her first husband.

After divorcing him due to his adultery, she lived alone and worked at various factory jobs for about fifteen years. She then met and married her second husband, who already had two grown sons. She has no children of her own. At the time of the interview, they had been married for twenty-five years. We conducted the interview sitting at her dining room table, which was piled with miscellaneous letters, knickknacks, and magazines at one end.

See chapters 2, 3, 4, and 6

Mrs. KINGSTON, interviewed in July 1995, at her embroidery store, squeezed next to a seafood shop on a busy street near the downtown area.

Born in the 1940s, she arrived in the United States in 1965 after her daughter was born.

The youngest daughter of a well-off family, she met her husband when he was the teacher of her English class. She later divorced him because of his affairs and raised their daughter alone. She was the founder and president of a military bride organization. She states that unlike other military brides, she didn't suffer because her parents-in-law were kind and well-off. At the time of the interview, she was approaching the age of sixty, living alone above her store and making a living by producing shirts, hats, jackets and other paraphernalia with embroidered logos for neighborhood sports teams, schools, clubs, and other small organizations.

See chapter 6.

MRS. LINBURG/MULLEN, interviewed in November 1996 at her home in a small, semirural town.

Born in 1929, she arrived with her husband in Seattle in 1951 by boat from Japan.

She divorced him after nine years due to his affair with an American woman, and remarried shortly thereafter. At the time of the interview, they had been married more than thirty-one years.

She is retired, but her husband, who is some years younger, continues to work. She has no children.

See chapters 2, 3, 4, 5, and 6.

MRS. MORGAN, interviewed in May 1995 in her home, a small townhouse on the air force base.

Born in the mid-1960s, she arrived in the United States in 1983. She has one son with her first husband, whom she divorced in 1989, and two sons with her second husband. She is the youngest of seven children and her father died a few years before she married. She attended college and lived with her mother as the last unmarried child. She was a member of the military bride church and we had talked often before the formal interview, which took place a week before she and her family were to move to Texas. We spent the entire day together. Her two younger sons, toddlers, were at home and her oldest son returned from elementary school just as the formal interview was finished.

See chapters 3, 4, 5, and 6.

MRS. MULLIGAN/VAUGHN, interviewed in 1995 at her home in a semi-rural area.

Born circa 1930, she arrived in 1960 with her second husband, who was an American soldier, their toddler son, and her teenage daughter from her first marriage to a Korean. She divorced him a few years later because he abused her daughter. She married her third husband when she was seeking a suitable father figure for her son. They built the home in which they now live. It was designed to accommodate two or more families, for it has a large basement with a kitchen in addition to bedrooms, living areas, and a kitchen on the first floor and more bedrooms on the second floor. They built this house so that she could better take care of the Amerasian families she sponsored for immigration. Her house is usually full with the latest newcomers. The families usually consist of an Amerasian man, his Korean wife, and their small children. She has not yet sponsored any Amerasian children and their mothers. She founded a regional military bride organization in the late 1970s, and in 1995 she was busy starting a military bride church in the basement of her home. A Korean minister and an American minister jointly held services in both languages. About ten families attended.

See chapters 2, 3, 4, 5, and 6.

MRS. ORELLANA, interviewed in 1995 and 1996 at her home, an apartment in a housing complex that is part of the air force base.

Born in 1966, she arrived in the United States in 1991. She and her husband have a toddler son. They met through her English club at college. He is the only son of Italian-American parents. She is a housewife and thinking about going to gemology school so that she can participate in the family jewelry business. She was a member of the military bride church, but left soon after to join an American church when she succeeded in persuading her Catholic husband to attend Protestant church with her. She was the only military bride I met who had graduated from college.

See chapters 2, 4, and 6.

MRS. PETERSON, interviewed in January 1995, at her apartment across the street from the Korean grocery and restaurant where she worked.

Born in 1962, she married an African American soldier and arrived in the United States in 1986. They have one son, age seven. At the time of the interview, she was in the process of divorcing her husband due to his affair with a white American woman. Many of our conversations were about her difficulties due to this woman and his affair, for they flaunted their relationship, which had begun when both were stationed in Germany. When I first met her, she had been separated from her husband for a year and she was working days at a Korean grocery store and evenings at a Korean restaurant. When her son came home from school, he would hang around the store with his mother. In between shifts at the store and restaurant, she would feed him dinner. Later, she would take a quick break from the restaurant to put him to bed. We often spoke while she worked at the store, and our formal interviews took place late at night after she finished work at the restaurant. Sometimes her son would wake up and, bleary-eyed, ask why we weren't asleep.

See chapters 2, 3, and 4.

MRS. PULASKI, interviewed in May 1995, at a small park near her home.

Born in the early 1950s, she arrived in the United States in 1984 and again in 1986. I often drove her and her son (10) and daughter (5) home from church and we shared many conversations. Recently divorced from her third husband, she was living on welfare and going to school to become a nurse's aid. She married her first husband, a Korean man, straight out of high school, primarily because her parents had recently died and she needed support. They had a daughter (now grown and herself married). She ran away when this daughter was four years old, because she could not tolerate her husband. She had a succession of menial jobs, including stints at camptowns in Pusan and in Kunsan. She met her second husband at one of the camptowns. They briefly came to the United States in 1984 and then went to his next post in Okinawa. There, they were divorced and she married another U.S. soldier, who was the son of a Korean mother and U.S. military father. They entered the United States in 1986. This interview was actually the second. The first interview was lost when my backpack containing the interview tape was stolen. Although other military brides I met were in more difficult situations, she had the most unstable life of the women I interviewed. She and her two children received no help from their father, and they lived in a studio apartment on a busy street near the military bride church.

See chapters 5 and 6.

MRS. RAMOS, interviewed in May 1995 at her apartment.

Born in the mid-1960s, she married a Puerto Rican in the U.S. military and arrived in the United States in 1987. Her husband died in a training accident at a base in Kansas a few months later, and she went to Puerto Rico for his funeral. She gave his family half the compensation she received from the Army because his family was even poorer than her own family in Korea. Her older sister had also married a U.S. soldier and she attended the military bride church. Her husband was a friend of her sister's husband. I knew this sister and her children well, but only later did I learn that the two women were sisters. Mrs. Ramos has a five-year-old son with another man whom she met after her husband's death, but they broke their engagement and never married. Her son lives with his father and visits her occasionally. She works as a hostess in a bar catering to Koreans. With her lack of English and job skills, she said, she has few options for employment.

See chapter 5.

MRS. WEINBERG, interviewed in February 1996 at her suburban home.

Born in the mid-1940s, she married her husband, an officer, in 1968 and arrived in the United States the following year. Her husband is Jewish and she converted to Judaism so that their two sons could also be Jewish. (Jewish identity is matrilineal, so the mothers must be Jewish in order for the children to be recognized as Jewish.) Of the woman interviewed, she was the only one who has never worked outside the home after her marriage.

See chapters 2, 3, 4, and 5.

A Note on Research

This study is based primarily on oral history interviews and fieldwork conducted from the fall of 1993 through the end of 1996 in the Delaware Valley and surrounding regions, including the Philadelphia metropolitan area and eastern Pennsylvania, New Jersey, and New York City. Research also included two 1997 trips to South Korea and visits to military camptowns in the Seoul area, including Itaewon, Uijongbu, and Tongduchon. Written sources include newspaper articles, community organization reports, U.S. military documents, and the personal papers of several military brides. But because written sources are scarce, my primary sources came from fieldwork. This includes formal, audiotaped oral history interviews with sixteen military brides who arrived in a forty-year time span from 1951 to 1991, as well as participant observation with approximately one hundred fifty military brides and their families. These people were found through personal contacts throughout the local Korean immigrant community who introduced me to military brides whom they knew.

Although the research was conducted in one geographical area, this is not a geographically bound community study. The study's focus is the history of Korean military brides and their life experiences, and much of the history and life experiences that the women discuss took place in locales throughout the United States, in Korea, and at U.S. military bases around the world. Only in chapters 5 and 6 does the Delaware Valley location assume specific importance, for in these chapters much of the discussion centers around the women's relationship with the mainstream Korean community in the area and with the development of their own regional associations. Nevertheless, these chapters also draw on the history of Korean military brides in other regions of the United States.

Only two women, to my knowledge, expressed explicit opposition to this study. The opposition of one woman at a regional association effectively prevented me from getting to know how the members of that association interacted at their monthly meetings, for like most Korean military bride associations, it operated by consensus. She felt that allowing a researcher at the association's members-only functions would make the functions stressful rather than relaxing and enjoyable. As this was a reasonable belief, I made no attempts to ask for a reconsideration or to plead my case. Other members of this association, however, spoke with me quite freely about both their own lives and the history of the association, and I attended functions that were open to nonmembers.

The opposition of the second woman arose from a reluctance to see the lives of military brides exposed to public view. She invited me to her home for dinner after church one Sunday. I thought she was either curious about or interested in participating in the research. She thought that I was a newly arrived military bride who needed befriending. Although the minister had announced my presence and the reason for it several weeks before, and I had been busily introducing myself to church members since then, she was unaware of my identity for she spent much of her time working in the church kitchen or the nursery. (This reminded me that the women had more interesting and important things to do amongst themselves than talk about the stranger who wanted to get to know them.) When I started to say, "As you know, I'm studying the lives of Korean women who married American soldiers and . . ." she was shocked and frankly expressed her sense of betrayal. She questioned the value of my research and noted that Koreans were quick to view military brides negatively. We came to an agreement: I would not ask for her help in the research, and she would not hinder my work. Instead, we would just be fellow church members. We were able to come to this agreement because, after a long conversation about my perspectives and goals for the research, she decided that the study would not be exploitative or sensationalized. Henceforth, we developed a friendly relationship and I treated her with the respect due an elder sister within Korean culture.

It was more common for husbands to object to their wives' contact with me. The reaction of Mrs. Ferriman's husband was typical of many other husbands, albeit more overtly so. He interrupted our taped interview by admonishing his wife to tell me the truth, and when I offered to interview him, he declined, saying that I wouldn't understand because I was not married. Another woman's husband harrumphed under his breath, "Can't understand a word they're saying. They oughtta speak English," as he came home and headed upstairs in the middle of his wife's conversation with me.

APPENDIX 2

Overview of Scholarly Treatment of Korean Military Brides

In framing the life experiences of Korean military brides within both Korean and American historical contexts and examining issues of hegemony, power, and resistance, this study is a radical break from existing studies of military brides. The overwhelming majority of the studies have been conducted by social service providers who are primarily interested in marital adjustment and conflict, incidence of domestic abuse, and strategies for providing better care. A number of chaplains and other social service providers associated with the military have produced studies on Korean women-U.S. soldier marriages and the services that the military should provide to assist these couples.[1] Ministers of Korean immigrant churches have also written about ways to minister to Korean military brides.[2] Some studies use statistical analysis to research narrowly defined issues. A typical study is a 1989 doctoral dissertation that examines factors in marital satisfaction among interracially married Korean women.[3]

A few studies have taken different approaches, but in them the experiences of the women are used primarily as research material for theoretical discussions about issues specific to a discipline. One anthropological study looks at the narrative strategies of two Korean military brides telling their life stories.[4] A communications study analyzes the American television and Korean video viewing habits of four different Korean populations in Texas, including first-generation immigrants, international students, second-generation Korean Americans, and military brides.[5]

The best known of the social service provider studies are those conducted by Bok-Lim Kim and Daniel Boo-Duk Lee, both of whom have spent twenty years or more working with Korean military brides seeking assistance.[6] Although both scholars are careful to note that many Korean military brides have happy, successful lives and marriages, they stress the difficulties that the women face in cultural adjustment, abuse from husbands, social isolation, and the resulting psychological damage. The portrait is of a population in extreme distress, even pathological, and in urgent need of external intervention. But since the women they studied were those who came to the attention of social service providers, this may not be an accurate reflection of the Korean military bride population as a whole.

A 1991 article written by an undergraduate is a refreshing departure from the other literature on Korean military brides. Haeyun Juliana Kim frames her article with the story of a second-generation Korean American woman, herself, getting to know the "women in shadows," women similar to those she remembers from church. She goes to a dinner with military brides in the Fort Devens, Massachusetts, area, and finds that they "could have been my aunts back in Korea."[7] After meeting with them regularly over a period of three months, she presents the stories of seven military brides.

Kim also makes an important assertion that indicates a shift in research perspective away from issues of social deviance and marital adjustment and toward the construction of history and community. She asserts that the military brides are Korean American women, which situates them as part of the Korean American community and its history. This perspective is tempered, however, by her characterization of them as "voices from the shadows." Although she situates them as Korean American women, she also keeps them at the margins of Korean American society. Despite this, her perspective places her work within an Asian American studies tradition of recovering and reconstructing a multi-linked past and thereby drawing marginalized and/or disparate populations into a coherent community. While the previous studies discussed are grounded in traditional disciplines such as sociology, social work, or anthropology and primarily address debates specific to those fields, her study attempts to chronicle the lives of marginalized peoples in the manner of the revisionist, groundbreaking scholarship embodied in fields such as ethnic studies and women's studies.[8]

With the exception of Bok-Lim Kim's work, none of the existing studies situate Korean military brides within the broader phenomenon of what I call international military brides, that is, women from around the world who have married American soldiers. This phenomenon began in earnest during World War II, when American soldiers began to fraternize with and marry women from Britain, France, Italy, and Germany as they were stationed in these countries.[9] These international marriages were largely limited to the immediate postwar period. By the 1960s, their numbers had drastically dwindled along with U.S. troop strength in Europe. With the postwar occupation of Japan, U.S. troops began to marry Japanese women. As Bok-Lim Kim demonstrates, marriages between women of a particular country and American soldiers followed the trajectory of U.S. military involvement in those countries. Thus, as the United States sent troops to Japan, Korea, the Philippines, and Vietnam, American soldiers brought home Japanese, Korean, Filipina, and Vietnamese wives.[10] Although most of the researchers mention that some of the women came from camptowns where women worked as prostitutes servicing American soldiers, none attempts to analyze how militarized prostitution affects marriages between local women and American soldiers or how it affects the lives of military brides.

Furthermore, none of the studies adequately situate the international military brides' experiences within the context of migration. Although Daniel Lee's work on Korean military brides has attempted to place them within Korean immigration history, he stresses a mainstream Korean immigrant perspective by seeing the women as important primarily for their contributions to Korean immigrant communities and their role as civilian ambassadors mediating Korea-U.S. relations at a social and cultural level.[11]

If the literature on military brides has been too narrow, the literature on Asian Americans fails to do much more than mention the existence of military brides. Both the landmark texts on the Asian American experience, Ronald Takaki's *Strangers from a Different Shore*, and Sucheng Chan's *Asian Americans: An Interpretive History*, devote no more than a few pages at most to a discussion of military brides from Asia. In both cases, the discussion is primarily about Chinese women who married Chinese American soldiers. I know of no monograph on Asian military brides other than Bok-Lim Kim's now out-of-print handbook for social service providers, *Women in Shadows*. Only two books contain lengthy sections on Asian military brides, and both focus on Japanese war brides.[12]

The literature on Korean Americans is even more neglectful. Two of the major texts on Korean Americans, Bong-Youn Choy's *Koreans in America* and Ilsoo Kim's *New Urban Immigrants: Koreans in New York*, which together chronicle Korean immigration from its turn of the century beginnings to its post-1965 boom, make only brief mention of Korean military brides.[13] The majority of monographs on Korean Americans published since the 1980s have focused on small business owners and their experiences with the ethnic economy, race relations, and the construction of identity.[14] Military brides are barely mentioned, if at all.

Scholarly attention in Korea to Korean military brides has likewise been minimal. Whatever attention has been given has tended to be from the mass media. Scholars like Sil Dong Kim (who in ensuing years became U.S.-based) have written journalistic accounts for the Korean media based on their research in the 1970s and 1980s, while scholars like Yoo Chul-In at Cheju University (who wrote his doctoral dissertation on the narrative strategies of two military brides) were consulted for a Korean television documentary on Korean military brides.[15] Neither scholar, as far as I can ascertain, has published in Korea his scholarly work on military brides. Indeed, I know of no serious scholarly work—be it an article, book chapter, or book—published in Korea that specifically deals with military brides. This lack of attention to military brides is particularly striking, given that the amount of Korean scholarship on Korean migration and on Koreans overseas has steadily increased over the past two decades.

NOTES

NOTES TO THE INTRODUCTION

1. Seen in the documentary *Women Outside*, by Hye-Jung Park and J. T. Takagi (Third World Newsreel, 1996).

2. For example, "War Brides Arriving in U.S.," *Life*, February 18, 1946, p. 27. A war bride transportation system was set up by the U.S. military to transport British war brides to the United States. See Jenel Virden, *Good-Bye, Piccadilly: British War Brides in America* (Urbana: University of Illinois Press, 1996), pp. 49–64.

3. Chinese American men in the armed forces also brought home Chinese women as brides. As citizens of China, an American ally during World War II, these women were exempt from immigration restrictions against Asians and about six thousand Chinese war brides came under the War Brides Act. This influx of women helped even skewed gender ratios in Chinese American communities. For a brief overview, see Sucheng Chan, *Asian Americans: An Interpretive History* (Philadelphia: Temple University Press, 1991), p. 140. Apparently, few of the Chinese war brides married non-Chinese Americans.

4. Daniel B. Lee, "Korean Women Married to Servicemen," in *Korean American Women Living in Two Cultures,* ed. Young In Song and Ailee Moon (Los Angeles: Academia Koreana, Keimyung-Baylo University Press, 1997), pp. 94–123.

5. The Korean War ended with a truce, not a peace treaty, and thus the United States remains officially at war on the Korean peninsula despite the absence of outright armed conflict. This is why South Korea is categorized as a combat zone by the U.S. military and soldiers posted there are given hardship pay.

6. See the work of historian Bruce Cumings for detailed analyses of U.S.-Korean relations since 1945, including his two-volume classic, *Origins of the Korean War* (Princeton: Princeton University Press, 1981 and 1990), and the modern history written for a general readership, *Korea's Place in the Sun: A Modern History* (New York: W. W. Norton, 1997).

7. Matchmaking has a long tradition in Korean culture, and it is common for Koreans to introduce people with the intent of seeing them get married. Thus military brides were not alone in offering to make such introductions. These offers came from many of the older Koreans I encountered.

8. I first heard this phrase during a talk Kelley gave at the University of Pennsylvania in 1993–94 about southern blacks, resistance, and the civil rights movement.

NOTES TO CHAPTER I

1. These statistics were most recently cited in Daniel B. Lee, "Korean Women Married to Servicemen," in *Korean American Women Living in Two Cultures,* ed. Young In Song and Ailee Moon (Los Angeles: Academia Koreana, Keimyung-Baylo University Press, 1997), pp. 96–97. Statistics on the actual number of Korean women who entered the United States as wives of U.S. military personnel are not kept by any single agency, but must be teased out of records kept by the U.S. Immigration and Naturalization Service, Seoul City Hall's records of marriages between Korean citizens and citizens of foreign countries, and records kept by the South Korean Emigration Office. Using these sources and others, Lee has compiled the most complete figures available on the subject.

2. For some statistics, see Chul-In Yoo, "Life Histories of Two Korean Women Who Marry American GIs," Ph.D. dissertation, University of Illinois at Urbana-Champaign, 1993; and Sawon Hong, "Another Look at Marriages between Korean Women and American Servicemen," *Korea Journal* (May 1982), pp. 21–30.

3. For a discussion of militarized prostitution around U.S. bases in Asia, see Cynthia Enloe, *Bananas, Beaches and Bases: Making Feminist Sense of International Politics* (Berkeley: University of California Press, 1989); Cynthia Enloe, *The Morning After: Sexual Politics at the End of the Cold War* (Berkeley: University of California Press, 1993); Saundra Pollock Sturdevant and Brenda Stoltzfus, *Let the Good Times Roll: Prostitution and the U.S. Military in Asia* (New York: New Press, 1992); and Katherine H. S. Moon, *Sex among Allies: Military Prostitution in U.S.-Korea Relations* (New York: Columbia University Press, 1997). While Sturdevant and Stoltzfus focus on U.S. bases in the Philippines, South Korea, and Okinawa, Enloe's discussion includes militarized prostitution sponsored not only by the United States, but also by Great Britain and other military powers.

4. My Sister's Place, untitled report on camptowns and camptown prostitution in South Korea, 1997, p 28. Hereafter referred to as My Sister's Place, 1997 report. My Sister's Place is the American name for Durae Bang, a community center for camptown women. Located in the Uijongbu camptown near Seoul, it is sponsored by Korea Church Women United.

5. Kevin Heldman, "On the Town with the U.S. Military," datelined Dec. 19, 1996, available on the Korea WebWeekly Internet web site, URL:<http://www.kimsoft.com/korea/us-army.htm>.

6. *Bbaet-bul* is the local nickname for the camptown, and means a swamplike area that, once entered is impossible to escape. It is also the title of a 1996 novel about camptown life written by Ahn Il Soon (Seoul: Gonggan Media).

7. Bok-Lim C. Kim, "Casework with Japanese and Korean Wives of Ameri-

cans," *Social Casework* (May 1972), p. 277; Bascom W. Ratliff, Harriet Faye Moon, and Gwendolyn A. Bonacci, "Intercultural Marriage: The Korean-American Experience," *Social Casework* (April 1978), p. 122; Sil Dong Kim, "Internationally Married Korean Women Immigrants: A Study in Marginality," Ph.D. dissertation, University of Washington, 1979, p. 5; Daniel Booduck Lee, "Military Transcultural Marriage: A Study of Marital Adjustment between American Husbands and Korean-Born Spouses," D.S.W. dissertation, University of Utah, 1980, p. 16.

8. Such marriages, when performed in Korea, are registered in Seoul with city officials, using forms provided by the U.S. Embassy as well as Korean forms used to register the marriages of all Korean citizens. The resulting marriage certificate, stamped and signed by both Korean and U.S. authorities, can then be used to apply for an immigration visa for the Korean spouse. However, the records kept by the City of Seoul do not indicate whether a Korean woman who marries an American citizen is from the camptowns, nor do they indicate how many of the American men are U.S. military personnel. The U.S. Embassy does not keep records of marriages between U.S. citizens and citizens of other countries. Conversations with a clerk at the Chongno-Gu Office, City of Seoul, in March 1997, and with a clerk at the U.S. Embassy in Seoul, Citizen Services Division, in July 1997.

9. Yoo, "Life Histories of Two Korean Women Who Marry American GIs," p. 36.

10. See Hong, "Another Look at Marriages between Korean Women and American Servicemen." Because the applications which soldiers must make to their commanding officers for permission to marry are not kept for longer than a year, Hong found it impossible to do more than examine the applications for the one year in which she conducted research.

11. My Sister's Place, 1997 report; Bok-Lim Kim, "Casework with Japanese and Korean Wives of Americans"; Yoo, "Life Histories of Two Korean Women Who Marry American GIs"; Sil Dong Kim, "Internationally Married Korean Women Immigrants"; Hong, "Another Look at Marriages between Korean Women and American Servicemen."

12. As quoted in Bok-Lim C. Kim, "Asian Wives of U.S. Servicemen: Women in Shadows," *Amerasia Journal*, no. 4 (1977), p. 235.

13. Heldman, "On the Town with the U.S. Military"; Bruce Cumings, "Silent but Deadly: Sexual Subordination in the U.S.-Korea Relationship," in *Let the Good Times Roll: Prostitution and the U.S. Military in Asia*, by Saundra Pollock Sturdevant and Brenda Stoltzfus (New York: New Press), 1992, pp. 169-75.

14. These quotes come from e-mails posted to the discussion list <moo-goonghwa@ucsd.edu> in mid-April 1999 and in the personal possession of the

author, who at that time was a member of the list. It is interesting to note that during this discussion the three ethnic Koreans (identifiable by their names, and including the author) who posted were angrily accused of being emotional, irrational, and anti-American for arguing that the U.S. military was partially responsible for camptown prostitution. The thread was prompted by the posting of an announcement of upcoming PBS broadcasts around the United States of the 1996 documentary of South Korean camptown women, *Women Outside,* directed by Hye-Jung Park and J. T. Takagi. This documentary was also dismissed by vocal members of the list as "emotional" and "propaganda."

15. John Dower, *War without Mercy: Race and Power in the Pacific War* (New York: Pantheon Books, 1993; originally published in 1986) has shown how racist depictions of the "Oriental enemy" were widely used during World War II. Lloyd Lewis, *The Tainted War: Culture and Identity in Vietnam Narratives* (Westport, Conn.: Greenwood Press, 1985), has noted that soldiers in all branches of the U.S. military recall being indoctrinated during their training with the idea that the enemy was Oriental and inferior.

16. Moon, *Sex among Allies,* p. 37.

17. *Pacific Stars and Stripes,* July 3, 1977, as quoted in Moon, *Sex among Allies,* p. 33.

18. Second Infantry Division, 102nd Military Intelligence Battalion Soldiers Book, 1987 rev. ed., pp. 14-15, available on the Internet for downloading, URL: http://members.xoom.com/cptango/102ndSolBk.PDF.

19. Moon, *Sex among Allies,* pp. 33-34.

20. Lynn Thiesmeyer, "U.S. Comfort Women and the Silence of the American Other," *Hitting Critical Mass: A Journal of Asian American Cultural Criticism,* vol. 3, no. 2 (Spring 1997), pp. 47-67.

21. Japan and the United States are not the only countries to engage in forcible prostitution for the benefit of their military. The Germans used Jewish women, as well as other women from countries they invaded, as sex slaves in military brothels during World War II; the French used Algerian women in "mobile field brothels" to service their troops in Vietnam (both countries were French colonies); and the Pakistani military kept military brothels stocked with captured Bengali women during their nine-month war in 1971-72. During World War II, U.S. General George S. Patton considered setting up military brothels for American troops, but abandoned the idea because he concluded that the uproar this would create among wives and mothers back in the United States would hurt the war effort. See Susan Brownmiller, *Against Our Will: Men, Women and Rape* (New York: Fawcett Columbine, 1975), pp. 63-64, 75-78, 82-83, and 92-93.

22. Thiesmeyer, "U.S. Comfort Women and the Silence of the American

Other"; Vietnam reference, Brownmiller, *Against Our Will,* pp. 94-97; Okinawa reference, Suzuyo Takazato and Harumi Miyashiro, "Crimes against Okinawan Women by American Soldiers since World War II," in *Appeal to Prioritize Women's Rights,* ed. Suzuyo Takazato and Keiko Itosu (Women's Group to Disallow the U.S. Military Bases, 1996); Korean War incident, Cumings, "Silent but Deadly," pp. 171-72; Philippines example, testimony of U.S. servicemen, ABC's "Prime Time Live," 5/13/1996; My Sister's Place, 1997 report; Korea Church Women United, *Great Father, Great Army: The USFK and Prostitution in Korea,* 1996; Moon, *Sex among Allies.*

23. It is instructive to note that systems of militarized prostitution are not a major issue around America's military installations in Europe. The local women who keep U.S. soldiers company are seen as girlfriends, not prostitutes. Prostitution itself is actively discouraged by the U.S. military in Europe. This says a great deal about the way "brown" and "white" women are differentially perceived. See Enloe, *Bananas, Beaches and Bases.*

24. My Sister's Place, 1997 report; Korea Church Women United, *Great Father, Great Army;* Katharine Moon, *Sex among Allies;* and Sturdevant and Stoltzfus, *Let the Good Times Roll.*

25. Cumings, "Silent but Deadly," p. 170.

26. Enloe, *Bananas, Beaches and Bases,* pp. 81-92; Cynthia Enloe, *Does Khaki Become You? The Militarization of Women's Lives* (Boston: South End Press, 1983).

27. It is worth noting here that while prostitution existed throughout Korea under Japanese colonialism, after 1945 it seems to have remained a problem only for the south. There is no evidence of prostitution in North Korea. See Cumings, "Silent but Deadly." Even during the Korean War, there seem to have been few women who followed North Korean or Chinese troops, in contrast to the hordes that followed U.S. and UN troops. This gives the lie to common American stereotypes of Korean women as promiscuous and carnal, and also indicates that post-1945 prostitution in South Korea is directly related to the presence of the U.S. military.

28. Hei Soo Shin, "Women's Sexual Services and Economic Development: The Political Economy of the Entertainment Industry and South Korean Dependent Development," Ph.D. dissertation, Rutgers University, 1991, pp. 42–44. The first chapters of Ilwoong Yoon, *Maechun: Jongguk Sachanggawa Changnyo Siltae (Prostitution: The Reality of Prostitution Districts and Prostitutes in Korea)* (Seoul: Dongkwang Press, 1987), also give an overview of the history of prostitution and female entertainers in Korea.

29. Jung-Mok Sohn, "Iljeha-ui Maech'unop: Kongch'ang-gwa Sach'ang (Prostitution under Japanese Rule in Korea: Legal and Illegal Red Light Dis-

tricts)," *Tosi Haengjong Yongu (Urban Administrative Review)*, no. 3 (1988), pp. 285-360 (Seoul: Seoul City University).

30. Ki-baik Lee, *A New History of Korea*, trans. Edward W. Wagner, with Edward J. Shultz (Cambridge, Mass.: Harvard University Press, 1984), pp. 346-59.

31. Sohn, "Iljeha-ui Maech'unop: Kongch'ang-gwa Sach'ang (Prostitution under Japanese Rule in Korea: Legal and Illegal Red Light Districts)." It should be noted here that the common notion that it is Confucian mores (that is, something specifically Asian and non-Western) that dictate female chastity in Asian countries may not be applicable. Studies of immigrant European women in the United States indicate, for example, that many who became prostitutes entered the field after having been "dirtied" by a former employer or other male. See Donna Gabaccia, *From the Other Side: Women, Gender and Immigrant Life in the U.S., 1820-1990* (Bloomington: Indiana University Press, 1994). Thus the phenomenon of women entering prostitution after experiencing a sexual violation appears to be related to patriarchal mores and a sexual double standard rather than specifically Confucian ones.

32. Kyu-Sik Kwon and Oh Myung-Kun, "Yullak Yosong-ui Silt'ae (Report on Prostitutes)," *Yosong Munje Yongu (Journal of Research on Women's Issues)*, no. 3 (1973), pp. 149-71 (Taegu, Korea: Hyosung Women's College).

33. George Hicks, *The Comfort Women* (Sydney, Australia: Allen and Unwin, 1995); Bahk Sunyoung and Ryu Baochoon, *I Could Not Destroy Myself (Na-neun Na-reul Jook-il-soo-ubtsudda)* (Seoul: Kipeun Sarang Press, 1995).

34. Bruce Cumings, *Origins of the Korean War*, vol. I (Princeton: Princeton University Press, 1981), details the U.S. military occupation of Korea and the policies and effects of the U.S. military government.

35. Korea Church Women United, *Great Army, Great Father*.

36. Much of what is described in *Silver Stallion* did take place during both the military government period (1945-48) and the war. My own aunts have described to me how women and girls were hidden every night during the war for fear of rape by U.S. soldiers. They and other Koreans who experienced the war also spoke of how U.S. soldiers would cry out "saekssi, saekssi," using the Korean word for maiden or bride as they looked for Korean women. This behavior was universally taken to mean that U.S. soldiers intended to violate Korean women and viewed them as sexual playthings. For a similar memory, see Chungmoo Choi, "Nationalism and Construction of Gender in Korea," in *Dangerous Women*, ed. Elaine H. Kim and Chungmoo Choi (New York: Routledge, 1998), pp. 9-32, especially p. 15.

37. Junghyo Ahn, *Silver Stallion* (New York: Soho Press, 1990).

38. My Sister's Place, 1997 report, pp. 31-32.

39. The DMZ (Demilitarized Zone) roughly approximates the 38th Parallel.

40. Korean Church Women United, *Great Army, Great Father*, pp. 31-32.

41. Katherine H. S. Moon, "International Relations and Women: A Case Study of United States-Korea Camptown Prostitution, 1971-1976," Ph.D. dissertation, Princeton University, 1994, pp. 41-42; and *Dong-A Ilbo*, 7/22/1962, as cited in Moon, p. 42.

42. When the Status of Forces Agreement (SOFA) between Korea and the United States was approved in 1966, local residents' hopes for compensation died completely. The agreement stipulated that the United States could use without charge any and all land necessary for its South Korean military operations.

43. My discussion of Songtan is taken from Oh Yun Ho, *Sikminji-ui Adul-ae-gae (To the Sons of the Colony)* (Seoul: Baiksan Sudang, 3d ed., 1994), pp. 140-42. The quote is from page 142 and is my translation from the original Korean.

44. Korea Church Women United, *Great Army, Great Father*, p. 33.

45. My Sister's Place, 1997 report, pp. 33-34.

46. Soldiers at first paid for their entertainment with a form of military scrip. When the United States introduced American dollars for use in the bases, soldiers paid in U.S. dollars. Then and now, prices at clubs and stores catering to U.S. soldiers have generally been calculated in American currency, not Korean.

47. Quoted in Moon, "International Relations and Women," pp. 70-71.

48. Eighth U.S. Army, Office of International Relations, "Human Factors Research: Part II, Troop-Community Relations," 1965, as cited in Moon, "International Relations and Women," p. 236.

49. According to a 1990 study of forty years of Korean government debate and policy on prostitution, the Korean government had double standards regarding domestic-oriented prostitution and foreign-oriented prostitution. The former was to be eliminated, for it was an immoral influence on Korean society; the latter was to be pragmatically tolerated, for it was an aid to national defense and the economy. In other words, the government supported camptown prostitution as a kind of compensation for the U.S. soldiers' presence in Korea and because it helped generate foreign exchange. Hyoung Cho and Pilwha Chang, "Perspectives on Prostitution in the National Assembly: 1948-89," *Women's Studies Review*, vol. 7 (December 1990) (Seoul: Korean Women Research Institute of Ewha Women's University).

50. Unless otherwise noted, the discussion of joint U.S.-Korea efforts to eradicate venereal disease and control camptown women comes from Moon, "International Relations and Women," and from Moon, *Sex among Allies*.

51. Moon, "International Relations and Women," p. 65.

52. The U.S. Status of Forces Agreement (SOFA) specifies what rights and privileges the U.S. military will enjoy in Korea, what responsibilities each government has regarding the U.S. forces in Korea, and what jurisdiction, if any, the

Korean government can exert over U.S. soldiers and other military employees who break Korean laws. The Joint Committee, established under SOFA, oversees the implementation of this agreement, which was first signed in 1966.

53. Women interviewed by Moon, *Sex among Allies,* and Sturdevant and Stoltzfus, *Let the Good Times Roll,* expressed this belief.

54. Quoted in Moon, "International Relations and Women," p. 142.

55. Quoted in Moon, "International Relations and Women," p. 240.

56. Quoted in Moon, "International Relations and Women," p. 259.

57. In addition to club women, camptowns also have streetwalkers. Their prices are lower than that of club women, as is their status among camptown women. In the camptown hierarchy, women who marry GIs have the highest status; next come women who have a steady GI boyfriend who supports them financially, that is, women in "contract live-in relationships"; next are the club women; and last are the streetwalkers. Among the streetwalkers, elderly women occupy the lowest status. This information comes from conversations with camptown women held during visits to My Sister's Place during February and March 1997.

58. Moon, "International Relations and Women," chapters 5 and 6; and *Sex among Allies,* chapters 3 and 4.

59. Sturdevant and Stoltzfus, *Let the Good Times Roll,* pp. 176-79; March 1997 interview with Myungboon Kim, staff worker at My Sister's Place.

60. The following discussion of camptown women and their routes to camptowns is taken from a March 1997 interview with Myungboon Kim, staff worker at My Sister's Place; My Sister's Place, 1997 report; Korea Church Women United, *Great Army, Great Father;* and Moon, "International Relations and Women."

61. The Korean government has had job training programs aimed at prostitutes as part of its efforts to eliminate prostitution, but since these efforts focus on rehabilitating the women rather than changing the social structures that encourage prostitution, the programs have had minimal success.

62. This description of camptown life and the club system comes from conversations with camptown women held at My Sister's Place during February and March 1997; Moon, "International Relations and Women," pp. 49-57; Moon, *Sex among Allies,* pp. 19-27; Sturdevant and Stoltzfus, *Let the Good Times Roll,* pp. 176-79; and a March 1997 interview with Myungboon Kim.

63. My Sister's Place, 1997 report, p. 17, my translation from the original Korean.

64. Yoon Chongmo, *Gobbi I* (Seoul: P'ulbit, 1988), pp. 31-32, my translation from the original Korean.

65. Although intended for U.S. troops stationed in South Korea, AFKN's

broadcasts were picked up by most television sets just like Korean networks, until a few years ago when broadcasting agreements were changed. AFKN programming brought American movies, sitcoms, comedy shows, and news to the Korean public.

66. Hyeon-Dew Kang, "Changing Image of America in Korean Popular Literature: With an Analysis of Short Stories between 1945-1975," *Korea Journal* (October 1976), pp. 19-33; Manwoo Lee, "Anti-Americanism and South Korea's Changing Perception of America," in *Alliance under Tension: The Evolution of South Korea-U.S. Relations*, ed. Manwoo Lee, Ronald D. McLaurin, and Chung-in Moon (Boulder, Colo.: Westview Press, 1988), pp. 7-27. America was implicated in the Kwangju massacre, carried out by South Korean troops, because America has been at the head of the military hierarchy that runs the joint ROK-U.S. forces. In other words, the Korean military was under the command of an American general in 1980, and thus the kind of massive troop movement that occurred during the massacre could only have been carried out with U.S. knowledge and approval. (This command structure officially changed in 1995, such that the commanding general of the joint forces is now a Korean.) For a discussion of U.S. government documents that confirms long-standing suspicions about the U.S. role in the massacre, see Tim Shorrock, "Ex-Leaders Go on Trial in Seoul," *Journal of Commerce*, Five Star edition, February 27, 1996, p. A1, and Tim Shorrock, "Debacle in Kwangju," *The Nation*, December 9, 1996, pp. 19-22.

67. See Bruce Cumings's 1998 address, "The Question of American Responsibility for the Suppression of the Chejudo Uprising," presented at the 50th Anniversary Conference of the April 3, 1948 Chejudo Rebellion, Tokyo, March 14, 1998.

68. See Stephen J. Epstein, "Wanderers in the Wilderness: Images of America in Ch'oe In-ho's Kipko p'urun pam," *Korea Journal*, vol. 35 (Winter 1995), pp. 72-79. While this may appear to be a more sympathetic reading of the camptown woman, it has its own problems, not least among them that this usage of the figure of the camptown woman is yet another way in which such women are objectified and their voices silenced, their life experiences used for someone else's purpose.

69. As violent crimes committed by American soldiers, such as the 1992 murder of Yoon Geum-Yi, are widely publicized, Koreans are becoming increasingly willing to condemn America and American soldiers. Nevertheless, this does not seem to be accompanied by a corresponding increase in sympathy for the camptown women.

70. My Sister's Place, 1997 report; and Sturdevant and Stoltzfus, *Let the Good Times Roll*.

71. See, for example, Gail Pheterson, ed., *A Vindication of the Rights of*

Whores (Seattle: Seal Press, 1989), and Frederique Delacoste and Priscilla Alexander, ed., *Sex Work: Writings by Women in the Sex Industry,* 2d ed. (Pittsburgh: Cleis Press, 1987).

72. Kang Suk-kyung, "Nat-gwa ggum (Days and Dreams)," in *Bam-gwa Yoram (Night and Cradle)* (Seoul: Min—sa, 1983, 1993), p. 25, my translation from the original Korean.

73. My Sister's Place, 1997 report, p. 13.

74. Because of the stigma, such children are often not registered in the family registry, the only way to register births and gain legal personhood in Korea. Because paternity usually cannot be proven and fathers rarely cooperate, the children cannot be registered with American authorities either. This in effect leaves them stateless. For an overview of the problems faced by Amerasian children in the camptowns, see Margo Okazawa-Rey, "Amerasian Children in GI Town: A Legacy of U.S. Militarism in South Korea," *Asian Journal of Women's Studies,* vol. 3, no. 1 (1997), pp. 71-102 (Seoul: Ewha Women's University Press).

75. Ms. Pak, as quoted in Sturdevant and Stoltzfus, *Let the Good Times Roll,* p. 209.

NOTES TO CHAPTER 2

1. For the classic study of the Korean War, see Bruce Cumings's two-volume *Origins of the Korean War* (Princeton: Princeton University Press, 1981 and 1990).

2. Although Public Law 271, also known as the War Brides Act, was passed in 1945 to allow soldiers to bring their wives to the United States, no provision was made for brides from Asian countries. At that time, immigration from Asia was legally prohibited as a result of several laws passed during the 1910s and 1920s. The exception was a small, token quota for China, a provision made in recognition of China's ally status during World War II and to forestall international charges of racism. Several amendments to Public Law 271 allowed Asian wives of soldiers to enter the United States, but these amendments expired within one or two years. (Ms. Cho appears to have entered the United States under one of these amendments.) It was not until 1952 that the law was changed to allow Asian wives of U.S. citizens entry into the United States without legal discrimination. For a discussion of the changes in the law, see Michael C. Thornton, "The Quiet Immigration: Foreign Spouses of U.S. Citizens, 1945–1985," in *Racially Mixed People in America,* ed. Maria P. P. Root (London: Sage Publications, 1992), pp. 64–76. For a general discussion of laws regarding women, immigration, and citizenship, see Candice Bredbenner, *A Nationality of Her Own:*

Women, Marriage and the Law of Citizenship (Berkeley: University of California Press, 1998).

3. Her response illustrates the changing views of marriage in South Korea, where romantic love gradually became a legitimate and sufficient reason for marriage. See Laurel Kendall, *Getting Married in Korea: Of Gender, Morality and Modernity* (Berkeley: University of California Press, 1996), for a brief history and a rich discussion of modern Korean marriage practices.

4. See Table 1 in Bok-Lim C. Kim, "Asian Wives of U.S. Servicemen: Women in Shadows," *Amerasia Journal*, no. 4 (1977), pp. 91–115. The original source is cited as U.S. Commissioner of Immigration and Naturalization, *Annual Reports, 1947–1975*, Table 6 (Washington, D.C.).

5. Kim, "Asian Wives of U.S. Servicemen."

6. A recent text by Bruce Cumings, *Korea's Place in the Sun: A Modern History* (New York: W. W. Norton, 1997) discusses economic conditions during that period. See especially chapters 4 through 6.

7. Cumings, *Korea's Place in the Sun*, p. 304.

8. This underground economy is still thriving, as evidenced in most Seoul marketplaces by piles of black market American goods obtained from PXs and commissaries, as well as by occasional newspaper reports of the arrest of black marketeers.

9. See Table 1 in Kim, "Asian Wives of U.S. Servicemen," pp. 91–115.

10. See George Ogle, *South Korea: Dissent within the Economic Miracle* (Atlantic Highlands, N.J.: Zed Books, 1990); and Martin Hart-Landsberg, *Rush to Development* (New York: Monthly Review Press, 1993), for discussions of the urbanization and proletarianization of Korea and the social upheavals that resulted in the mass migration of poverty-stricken young women into urban areas. The 1997 report by My Sister's Place discusses how this urbanization influenced the dispersal of many young women into camptowns.

11. There are no birth certificates, marriage certificates, divorce certificates, and the like, as in the United States. Instead, all such events are recorded in each family's Family Register, and official copies of this register are required to marry, divorce, immigrate, prove one's identity, and so on.

12. Katherine H. S. Moon, "International Relations and Women: A Case Study of United States-Korea Camptown Prostitution, 1971–1976," Ph.D. dissertation, Princeton University, 1994, p. 43.

13. See Table 1 in Kim, "Asian Wives of U.S. Servicemen"; and Table 1 in Daniel B. Lee, "Korean Women Married to Servicemen," in *Korean American Women Living in Two Cultures*, ed. Young In Song and Ailee Moon (Los Angeles: Academia Koreana, Keimyung-Baylo University Press, 1997), pp. 94–123.

14. For a study of the lives of factory women in Korea, see Royal Asiatic Society, Korea Branch, *Yogong: Factory Girl* (Seoul: Royal Asiatic Society, Korea Branch, 1988).

15. Hart-Landsberg, *Rush to Development,* pp. 177–82.

16. *Unni,* an honorific used by women to refer to and address their elder sisters, is also used among young women as a form of address for slightly older women.

17. See Table 1 in Lee, "Korean Women Married to Servicemen."

18. See Ilsoo Kim, *New Urban Immigrants: The Korean Community in New York* (Princeton: Princeton University Press, 1981), for a lengthy discussion of Korean emigration.

19. See Nancy Abelmann and John Lie, *Blue Dreams: Korean Americans and the Los Angeles Riots* (Cambridge, Mass.: Harvard University Press, 1995), pp. 56–77, for a discussion of modernity, transnationalism, and the American fever. See Kim, *New Urban Immigrants,* chapters 1 through 3, for a discussion of the multiple factors (economics, government policy, and the like) that created a desire among Koreans to emigrate to America.

20. See Table 1 in Lee, "Korean Women Married to Servicemen."

21. Lee, "Korean Women Married to Servicemen."

22. Personal interview with Yvonne Park, Deputy Director, U.S.O. Seoul, on February 26, 1997, in Seoul.

23. For example, *Chukeum-eul Nomo Sidaeui Odum-eul Nomo,* an eyewitness account of the uprising and massacre, was published in 1985. Although banned, the book circulated widely in the student movement. The English translation by Jai-Euii Lee is *Kwangju Diary: Beyond Death, Beyond the Darkness of the Age* (Berkeley: University of California Press, 1999).

24. Until the mid-1990s, the commander of joint U.S.-ROK forces was always an American. Since the only Korean forces were part of the joint forces, this in effect left supreme command of the Korean military in the hands of the United States. Documents recently uncovered by journalist Tim Shorrock through the Freedom of Information Act reveal that the students were basically correct in their speculations about U.S. involvement in the massacre. See Tim Shorrock, "Ex-Leaders Go on Trial in Seoul," *Journal of Commerce,* Five Star edition, February 27, 1996, p. A1; and "Debacle in Kwangju," *The Nation,* December 9, 1996, pp. 19–22. For an anthology of scholarly articles about the Kwangju uprising and massacre, see Donald N. Clark, ed., *The Kwangju Uprising: Shadows over the Regime in South Korea* (Boulder, Colo.: Westview Press, 1988).

25. For a brief account of the politics, student and labor demonstrations, and the democracy movement in Korea during the 1980s, see Cumings, *Korea's Place in the Sun,* pp. 377–93.

26. In 1977, the INS stopped keeping track of immigrants who entered as wives of U.S. citizens. Thus no INS records are available that indicate how many other Korean women entered with Mrs. Orellana. Data compiled by Daniel B. Lee using Korean sources do not go past 1989, and I was unable to find any other data in the secondary literature.

27. See Paul Messaris and Jisuk Woo, "Image vs. Reality in Korean Americans' Responses to Mass-Mediated Depictions of the United States," *Critical Studies in Mass Communication,* vol. 8 (1991), pp. 74–90, for a discussion of Korean immigrants' views of America before coming to the United States. In their study of forty-one Korean immigrants, the researchers found that images of wealth, freedom, and opportunity were dominant, and that the immigrants spoke of viewing America as a paradise or land where dreams came true. Significantly, the researchers also found that the interviewees felt that their experience of reality did not live up to these images.

28. J. M. Blaut, *The Colonizer's Model of the World* (New York: Guilford Press, 1993).

29. Frantz Fanon, *Black Skin, White Masks,* trans. Charles Lam Markmann, originally published in French in 1952 (New York: Grove Weidenfeld, 1967); Aime Cesaire, *Discourse on Colonialism,* trans. Joan Pinkham, originally published in French in 1955 (New York: Monthly Review Press, 1972); Albert Memmi, *The Colonizer and the Colonized,* trans. Howard Greenfield, originally published in French in 1957 (Boston: Beacon Press, 1967).

30. The following discussion of English and its importance in South Korea is drawn from accounts of Korean acquaintances, friends, and family who lived through the periods in question, my own knowledge of the South Korean educational system through involvement in English education and publishing, and two articles on English education in Korea in the Korean news monthly *Mal,* September 1997, pp. 126–29, and April 1998, pp. 194–97.

31. Although Korea has long had a centralized education system, the South Korean government did not officially begin a centralized program until 1954 when it introduced mandatory textbooks in what is called the First National Curriculum. The curriculum is revised every few years and national textbooks are rewritten accordingly. South Korea is currently in the middle of the Sixth National Curriculum, which was promulgated in 1999.

32. Lee, Table 1 in "Korean Women Married to Servicemen."

NOTES TO CHAPTER 3

1. Aihwa Ong, *Spirits of Resistance and Capitalist Discipline: Factory Women in Malaysia* (Albany: State University of New York Press, 1987). Similarly, Robin

D. G. Kelley, in *Race Rebels: Culture, Politics and the Black Working Class* (New York: Free Press, 1996) and *Hammer and Hoe: Alabama Communists during the Great Depression* (Chapel Hill: University of North Carolina Press, 1990) describes disguised resistance among African Americans and how under the right circumstances it can blaze into outright rebellion.

2. James C. Scott, *Domination and the Arts of Resistance* (New Haven, Conn.: Yale University Press, 1990), pp. 19 and 190. See also his *Weapons of the Weak: Everyday Forms of Peasant Resistance* (New Haven, Conn.: Yale University Press, 1985).

3. This resonates with scholarship on imperialism and race, which has delineated the ways in which colonizers viewed the colonized as less than human, and has also shown that this view lingers long after the official colonizer-colonized relationship ends. In *War without Mercy*, John W. Dower shows how both the United States and Japan caricaturized and racialized each other. His analysis reveals, however, that while the United States depicted the Japanese enemy as subhuman, Japan's racialization strategy depended on defining the United States as evil. He also notes that the U.S. characterization of the Japanese as beastlike and subhuman extended to include other Asians, most notably during wars in Korea and Vietnam, and was linked to a general Western tendency to characterize non-white peoples as subhuman. See John W. Dower, *War without Mercy: Race and Power in the Pacific War* (New York: Pantheon Books, 1993). Originally published in 1986.

4. For various discussions of race, see Barbara J. Fields, "Race and Ideology in American History," in *Region, Race and Reconstruction: Essays in Honor of C. Vann Woodward*, ed. J. Morgan Kousser and James M. McPherson (New York: Oxford University Press, 1982), 143–47; Henry Louis Gates, Jr., "Introduction: Writing 'Race' and the Difference It Makes," in *"Race," Writing and Difference*, ed. Henry Louis Gates, Jr. (Chicago: University of Chicago Press, 1986) pp. 1–20; and Evelyn Brooks Higginbotham, "African American Women's History and the Metalanguage of Race," *Signs: Journal of Women in Culture and Society*, vol. 17, no. 2 (1992), pp. 251–74.

5. Ronald Takaki has shown how racial categories operated throughout the history of North America, from colonial times to the twentieth century, to repeatedly confer economic, political, social, and cultural privilege to whites at the expense of others. See Ronald Takaki, *Iron Cages: Race and Culture in Nineteenth-Century America* (New York: Oxford University Press, 1979; 2d ed., 1990); and "Reflections on Racial Patterns in America," in *From Different Shores: Perspectives on Race and Ethnicity in America*, ed. Ronald Takaki (New York: Oxford University Press, 1987), pp. 26–38.

Michael Omi and Howard Winant persuasively argue that American society

has responded to antiracist movements such as the civil rights struggle by simply forming a different racial formation, one that accommodates some demands
but leaves intact the underlying foundation of inequality based on racial categories. Arguing against paradigms of ethnicity, class, and nation that seek to explain race and racism as by-products of allegedly more fundamental discrimina-
tions, they demonstrate that race and racism have a separate dynamics that cannot be explained by these other paradigms. They also argue that the terrain on
which racial formation occurs is broad, encompassing every possible aspect of
human experience and activity from what they call the macrolevel of the public
sphere to the microlevel of everyday personal experience. See Michael Omi and
Howard Winant, *Racial Formations in the United States* (New York: Routledge,
1994).

Feminist scholars such as Patricia Hill Collins and bell hooks go a step further
than either Takaki or Omi and Winant, taking the case of black women in America to show how race and gender are linked in the domination and oppression of
women of color. They show, for example, how stereotypes such as the Mammy
and the Jezebel are both raced and gendered and are continually reconstituted
to discipline black women and keep them in their "proper place." Similarly,
stereotypes of Asian women as the docile, hyperfeminine, and submissive Lotus
Blossom and as the conniving, aggressive, and dangerous Dragon Lady function
to demand that Asian women fulfill particular roles deemed "natural" and
"proper." See Patricia Hill Collins, *Black Feminist Thought: Knowledge, Consciousness, and the Politics of Empowerment* (New York: Routledge, 1990); and
bell hooks, *Ain't I a Woman? Black Women and Feminism* (Boston: South End
Press, 1981).

A common thread in these analyses is the insight that racism operates at multiple levels, affecting even the most mundane daily experiences and the most
personal human interactions. Furthermore, the racism is often hidden, natural-
ized in what Stuart Hall calls inferential racism, and E. San Juan, Jr., calls covert
racism: attitudes and behaviors inscribed with racist premises as unquestioned
assumptions, thus allowing racism to be practiced without revealing the racist
predicates on which it is grounded. See E. San Juan, Jr., *Racial Formations, Critical Transformations: Articulations of Power in Ethnic and Racial Studies in the
United States* (Atlantic Highlands, N.J.: Humanities Press International, 1992), p.
40; and Stuart Hall, "The Whites of Their Eyes: Racist Ideologies and the
Media," in *Silver Linings*, ed. George Bridges and Rosalind Brunt (London:
Lawrence and Wishart, 1981), p. 36.

6. For discussions of Orientalism and stereotypes of Asian women, see,
among others: Renee E. Tajima, "Lotus Blossoms Don't Bleed: Images of Asian
Women," in *Making Waves: An Anthology of Writings by and about Asian*

American Women, ed. Asian Women United of California (Boston: Beacon Press, 1989), pp. 308–18; L. Hyun-Yi Kang, "The Desiring of Asian Female Bodies," *Visual Anthropology Review*, vol. 9, no. 1 (Spring 1993), pp. 5–21; Gina Marchetti, *Romance and the "Yellow Peril": Race, Sex, and Discursive Strategies in Hollywood Fiction* (Berkeley: University of California Press, 1993), and Aki Uchida, "The Orientalization of Asian Women in America," *Women's Studies International Forum*, vol. 21, no. 2 (1998), pp. 161–74.

7. Darrell Y. Hamamoto, *Monitored Peril: Asian Americans and the Politics of TV Representation* (Minneapolis: University of Minnesota Press, 1994); Marchetti, *Romance and the Yellow Peril*, Kang, "The Desiring of Asian Female Bodies"; and Yoki Yoshikawa, "The Heat Is on *Miss Saigon*: Organizing across Race and Sexuality," in *The State of Asian America: Activism and Resistance in the 1990s*, ed. Karin Aguilar-San Juan (Boston: South End Press, 1994), pp. 275–94.

8. Rosina Lippi-Green, *English with an Accent: Language, Ideology, and Discrimination in the United States* (New York: Routledge, 1997). See especially chapters 9 (The real trouble with Black English) and 11 (The stranger within the gates). Lippi-Green also discusses numerous legal cases of language discrimination, especially accent discrimination, in which Asian immigrants and Asian Americans lost jobs, were fired, or were otherwise discriminated against on the basis of the way they spoke English. See chapter 8 (Language ideology in the workplace and the judicial system).

9. I am setting aside the question of how "Koreanness" can be defined and exactly what "Koreanness" is, for that is beyond the scope of my study. Instead, I would argue that the term itself is dynamic, fluid, polyvocal, and contested, holding many meanings depending on context and intent. With that caveat, I use the term broadly and loosely to refer to the beliefs, behaviors, lifestyles, expressions, and the like that are associated with being Korean by many Koreans themselves, including the women in this study, as well as by Americans.

10. Daniel Y. Moon, "Ministering to Korean Wives of Servicemen," in *Korean Women in a Struggle for Humanization*, ed. Harold Hakwon Sunoo and Dong Soo Kim (Memphis, Tenn.: Association of Korean Christian Scholars in North America, 1978), p. 107.

11. Lisa Lowe, *Immigrant Acts: On Asian American Cultural Politics* (Durham: Duke University Press, 1996), especially the first chapter, and Gary Okihiro, *Margins and Mainstreams: Asians in American History and Culture* (Seattle: University of Washington Press, 1994), both talk about the ways in which Asians have been constructed and treated as the perpetual alien.

12. This kind of reasoning, for example, was behind the arrest in the wake of Pearl Harbor of Japanese immigrants who were cultural leaders within their

communities. Those who practiced and taught the Japanese language, Japanese dance, and other forms of cultural expression, it was assumed, were disloyal to America.

13. While most children experienced anti-Asian slurs, this son of a Korean mother and Jewish American father experienced slurs in which anti-Asian and anti-Semitic prejudices were combined. Similarly, women who married African American soldiers reported that their children were called names such as "slant-eyed nigger." In the experiences recounted to me, the attackers were always white, with one exception. One woman who had married an African American and settled in an African American neighborhood after her divorce, said that her son from the marriage would occasionally be harrassed as a "chink" or a "gook" by the other African American children. No one had experienced similar slurs from other Koreans, but I believe that this was due primarily to lack of contact with other Koreans.

14. See the essays in Mari J. Matsuda, Charles R. Lawrence III, Richard Delgado, and Kimberlé Williams Crenshaw, *Words That Wound* (Boulder, Colo.: Westview Press, 1993). The definition of "assaultive speech" comes from p. 1.

15. Koreans count the length of pregnancy as ten months, in which each month equals four weeks. The total span of forty weeks corresponds with the medical definition of the length of human pregnancy.

16. Quoted in Dongsook Park Kim, "The Meanings of Television Viewing: An Interpretive Analysis of Four Korean Groups in the U.S.," Ph.D. dissertation, University of Texas at Austin, 1990, p. 257.

17. See the disscussion of survey results and marital conflict in Don Chang Lee, "Intermarriage and Spouse Abuse: Korean Wife and American Husband," in *Koreans in America: Dreams and Realities*, ed. Hyung-chan Kim and Eun Ho Lee (Seoul: Institute of Korean Studies, 1990), pp. 133–50.

18. Venny Villapando, "The Business of Selling Mail-Order Brides," in *Making Waves: An Anthology of Writings by and about Asian American Women*, ed. Asian Women United of California, (Boston: Beacon Press, 1989), pp. 318–36. For a first-person account that positions the Asian woman as the gentle but strong spirit that saves weary American men and rejuvenates the American family through traditional Asian values that turn out to be traditional American values lost in the rampant individualism of modern society, see Wanwadee Larson, *Confessions of a Mail Order Bride* (Far Hills, N.J.: New Horizon Press, 1989).

19. Numerous scholars have analyzed these segmentations in the U.S. labor market. Among them, see Teresa L. Amott and Julie A. Matthaei, *Race, Gender and Work* (Boston: South End Press, 1991); Evelyn Nakano Glenn, *Issei, Nisei, War Bride: Three Generations of Japanese Women in Domestic Service* (Philadel-

phia, Temple University Press, 1986); and Lucie Cheng and Edna Bonacich, ed., *Labor Immigration under Capitalism* (Berkeley: University of California Press, 1984).

20. See Evelyn Nakano Glenn and Ching Kwan Lee, "Factory Regimes of Chinese Capitalism: Different Cultural Logics of Labor Control," in *Ungrounded Empires: The Cultural Politics of Modern Chinese Transnationalism,* ed. Aihwa Ong and Donald Nonini (New York: Routledge, 1997), pp. 115–42.

21. The self-described in-between position of Korean military brides evokes the term borderlands, used by Gloria Anzaldua to describe the hybrid, liminal histories and position of Mexican Americans. First popularized by her book *Borderland/La Frontera: The New Mestiza* (San Francisco: Aunt Lute Books, 1987), the term borderlands has now become a trope to describe the experiences of migrants negotiating two or more cultural, geographical, and national contexts.

22. This is a Korean saying for describing a luxurious life of plenty, and has often been used in reference to America.

NOTES TO CHAPTER 4

1. Roland Barthes, "Toward a Psychosociology of Contemporary Food Consumption," in *Food and Culture,* ed. Carole Counihan and Penny Van Esterik (New York: Routledge, 1997), p. 21, notes that "food sums up and transmits a situation; it constitutes information; it signifies."

2. The "imagined community" of the United States, that is, its dominant self-identity, has long been one of immigrants who have exchanged their worn-out, old cultures for the new, modern culture of America and a new, better life as Americans. Although sometimes modified with cultural pluralism or multiculturalism so that the melting pot becomes a mosaic or a salad or any number of other metaphors for mixtures as coherent wholes, the ideal of Americanization, one that posits a white America and things white American as superior, has remained strong throughout the twentieth century. One important measure of Americanization has been food.

3. Min Pyong Gap et al., *Migug Sok-eu Hangugin (Koreans in America)* (Seoul: Yurim Munhwa Sa, 1991), p. 180; and Eui-Young Yu, "Ethnic Identity and Community Involvement of Younger-Generation Korean Americans," in *Korean Studies: New Pacific Currents,* ed. Dae-Sook Suh (Honolulu: University of Hawaii Press, 1994), pp. 263–82. The other aspect that the second generation wanted to preserve was respect for elders.

4. Han Kyung-Koo, "Some Foods Are Good to Think: Kimchi and the Epitomization of National Character," *Hankuk Munhwa Inryuhak,* vol. 26 (1994), pp. 51–68.

5. Spaghetti became a popular foreign dish among many Koreans, perhaps because it contains garlic and because noodles topped with sauce is a familiar form of food to Koreans. For many bachelor students from Korea during the 1960s and 1970s, opening a can of spaghetti sauce, adding some garlic, and boiling noodles was their first introduction to feeding themselves in America.

6. It is common for Korean women to know only the rudimentary basics of cooking when they marry and to learn how to cook as young wives under the direction of their mothers-in-law. For military brides, marriage to an American can thus mean that they never learn to cook Korean food.

7. *Unni* is an honorific used by women to address their elder sisters. It is common for Korean women to call older women by this familial term. Among military brides, the usage of this term is often accompanied by the development of fictive kin relationships.

8. Some Korean Americans, on the other hand, say that Korean food in Korea does not taste as good as Korean food in America. Having grown up with easy access to Koreatowns and with Korean food served daily in their homes, these Korean Americans are also expressing their homesickness, but with a particular transnational twist as racial and ethnic minorities who grew up outside of their ancestral country of origin.

9. Donna Gabaccia, *We Are What We Eat* (Cambridge, Mass.: Harvard University Press, 1998), pp. 122–48. See also George Sanchez, "'Go after the Women': Americanization and the Mexican Immigrant Woman, 1915–1929," in *Unequal Sisters: A Multicultural Reader in U.S. Women's History,* ed. Vicki L. Ruiz and Ellen Carol Dubois (New York: Routledge, 1990), pp. 284–97.

10. For discussions of the ways in which food preparation is gendered, see, among others: Marjorie L. DeVault, *Feeding the Family: The Social Organization of Caring as Gendered Work* (Chicago: University of Chicago Press, 1991); Jacqueline Burgoyne and David Clarke, "You Are What You Eat: Food and Family Reconstitution," in *The Sociology of Food and Eating,* ed. Anne Murcott (Aldershot, England: Gower Publishing House, 1983); Janet Theophano and K. Curtis, "Sisters, Mothers and Daughters: Food Exchanged and Reciprocity in an Italian-American Community," in *Diet and Domestic Life in Society,* ed. A. Sharman, J. Theopano, K. Curtis, and E. Messer (Philadelphia: Temple University Press, 1991); and M. Ekstrom, "Class and Gender in the Kitchen," in *Palatable Worlds: Sociocultural Food Studies,* ed. E. L. Furst, R. Prattala, M. Ekstrom, L. Holm, and U. Kjaernes (Oslo: Solum Forlag, 1991).

For discussions of the role of food in the expression of identity, see Linda Keller Brown and Kay Mussell, ed., *Ethnic and Regional Foodways in the United States: The Performance of Group Identity* (Knoxville, Tenn.: University of Tennessee Press, 1984).

11. Lisa Heldke calls this phenomenon "cultural food colonialism." See "Let's Eat Chinese: Cultural Food Colonialism," presented at the Midwestern Conference of the Society for Women in Philosophy, Spring 1993, and quoted in Uma Narayan, *Dislocating Cultures: Identities, Traditions, and Third World Feminism* (New York: Routledge, 1997), pp. 178–88.

12. Stephanie Coontz, *The Way We Never Were: American Families and the Nostalgia Trap* (New York: Basic Books, 1992), shows that such a bygone era may never really have existed and that the traditional American family ideal of the housewife was never realized by more than a minority of American women.

13. Daniel Y. Moon, "Ministering to 'Korean Wives' of Servicemen," in *Korean Women in a Struggle for Humanization*, ed. Harold Hakwon Sunoo and Dong Soo Kim (Memphis, Tenn.: Association of Korean Christian Scholars in North America, 1978), pp. 97–116.

14. Min Pyong Gap et al., *Migug Sok-eu Hangugin (Koreans in America)* (Seoul: Yurim Munhwa Sa, 1991), pp. 179–80.

15. Donna Gabaccia succinctly outlines such beliefs in *From the Other Side: Women, Gender and Immigrant Life in the U.S., 1820–1990* (Bloomington: Indiana University Press, 1994).

16. For studies of whiteness as a racial and cultural identity in the United States and the advantages that whiteness confers, see Ruth Frankenberg, *White Women, Race Matters: The Social Construction of Whiteness* (Minneapolis: University of Minnesota Press, 1993; David Roediger, *The Wages of Whiteness* (New York: Verso, 1991); Noel Ignatiev, *How the Irish Became White* (New York: Routledge, 1995); and George Lipsitz, *The Possessive Investment in Whiteness: How White People Profit from Identity Politics* (Philadelphia: Temple University Press, 1998). They are part of a growing literature on whiteness that also includes Matthew Frye Jacobson, *Whiteness of a Different Color: European Immigrants and the Alchemy of Race* (Cambridge, Mass.: Harvard University Press, 1998); Karen Brodkin, *How Jews Became White Folks and What That Says about Race in America* (New Brunswick, N.J.: Rutgers University Press, 1998); and Ruth Frankenberg, ed., *Displacing Whiteness: Essays in Social and Cultural Criticism* (Durham, N.C.: Duke University Press, 1997).

17. See Laurel Kendall and Mark Peterson, ed., *Korean Women: View from the Inner Room* (New Haven, Conn.: East Rock Press, 1983) Sandra Mattielli, ed., *Virtues in Conflict: Tradition and the Korean Woman Today* (Seoul: Royal Asiatic Society, Korea Branch, 1977); Yung-Chung Kim, ed. and trans., *Women of Korea*, by the Committee for the Compilation of the History of Korean Women (Seoul: Ewha Women's University Press, 1976); and Alternative Culture, ed., *Jubu: Geu Makhim-gwa Teu-im (Housewife: That Closing and Opening)* (Seoul: Alternative Culture Press, 1990).

18. Sidney Mintz, *Tasting Food, Tasting Freedom* (Boston: Beacon Press, 1996), has observed that America does not have a cuisine per se but a distinctive way of eating characterized by fast food, instant food, frozen food, canned food, and other ready-to-eat and easy-to-prepare edibles.

19. Richard D. Alba, *Ethnic Identity: The Transformation of White America* (New Haven, Conn.: Yale University Press, 1990), pp. 79–80, 85–86. See also Mary C. Waters, *Ethnic Options: Choosing Identities in America* (Berkeley: University of California Press, 1990).

20. Mary Douglas, "Deciphering a Meal," in *Food and Culture,* ed. Carole Counihan and Penny Van Esterik (New York: Routledge, 1997), pp. 36–54.

21. My description of the structure of Korean meals is based on my life experience eating meals in middle-class Korean families in Korea and in America, plus discussions with other Korean women about what constitutes a proper Korean meal. Fancy Korean meals served in restaurants vary in structure, and some include courses.

22. My description of the structure of American meals is based on my life experience in America, plus discussions with American women about what makes a proper meal.

23. Gabaccia, *We Are What We Eat,* discusses the incorporation of ethnic food items into American culture.

24. Kim Yumee, *Migug Hakgyo-ei Hangug Aideul (Korean Children in American Schools)* (Seoul: Il Sa Jun Suh Books, 1988), pp. 69–75.

25. Sil Dong Kim, "Internationally Married Korean Women Immigrants: A Study in Marginality," Ph.D. dissertation, University of Washington, 1979, p. 110.

26. Similarly, Indochinese and Hmong immigrant women speak of eating their native foods as a means of healing the illnesses and emotional traumas that come from the stress of cultural change. See Gabaccia, *From the Other Side,* p. 121.

NOTES TO CHAPTER 5

1. *Han* is sometimes referred to as the defining characteristic of Koreans. Elaine Kim uses the concept of *han* to link the history of Korean Americans to that of Koreans on the peninsula as she reflects on the meaning and effect of the 1992 Los Angeles civil unrest in "Home Is Where the *Han* Is," in *Reading Rodney King, Reading Urban Uprising,* ed. Robert Gooding-Williams (New York: Routledge, 1993), pp. 215–35. For a discussion of *han* in the context of post-1945 Korea and the problem of national division and reunification, see Roy Richard Grinker, "Loss, Mourning and Resentment: *Han,*" in *Korea and Its Futures: Uni-*

fication and the Unfinished War (New York: Macmillan, 1998). For a discussion of *han* from a Korean American Christian viewpoint, see Andrew Sung Park, *The Wounded Heart of God: The Asian Concept of Han and the Christian Doctrine of Sin* (Nashville, Tenn.: Abingdon Press, 1994).

2. *Chusok* is an annual holiday observed on the fifteenth day of the eighth month of the lunar calendar, a day that usually falls in September or early October. Along with the lunar New Year, it is the most important holiday in Korea and is commemorated with family gatherings and visits to the graves of ancestors.

3. Alejandro Portes and Alex Stepick, *City on the Edge: The Transformation of Miami* (Berkeley: University of California Press, 1993) discuss the ways in which Cuban and Haitian immigrants dissociate themselves from American blacks in their search for economic security and social acceptance. A brief history of African Americans published in the wake of the 1992 Los Angeles turmoil attempted to teach first-generation Korean immigrants about African Americans. It has been used in study seminars in Los Angeles, New York, and Philadelphia, and urged upon parents by their children. The book is Edward Chang (Jang Tae-han), *Heukin: Geudeulee Nugu Inga? (Blacks: Who Are They?)* Seoul: Korea Economic Daily, 1993.

4. This does not mean that Korean parents welcome foreign daughters-in-law more readily than they welcome foreign sons-in-law, but rather that men who marry foreigners do not encounter the social ostracism, contempt, and prejudice that the women do.

5. This view was expressed by many of the men Elaine Kim interviewed in her article, "Men's Talk: A Korean American View of South Korean Constructions of Women, Gender and Masculinity," in Elaine Kim and Chungmoo Choi, ed., *Dangerous Women: Gender and Korean Nationalism* (New York: Routledge, 1998), pp. 67–118.

6. Jiemin Bao, "Same Bed, Different Dreams: Intersections of Ethnicity, Gender, and Sexuality among Middle- and Upper-Class Chinese Immigrants in Bangkok," *positions: east asia cultural critique,* vol. 6, no. 2 (Fall 1998), p. 482.

7. The exception has been within the student movement and other nationalist social movements, where both men have been criticized for being overly influenced by foreigners and lacking in patriotism. In this context, their marriages to foreign women have been cited as evidence of their westernization. Notably, however, these criticisms are limited to the question of patriotism and westernization, and do not bring up the issues of morality or pollution that are so central to the negative image of Korean women who marry foreigners.

8. Agnes Davis Kim, *I Married a Korean* (New York: John Day, 1953).

9. Daniel B. Lee, "Korean Women Married to Servicemen," in *Korean Ameri-*

can Women Living in Two Cultures, ed. Young In Song and Ailee Moon (Los Angeles: Academia Koreana, Keimyung-Baylo University Press, 1997), p. 97.

10. *Mal*, August 1988, p. 109.

11. During that same twenty-year period, thousands of Korean children immigrated to the United States when they were adopted by Americans. Although the data are not complete, the number of adoptees is most likely much greater than that of military brides.

12. Lee, "Korean Women Married to Servicemen," pp. 96–97.

13. Koreans, mostly students, were present in the city as early as the 1910s, but a sizable community did not form until decades later. See Jae-Hyup Lee, "Identity and Social Dynamics in Ethnic Community: Comparative Study on Boundary Making among Asian Americans in Philadelphia," Ph.D. dissertation, University of Pennsylvania, 1994; and Changhee Lee, *Philadelphia Haninsa, 1945–1995 (History of Koreans in Philadelphia, 1945–1995)* (Philadelphia: Korean Association of Philadelphia, 1995).

14. "1.5 generation" is a term first used to refer to Koreans who immigrated as young children. The term connotes the particular in-between status of many of these immigrants, whose formative years were split between Korea and America. Its usage has now broadened to include other Asians who immigrated as young children.

15. See Kyeyoung Park, *The Korean American Dream: Immigrants and Small Business in New York City* (Ithaca, N.Y.: Cornell University Press, 1997); In-Jin Yoon, *On My Own: Korean Business and Race Relations in America* (Chicago: University of Chicago Press, 1997); Min Pyong Gap, *Caught in the Middle: Korean Communities in New York and Los Angeles* (Berkeley: University of California Press, 1996); Ivan Light and Edna Bonacich, *Immigrant Entrepreneurs: Koreans in Los Angeles, 1965–1982* (Berkeley: University of California Press, 1988); and Ilsoo Kim, *New Urban Immigrants: The Korean Community in New York* (Princeton: Princeton University Press, 1981).

16. *Tweegee* is a derogatory term for mixed-blood Koreans.

17. "To lie down and spit" is a Korean saying referring to the act of criticizing or bad-mouthing others who are connected to oneself, such as family, fellow Koreans, fellow workers, and so on. Such behavior is considered to backfire—much as spit falls back on one's face—because it reveals a person's bad character or weaknesses.

18. "Gugjae Gyulhon Yosong: Geu Myung-gwa Ahm, 1, 2 Hwe (Internationally Married Women: The Light and the Darkness, Parts I and II)," *PD Such'up (Producer's Diary)*, MBC, Seoul, Korea, broadcast September 27, 1994, and October 4, 1994.

19. The killing and the riots were extensively covered in the South Korean

press. There were two main reactions, pity at the plight of fellow Koreans, and horror at the cruelty committed by a fellow Korean. South Koreans could not seem to get over what they perceived to be a fatal altercation over a mere bottle of orange juice. Soon Ja Du—and by extension the Korean immigrant community at large—was portrayed as a grasping, petty person who valued money over human life. That this incident occurred at a time when South Koreans themselves were concerned about the ways in which capitalist values had changed lifestyles and priorities may partially explain this reaction.

20. Front page stories appeared throughout 1996 in the newspaper *Dong-A Ilbo*, Philadelphia edition.

21. "Serujin Choht Bool: Yi Young-ok aegae ohnjung-eul (A Fading Candle: A Warm Heart to Ms. Lee Young-ok)." *Dong-A Ilbo*, Philadelphia edition, February 3, 1996, p. 1.

22. "Dadeuthan Sohngil, Ahshiwoon Gyopo Yoin (A Warm Helping Hand, An Unfortunate Korean Woman)." *Dong-A Ilbo*, Philadelphia edition, August 1, 1995, p. 3.

23. "Hangugin-ae Adeul Iudda (The Son of a Korean)." *Korea Times*, Atlanta edition, October 15, 1997, p. B7.

24. Lisa Lowe, *Immigrant Acts: On Asian American Cultural Politics* (Durham: Duke University Press, 1996), pp. 1–36.

25. Chon S. Edwards (Song Jun-Gi), *Na-do Hangug-ui Ddal (I Am also a Daughter of Korea)* (Seoul: Mirae Munhwasa Press, 1988).

NOTES TO CHAPTER 6

1. Women in North Korea may well have done the same, but as I am not aware of any studies that discuss this in any depth beyond mentioning the activities of women's organizations sponsored by the government, I limit my discussion of women's organizations in post-1945 Korea to the south.

2. Yi Soong Sun et al., "Housewife Movement," in *Jubu: Geu Makhim-gwa Teuim (Housewife: That Closing and Opening)*, ed. Ddo Hana-eu Munhwa (Seoul: Ddo Hana-eu Munhwa Press, 1990), pp. 308–20.

3. A group of Korean ministers have begun holding annual conferences to discuss the question of how best to minister to military brides. Their second annual conference was held in Las Vegas in 1997.

4. Taking their cue from Anderson, other scholars have analyzed the role of broadcast media in the construction of "imagined community." For example, see Purnima Mankekar, "Television Tales and a Woman's Rage: A Nationalist Recasting of Draupadi's 'Disrobing,'" *Public Culture*, vol. 5, no. 3 (Spring 1993), pp. 469–92.

5. Both Katherine Moon in *Sex among Allies* (New York: Columbia University Press, 1997), and Saundra Pollock Sturdevant and Brenda Stoltzfus in *Let the Good Times Roll: Prostitution and the U.S. Military in Asia* (New York: New Press, 1992) discuss how racial boundaries among U.S. troops are replicated among camptown women. See especially pp. 84–92 in *Sex among Allies*, where Moon discusses how racial conflict between black and white soldiers that in part stemmed from the social issues of the 1960s and 1970s was displaced onto the women, who were seen by the military authorities as the cause of these problems and targeted for antidiscrimination education.

6. Lisa Lowe, "Imagining Los Angeles in the Production of Multiculturalism," in *Immigrant Acts: On Asian American Cultural Politics* (Durham: Duke University Press, 1996), pp. 84–96. See also E. San Juan, Jr., "The Cult of Ethnicity and the Fetish of Pluralism," in his *Racial Formations, Critical Transformations: Articulations of Power in Ethnic and Racial Studies in the United States* (Atlantic Highlands, N.J.: Humanities Press, 1992), pp. 31–41.

7. Israel Zangwill's play, *The Melting Pot,* opened in 1908 to great acclaim. The concept of the melting pot was also dramatized in performances at the Ford English School. See Jonathan Schwartz, "Henry Ford's Melting Pot," in *Ethnic Groups in the City,* ed. Otto Feinstein (Lexington, Mass.: Heath Lexington, 1971), pp. 192–93. The melting pot idea itself is older and can be traced back to J. Hector St. John Crevecoeur's 1782 *Letters from an American Farmer*, especially the essay, "What Is an American?" in which he extols the "new man" being formed out of Europe's various "races." It is important to note here that the melting pot was originally conceived to be both male and European, that is, both Crevecoeur and Zangwill envisioned the American as being created from the mixing of male Europeans. Africans, Asians, or others designated as nonwhite and non-European, as well as women of any race, were distinctly absent. For pointing me to these references, I thank my colleagues on the e-mail discussion list H-Ethnic, especially Dietrich Herrmann of Dresden, Germany.

8. Hazel Carby, "Multiculture," *Screen Education,* vol. 34 (Spring 1980), pp. 62–70.

9. Kyeyoung Park, "'I Really Do Feel I'm 1.5!': The Construction of Self and Community by Young Korean Americans," in *Amerasia Journal,* vol. 25, no. 1 (1999), pp. 139–63.

10. Kari Ruth, "Dear Luuk," in *Seeds from a Silent Tree: An Anthology by Korean Adoptees,* ed. Tonya Bishoff and Jo Rankin, (San Diego, Calif.: Pandal Press, 1998), p. 144.

11. bell hooks, *Outlaw Culture: Resisting Representations* (New York: Routledge, 1994), p. 234.

1. For example, Bascom W. Ratliff, Harriet Faye Moon, and Gwendolyn A. Bonacci, "Intercultural Marriage: The Korean-American Experience," *Social Casework* (April 1978), pp. 221–26; Frank D. Richardson, "Ministries to Asian Wives of Servicemen: A 1975 Inquiry," *Military Chaplains' Review* (Winter 1976), pp. 1–14.

2. See, for example, Daniel Y. Moon, "Ministering to Korean Wives of Servicemen," in *Korean Women In a Struggle for Humanization*, ed. Harold Hakwon Sunoo and Dong Soo Kim (Memphis, Tenn.: Association of Korean Christian Scholars in North America, 1978), pp. 97–116.

3. Jung Ja Rho, "Multiple Factors Contributing to Marital Satisfaction in Korean-American Marriages and Correlations With Three Dimensions of Family Life," Ph.D. dissertation, Kansas State University, 1989.

4. Chul-In Yoo, "Life Histories of Two Korean Women Who Marry American GIs," Ph.D. dissertation, University of Illinois at Urbana-Champaign, 1993.

5. Dongsook Park Kim, "The Meanings of Television Viewing: An Interpretive Analysis of Four Korean Groups in the U.S.," Ph.D. dissertation, University of Texas at Austin, 1990.

6. The best-known work is Bok-Lim Kim et al., *Women in Shadows: A Handbook for Service Providers Working with Asian Wives of U.S. Military Personnel* (La Jolla, Calif.: National Committee Concerned with Asian Wives of U.S. Servicemen, 1981). Refer to Bibliography for a representative sample of other publications by Kim and Lee.

7. Haeyun Juliana Kim, "Voices from the Shadows: The Lives of Korean War Brides," *Amerasia*, vol. 17, no. 1 (1991), p. 16.

8. An early example of such scholarship within Asian American studies is Victor G. Nee and Brett de Bary Nee, *Longtime Californ'* (Stanford: Stanford University Press, 1986; originally published in 1972), a study of San Francisco Chinatown.

9. Elfrieda Berthiaume Shukert and Barbara Smith Scibetta, *War Brides of World War II* (New York: Penguin Books, 1989); Jenel Virden, *Good-Bye, Piccadilly: British War Brides in America* (Urbana: University of Illinois Press, 1996). All three of these authors are themselves the children of World War II war brides. As they point out, the war bride phenomenon did not begin in World War II, for American soldiers married local women during previous wars, especially World War I.

10. They also left behind entire generations of children they fathered but never claimed, Amerasians who, along with their mothers, have been subject to

discrimination and rejection. Margo Okazawa-Rey discusses the contemporary Korean situation in "Amerasian Children in GI Town: A Legacy of U.S. Militarism in South Korea," *Asian Journal of Women's Studies*, vol. 3, no. 1 (1997), pp. 71–102 (Seoul: Ewha Women's University Press). Chung Hoang Chuong and Le Van discuss the experiences of Vietnamese Amerasians relocated in the 1980s to the United States in *The Amerasians from Vietnam: A California Study* (Folsom, Calif.: Southeast Asia Community Resource Center, 1994). An Internet web site (URL: www.famas.org) is devoted to publicizing Filipino Amerasians and lobbying for amendment of the Amerasian immigration law to include Filipino Amerasians. The law allowed only Amerasians from Korea and certain Southeast Asian countries, countries where the United States went to war, to immigrate to the United States.

11. Daniel B. Lee, "Transcultural Marriage and Its Impact on Korean Immigration," in *Korean-American Women: Toward Self-Realization*, ed. Inn Sook Lee (Mansfield, Ohio: Association of Korean Christian Scholars in North America, 1985), pp. 42–64.

12. Evelyn Nakano Glenn, *Issei, Nisei, War Bride: Three Generations of Japanese American Women in Domestic Service* (Philadelphia: Temple University Press, 1986); Paul Spickard, *Mixed Blood: Intermarriage and Ethnic Identity in Twentieth-Century America* (Madison, Wis.: University of Wisconsin Press, 1989).

13. Bong-Youn Choy, *Koreans in America* (Chicago: Nelson-Hall, 1979); Ilsoo Kim, *New Urban Immigrants: The Korean Community in New York* (Princeton: Princeton University Press, 1981).

14. Nancy Abelmann and John Lie, *Blue Dreams: Korean Americans and the Los Angeles Riots* (Cambridge, Mass.: Harvard University Press, 1995); Ivan Light and Edna Bonacich, *Immigrant Entrepreneurs: Koreans in Los Angeles, 1965–1982* (Berkeley: University of California Press, 1988); Min Pyong Gap, *Caught in the Middle: Korean Communities in New York and Los Angeles* (Berkeley: University of California Press, 1996); Kyeyoung Park, *The Korean American Dream: Immigrants and Small Businesses in New York City* (Ithaca, N.Y.: Cornell University Press, 1997); In-Jin Yoon, *On My Own: Korean Businesses and Race Relations in America* (Chicago: University of Chicago Press, 1997).

15. Sil Dong Kim, "Ko-jaengi byungsa-wa honin-han hanguk yuhja chilman-myung-eu sijib sari (The Marriage Life of Korean Women Who Married the Big-Nosed Soldiers)," in *Bburi Gipun Namu (Deep-Rooted Tree)*, October 1979, pp. 60–67; and "Gugjae Gyulhon Yosong: Geu Myung-gwa Ahm, 1, 2 Hwe (Internationally Married Women: The Light and the Darkness, Parts I and II)," *PD Such'up (Producer's Diary)*, MBC, Seoul, Korea, broadcast September 27, 1994, and October 4, 1994.

BIBLIOGRAPHY

ENGLISH LANGUAGE SOURCES

Abelmann, Nancy, and John Lie. *Blue Dreams: Korean Americans and the Los Angeles Riots.* Cambridge, Mass.: Harvard University Press, 1995.

Aguilar-San Jaun, Karin. *The State of Asian America: Activism and Resistance in the 1990s.* Boston: South End Press, 1994.

Ahn, Junghyo. *Silver Stallion.* New York: Soho Press, 1990 (first published in Korean in 1986, translated by the author).

Alba, Richard D. *Ethnic Identity: The Transformation of White America.* New Haven: Yale University Press, 1990.

Amott, Teresa L., and Julie A. Matthaei. *Race, Gender and Work.* Boston: South End Press, 1991.

Anderson, Benedict. *Imagined Communities: Reflections on the Origin and Spread of Nationalism.* New York: Verso, rev. ed., 1991.

Anzaldua, Gloria. *Borderland/La Frontera: The New Mestiza.* San Francisco: Aunt Lute Books, 1987.

Asian Women United of California, ed. *Making Waves: An Anthology of Writings by and about Asian American Women.* Boston: Beacon Press, 1989.

Bak, Sangmee. "McDonald's in Seoul: Food Choices, Identity and Nationalism." In *Golden Arches East: McDonald's in East Asia,* ed. James L. Watson. Stanford: Stanford University Press, 1997.

Bao, Jiemin. "Same Bed, Different Dreams: Intersections of Ethnicity, Gender, and Sexuality among Middle- and Upper-Class Chinese Immigrants in Bangkok." *positions: east asia cultural critique,* vol. 6, no.2 (Fall 1998), pp. 475–502.

Barthes, Roland. "Toward a Psychosociology of Contemporary Food Consumption." In *Food and Culture,* ed. Carole Counihan and Penny Van Esterik. New York: Routledge, 1997.

Beardsworth, Alan, and Teresa Keil. *Sociology on the Menu.* New York: Routledge, 1997.

Blaut, J. M. *The Colonizer's Model of the World.* New York: Guilford Press, 1993.

Bredbenner, Candice. *A Nationality of Her Own: Women, Marriage and the Law of Citizenship.* Berkeley: University of California Press, 1998.

Brewer, Brooke Lilla. "Interracial Marriage: American Men Who Marry Korean Women." Ph.D. dissertation, Syracuse University, 1982.

Brodkin, Karin. *How Jews Became White Folks and What That Says about Race in America.* New Brunswick, N.J.: Rutgers University Press, 1998.

Brown, Linda Keller, and Kay Mussell, ed. *Ethnic and Regional Foodways in the United States: The Performance of Group Identity.* Knoxville, Tenn.: University of Tennessee Press, 1984.

Brownmiller, Susan. *Against Our Will: Men, Women and Rape.* New York: Fawcett Columbine, 1975.

Burgoyne, Jacqueline, and David Clarke. "You Are What You Eat: Food and Family Reconstitution." In *The Sociology of Food and Eating,* ed. Anne Murcott. Aldershot, England: Gower Publishing House, 1983.

Butler, Judith. *Gender Trouble.* New York: Routledge, 1990.

Callaway, Helen. *Gender, Culture and Empire: European Women in Colonial Nigeria.* Urbana: University of Illinois Press, 1987.

Campomanes, Oscar V. "New Formations of Asian American Studies and the Question of U.S. Imperialism." *positions: east asia cultural critique,* vol. 5, no. 2 (Fall 1997), pp. 523–50.

Carby, Hazel. "Multiculture." *Screen Education,* vol. 34 (Spring 1980), pp. 62–70.

Cesaire, Aime. *Discourse on Colonialism.* Trans. Joan Pinkham. Originally published in French in 1955. New York: Monthly Review Press, 1972.

Chan, Sucheng. *Asian Americans: An Interpretive History.* Philadelphia: Temple University Press, 1991.

Cheng, Lucie, and Edna Bonacich, ed. *Labor Immigration under Capitalism.* Berkeley: University of California Press, 1984.

Choi, Chungmoo. "Nationalism and the Construction of Gender in Korea." In *Dangerous Women,* ed. Elaine H. Kim and Chungmoo Choi. New York: Routledge, 1998, pp. 9–32.

Choy, Bong-Youn. *Koreans in America.* Chicago: Nelson-Hall, 1979.

Chuong, Chung Hoang, and Le Van. *The Amerasians from Vietnam: A California Study.* Folsom, Calif.: Southeast Asia Community Resource Center, 1994.

Clark, Donald N., ed. *The Kwangju Uprising: Shadows over the Regime in South Korea.* Boulder, Colo.: Westview Press, 1988.

Collins, Patricia Hill. *Black Feminist Thought: Knowledge, Consciousness, and the Politics of Empowerment.* New York: Routledge, 1990.

Coontz, Stephanie. *The Way We Never Were: American Families and the Nostalgia Trap.* New York: Basic Books, 1992.

Counihan, Carole, and Penny Van Esterik, ed. *Food and Culture: A Reader.* New York: Routledge, 1997.

Crevecoeur, J. Hector St. John. *Letters from an American Farmer.* 1782.

Cumings, Bruce. *Origins of the Korean War,* 2 vols. Princeton: Princeton University Press, 1981 and 1990.

———. "Silent but Deadly: Sexual Subordination in the U.S.-Korea Relationship." In *Let the Good Times Roll: Prostitution and the U.S. Military in Asia,* ed. Saundra Pollock Sturdevant and Brenda Stoltzfus. New York: New Press, 1992, pp. 169–75.

———. *Korea's Place in the Sun: A Modern History*. New York: W. W. Norton, 1997.

Delacoste, Frederique, and Prescilla Alexander, ed. *Sex Work: Writings by Women in the Sex Industry*, 2d ed. Pittsburgh: Cleis Press, 1987.

DeVault, Marjorie L. *Feeding the Family: The Social Organization of Caring as Gendered Work*. Chicago: University of Chicago Press, 1991.

Douglas, Mary. "Deciphering a Meal." In *Food and Culture*, ed. Carole Counihan and Penny Van Esterik. New York: Routledge, 1997, pp. 36–54.

Dower, John W. *War without Mercy: Race and Power in the Pacific War*. New York: Pantheon Books, 1993. Originally published in 1986.

Ekstrom, M. "Class and Gender in the Kitchen." In *Palatable Worlds: Sociocultural Food Studies*, ed. E. L. Furst, R. Prattala, M. Ekstrom, L. Holm, and U. Kijaernes. Oslo: Solum Forlag, 1991.

Enloe, Cynthia. *Does Khaki Become You? The Militarization of Women's Lives*. Boston: South End Press, 1983.

———. *Bananas, Beaches and Bases: Making Feminist Sense of International Politics*. Berkeley: University of California Press, 1989.

———. *The Morning After: Sexual Politics at the End of the Cold War*. Berkeley: University of California Press, 1993.

Epstein, Stephen J. "Wanderers in the Wilderness: Images of America in Ch'oe In-ho's Kipko p'urun pam." *Korea Journal*, vol. 35 (Winter 1995), pp. 72–79.

Fanon, Fritz. *Black Skin, White Masks*. Trans. Charles Lam Markmann. New York: Grove Weidenfeld, 1967. Originally published in French in 1952.

Fenkl, Heinz Insu. *Memories of My Ghost Brother*. New York: Penguin Books, 1996.

Fields, Barbara J. "Race and Ideology in American History." In *Region, Race and Reconstruction: Essays in Honor of C. Vann Woodward*, ed. J. Morgan Kousser and James M. McPherson. New York: Oxford University Press, 1982, pp. 143–47.

Foucault, Michel. "Afterword: The Subject and Power." In *Michel Foucault: Beyond Structuralism and Hermeneutics*, ed. Hubert L. Dreyfuss and Paul Rabinow. Chicago: University of Chicago Press, 2d ed., 1983.

Frankenberg, Ruth. *White Women, Race Matters: The Social Construction of Whiteness*. Minneapolis: University of Minnesota Press, 1993.

———, ed. *Displacing Whiteness: Essays in Social and Cultural Criticism*. Durham, N.C.: Duke University Press, 1997.

Gabaccia, Donna. *From the Other Side: Women, Gender and Immigrant Life in the U.S., 1820–1990*. Bloomington: Indiana University Press, 1994.

Gabaccia, Donna. *We Are What We Eat*. Cambridge, Mass.: Harvard University Press, 1998.

Galbraith, Hemming L., and Robert S. Barnard, Jr. "A Survey of Korean-American Marriage Applicants." *Military Chaplains' Review* (Winter 1981), pp. 51–61.

Gates, Henry Louis, Jr. "Introduction: Writing 'Race' and the Difference It Makes." In *"Race," Writing and Difference*, ed. Henry Louis Gates, Jr. Chicago: University of Chicago Press, 1986, pp. 1–20.

Glenn, Evelyn Nakano. *Issei, Nisei, War Bride: Three Generations of Japanese American Women in Domestic Service*. Philadelphia: Temple University Press, 1986.

Glenn, Evelyn Nakano, and Ching Kwan Lee. "Factory Regimes of Chinese Capitalism: Different Cultural Logics of Labor Control." In *Ungrounded Empires: The Cultural Politics of Modern Chinese Transnationalism*, ed. Aihwa Ong and Donald Nonini. New York: Routledge, 1997, pp. 115–42.

Gramsci, Antonio. *Selections from the Prison Notebooks*, ed. and trans. Quintin Hoare and Geoffrey Nowell Smith. New York: International Publishers, 1997. Originally published in 1971.

Grinker, Roy Richard. *Korea and Its Futures: Unification and the Unfinished War*. New York: MacMillan, 1998.

Hall, Stuart. "The Whites of Their Eyes: Racist Ideologies and the Media." In *Silver Linings*, ed. George Bridges and Rosalind Brunt. London: Lawrence and Wishart, 1981.

———. "Gramsci's Relevance for the Study of Race and Ethnicity." In *Stuart Hall: Critical Dialogues in Cultural Studies*, ed. David Morley and Kuan-Hsing Chen. London: Routledge, 1996.

Hamamoto, Darrell Y. *Monitored Peril: Asian Americans and the Politics of TV Representation*. Minneapolis: University of Minnesota Press, 1994.

Harris, Marvin. *Good to Eat*. New York: Simon and Schuster, 1985.

Hart-Landsberg, Martin. *Rush to Development*. New York: Monthly Review Press, 1993.

Heldman, Kevin. "On the Town with the U.S. Military." Datelined Dec. 19, 1996, available on the Korea WebWeekly Internet web site, URL: <http://www.kimsoft.com/korea/us-army.htm>.

Hicks, George. *The Comfort Women*. Sydney, Australia: Allen and Unwin, 1995.

Higginbotham, Evelyn Brooks. "African American Women's History and the Metalanguage of Race." *Signs: Journal of Women in Culture and Society*, vol. 17, no. 2 (1992), pp. 251–74.

Hong, Sawon. "Another Look at Marriages between Korean Women and American Servicemen." *Korea Journal* (May 1982), pp. 21–30.

hooks, bell. *Ain't I a Woman? Black Women and Feminism*. Boston: South End Press, 1981.

————. "Eating the Other." In *Black Looks: Race and Representation*. Boston: South End Press, 1992, pp. 21–40.

————. *Outlaw Culture: Resisting Representations*. New York: Routledge, 1994.

Ignatiev, Noel. *How the Irish Became White*. New York: Routledge, 1995.

Jacobson, Matthew Frye. *Whiteness of a Different Color: European Immigrants and the Alchemy of Race*. Cambridge, Mass.: Harvard University Press, 1998.

Jeffords, Susan. *The Remasculinazation of the United States*. Bloomington: Indiana University Press, 1989.

Jeong, Gyung Ja, and Walter R. Schumm. "Family Satisfaction in Korean/American Marriages: An Exploratory Study of the Perceptions of Korean Wives." *Journal of Comparative Family Studies*, vol. 21, no. 3 (Autumn 1990), pp. 325–36.

Kang, Hyeon-Dew. "Changing Image of America in Korean Popular Literature: With an Analysis of Short Stories between 1945–75." *Korea Journal* (October 1976), pp. 19–33.

Kang, L. Hyun-Yi. "The Desiring of Asian Female Bodies." *Visual Anthropology Review*, vol. 9, no. 1 (Spring 1993), pp. 5–21.

Kelley, Robin D. G. *Hammer and Hoe: Alabama Communists during the Great Depression*. Chapel Hill: University of North Carolina Press, 1990.

————. *Race Rebels: Culture, Politics and the Black Working Class*. New York: Free Press, 1996.

Kendall, Laurel. *Getting Married in Korea: Of Gender, Morality and Modernity*. Berkeley: University of California Press, 1996.

Kendall, Laurel, and Mark Peterson, ed. *Korean Women: View from the Inner Room*. New Haven, Conn.: East Rock Press, 1983.

Kim, Anges Davis. *I Married a Korean*. New York: John Day, 1953.

Kim, Bok-Lim C. "Casework with Japanese and Korean Wives of Americans." *Social Casework* (May 1972), p. 277.

————. "Asian Wives of U.S. Servicemen: Women in Shadows." *Amerasia Journal*, no. 4 (1977), pp. 91–115.

————. "Pioneers in Intermarriage: Korean Women in the United States." In *Korean Women in a Struggle for Humanization*, ed. Harold Hakwon Sunoo and Dong Soo Kim. Memphis, Tenn.: Association of Korean Christian Scholars in North America, 1978, pp. 59–95.

Kim, Bok-Lim C. et al. *Women in Shadows: A Handbook for Service Providers Working with Asian Wives of U.S. Military Personnel*. La Jolla, Calif.: National Committee Concerned with Asian Wives of U.S. Servicemen, 1981.

Kim, Dongsook Park. "The Meanings of Television Viewing: An Interpretive

Analysis of Four Korean Groups in the U.S." Ph.D. dissertation, University of Texas at Austin, 1990.

Kim, Elaine. "Home Is Where the *Han* Is." In *Reading Rodney King, Reading Urban Uprising,* ed. Robert Gooding-Williams, pp. 215–35. New York: Routledge, 1993.

———. "Men's Talk: A Korean American View of South Korean Constructions of Women, Gender and Masculinity." In *Dangerous Women: Gender and Korean Nationalism,* ed. Elaine Kim and Chungmoo Choi. New York: Routledge, 1998, pp. 67–118.

Kim, Elaine, and Chungmoo Choi, ed. *Dangerous Women: Gender and Korean Nationalism.* New York: Routledge, 1998

Kim, Haeyun Juliana. "Voices from the Shadows: The Lives of Korean War Brides." *Amerasia,* vol. 17, no. 1 (1991), pp. 15–30.

Kim, Hyun Sook, and Pyong Gap Min. "The Post-1965 Korean Immigrants: Their Characteristics and Settlement Patterns." *Korea Journal of Population and Development,* vol. 21, no. 2 (1992), pp. 121–43.

Kim, Hyung-chan, and Eun Ho Lee, ed. *Koreans in America: Dreams and Realities.* Seoul: Institute of Korean Studies, 1990.

Kim, Ilsoo. *New Urban Immigrants: The Korean Community in New York.* Princeton: Princeton University Press, 1981.

Kim, Sil Dong. "Internationally Married Korean Women Immigrants: A Study in Marginality." Ph.D. dissertation, University of Washington, 1979.

Kim, Yung-Chung, ed. and trans. *Women of Korea,* by the Committee for the Compilation of the History of Korean Women. Seoul: Ewha Women's University Press, 1976.

Kwak, Tae-Hwan, and Seong Hyong Lee, ed. *The Korean-American Community: Present and Future.* Seoul: Kyungnam University Press, 1991.

Larson, Wanwadee. *Confessions of a Mail Order Bride.* Far Hills, N.J.: New Horizon Press, 1989.

Lee, Ching Kwan. "Factory Regimes of Chinese Capitalism: Different Cultural Logics of Labor Control." In *Ungrounded Empires: The Cultural Politics of Modern Chinese Transnationalism,* ed. Aihwa Ong and Donald Nonini. New York: Routledge, 1997, pp. 115–42.

Lee, Daniel Booduck. "Military Transcultural Marriage: A Study of Marital Adjustment between American Husbands and Korean-Born Spouses." Department of Social Work dissertation, University of Utah, 1980.

———. "Transcultural Marriage and Its Impact on Korean Immigration." In *Korean-American Women: Toward Self-Realization,* ed. Inn Sook Lee. Mansfield, Ohio: Association of Korean Christian Scholars in North America, 1985, pp. 42–64.

———. "Transculturally Married Korean Women in the U.S.: Their Contributions and Sufferings." In *The Korean-American Community: Present and Future*, ed. Tae-Hwan Kwak and Seong Hyong Lee. Seoul: Kyungnam University Press, 1991, pp. 287–316.

———. "Korean Women Married to Servicemen." In *Korean American Women Living in Two Cultures*, ed. Young In Song and Ailee Moon. Los Angeles: Academia Koreana, Keimyung-Baylo University Press, 1997, pp. 94–123.

Lee, Don Chang. "Intermarriage and Spouse Abuse: Korean Wife-American Husband." In *Koreans in America: Dreams and Realities*, ed. Hyung-chan Kim and Eun Ho Lee. Seoul: Institute of Korean Studies, 1990.

Lee, Inn Sook, ed. *Korean-American Women: Toward Self-Realization*. Mansfield, Ohio: Association of Korean Christian Scholars in North America, 1985.

Lee, Jae-Hyup. "Identity and Social Dynamics in Ethnic Community: Comparative Study on Boundary Making among Asian Americans in Philadelphia." Ph.D. dissertation, University of Pennsylvania, 1994.

Lee, Jai-Eui. *Kwangju Diary: Beyond Death, Beyond the Darkness of the Age* [translation of *Chukeum-eul Nomo Sidaeui Odum-eul Nomo*]. Berkeley: University of California Press, 1999.

Lee, Ki-baik. *A New History of Korea*, trans. Edward W. Wagner, with Edward J. Schultz. Cambridge, Mass.: Harvard University Press, 1984.

Lee, Manwoo. "Anti-Americanism and South Korea's Changing Perception of America." In *Alliance under Tension: The Evolution of South Korea-U.S. Relations*, ed. Manwoo Lee, Ronald D. McLaurin, and Chung-in Moon. Boulder, Colo.: Westview Press, 1988, pp. 7–27.

Lewis, Lloyd B. *The Tainted War: Culture and Identity in Vietnam Narratives*. Westport, Conn.: Greenwood Press, 1985.

Light, Ivan, and Edna Bonacich. *Immigrant Entrepreneurs: Koreans in Los Angeles, 1965–1982*. Berkeley: University of California Press, 1988.

Lippi-Green, Rosina. *English with an Accent: Language, Ideology, and Discrimination in the United States*. New York: Routledge, 1997.

Lipsitz, George. *The Possessive Investment in Whiteness: How White People Profit from Identity Politics*. Philadelphia: Temple University Press, 1998.

Lowe, Lisa. *Immigrant Acts: On Asian American Cultural Politics*. Durham: Duke University Press, 1996.

MacClancy, Jeremy. *Consuming Culture*. New York: Holt, 1992.

Mankekar, Purnima. "Television Tales and a Woman's Rage: A Nationalist Recasting of Draupadi's 'Disrobing.'" *Public Culture*, vol. 5, no. 3 (1993), pp. 469–92.

Marchetti, Gina. *Romance and the "Yellow Peril": Race, Sex, and Discursive Strategies in Hollywood Fiction*. Berkeley: University of California Press, 1993.

Matsuda, Mari, J., Charles R. Lawrence III, Richard Delgado, and Kimberlé Williams Crenshaw. *Words That Wound*. Boulder, Colo.: Westview Press, 1993.

Matsui, Yayori. *Women's Asia*. Atlantic Highlands, N.J.: Zed Books, 1989.

Matielli, Sandra, ed. *Virtues in Conflict: Tradition and the Korean Woman Today*. Seoul: Royal Asiatic Society, Korea Branch, 1977.

Memmi, Albert. *The Colonizer and the Colonized*. Trans. Howard Greenfield. Boston: Beacon Press, 1967. Originally published in French in 1957.

Messaris, Paul, and Jisuk Woo. "Image vs. Reality in Korean Americans' Responses to Mass-Mediated Depictions of the United States." *Critical Studies in Mass Communication*, vol. 8 (1991), pp. 74–90.

Mies, Marie. *Patriarchy and the Accumulation of Capital on a World Scale*. London: Zed Books, 1986.

Mies, Marie, Veronica Bennholdt-Thomson, and Claudia von Werlhof. *Women: The Last Colony*. Atlantic Highlands, N.J.: Zed Books, 1988.

Min, Pyong Gap. *Caught in the Middle: Korean Communities in New York and Los Angeles*. Berkeley: University of California Press, 1996.

Mintz, Sidney. *Tasting Food, Tasting Freedom*. Boston: Beacon Press, 1996.

Moallem, Minoo, and Iain A. Boal. "Multicultural Nationalism and the Politics of Inauguration." In *Between Woman and Nation: Nationalisms, Transnational Feminisms and the State*, ed. Caren Kaplan, Norma Alarcon, Minoo Moallem. Raleigh, N.C.: Duke University Press, 1999, pp. 243–63.

Moon, Daniel Y. "Ministering to Korean Wives of Servicemen." In *Korean Women in a Struggle for Humanization*, ed. Harold Hakwon Sunoo and Dong Soo Kim. Memphis, Tenn.: Association of Korean Christian Scholars in North America, 1978, pp. 97–116.

Moon, Katherine H. S. "International Relations and Women: A Case Study of United States-Korean Camptown Prostitution, 1971–1976." Ph.D. dissertation, Princeton University, 1994.

———. *Sex among Allies: Military Prostitution and U.S.-Korea Relations*. New York: Columbia University Press, 1997.

Murcott, Anne, ed. *The Sociology of Food and Eating*. Aldershot, England: Gower Publishing House, 1983.

Naficy, Hamid. *The Making of Exile Cultures: Iranian Television in Los Angeles*. Minneapolis: University of Minnesota Press, 1993.

Narayan, Uma. *Dislocating Cultures: Identities, Traditions, and Third World Feminism*. New York: Routledge, 1997.

Nee, Victor G., and Brett de Bary Nee. *Longtime Californ'*. Stanford: Stanford University Press, 1986. Originally published in 1972.

Ogle, George. *South Korea: Dissent within the Economic Miracle*. Atlantic Highlands, N.J.: Zed Books, 1990.

Okazawa-Rey, Margo. "Amerasian Children in GI Town: A Legacy of U.S. Militarism in South Korea." *Asian Journal of Women's Studies,* vol. 3, no. 1 (1997), pp. 71–102. Seoul: Ewha Women's University Press.

Okihiro, Gary. *Margins and Mainstreams: Asians in American History and Culture.* Seattle: University of Washington Press, 1994.

Omi, Michael, and Howard Winant. *Racial Formations in the United States.* New York: Routledge, 1994.

Ong, Aihwa. *Spirits of Resistance and Capitalist Discipline: Factory Women in Malaysia.* Albany: State University of New York Press, 1987.

———. "On the Edge of Empires: Flexible Citizenship among Chinese in Diaspora." *positions: east asia cultural critique,* vol. 1, no. 3 (1993), pp. 745–78.

Park, Andrew Sung. *The Wounded Heart of God: The Asian Concept of Han and the Christian Doctrine of Sin.* Nashville, Tenn.: Abingdon Press, 1994.

Park, Kyeyoung. *The Korean American Dream: Immigrants and Small Businesses in New York City.* Ithaca, N.Y.: Cornell University Press, 1997.

———. "'I Really Do Feel I'm 1.5!': The Construction of Self and Community by Young Korean Americans." *Amerasia Journal,* vol. 25, no. 1 (1999), pp. 139–69.

Park, Young Mi. "U.S. Military Presence in Korea and Its Effects on Korean Women: A Theological Reflection on Prostitution and Marriage." M. Div. thesis, Harvard Divinity School, Harvard University.

Pascoe, Peggy. "Race, Gender and Intercultural Relationships: The Case of Interracial Marriage." *Frontiers: A Journal of Women Studies,* vol. 12, no. 1 (1991), pp. 5–18.

Pheterson, Gail, ed. *A Vindication of the Rights of Whores.* Seattle: Seal Press, 1989.

Portes, Alejandro, and Alex Stepick. *City on the Edge: The Transformation of Miami.* Berkeley: University of California Press, 1993.

Ratliff, Bascom W., Harriet Faye Moon, and Gwendolyn A. Bonacci. "Intercultural Marriage: The Korean-American Experience." *Social Casework* (April 1978), pp. 221–26.

Ray, Krishnendu. "Meals, Migration and Modernity: Domestic Cooking and Bengali Indian Ethnicity in the United States." *Amerasia Journal,* vol. 24, no. 1 (1998): 105–27.

Rho, Jung Ja. "Multiple Factors Contributing to Marital Satisfaction in Korean-American Marriages and Correlations with Three Dimensions of Family Life." Ph.D. dissertation, Kansas State University, 1989.

Richardson, Frank D. "Ministries to Asian Wives of Servicemen: A 1975 Inquiry." *Military Chaplain' Review* (Winter 1976), pp. 1–14.

Roediger, David. *The Wages of Whiteness.* New York: Verso, 1991.

Royal Asiatic Society, Korea Branch. *Yogong: Factory Girl.* Seoul: Royal Asiatic Society, Korea Branch, 1988.

Ruth, Kari. "Dear Luuk." In *Seeds from a Silent Tree: An Anthology by Korean Adoptees,* ed. Tonya Bishoff and Jo Rankin. San Diego, Calif.: Pandal Press, 1998.

Saenz, Rogelio, Sean-Shong Hwang, and Benigno E. Aguirre. "In Search of Asian War Brides." *Demography,* vol. 31, no. 3 (August 1994), pp. 549–59.

Sanchez, George. "'Go after the Women': Americanization and the Mexican Immigrant Woman, 1915–1929." In *Unequal Sisters: A Multicultural Reader in U.S. Women's History,* ed. Vicki L. Ruiz and Ellen Carol Dubois. New York: Routledge, 1990, pp. 284–97.

San Juan, Jr., E. *Racial Formations, Critical Transformations: Articulations of Power in Ethnic and Racial Studies in the United States.* Atlantic Highlands, N.J.: Humanities Press International, 1992.

Schwartz, Jonathan. "Henry Ford's Melting Pot." In *Ethnic Groups in the City,* ed. Otto Feinstein. Lexington, Mass.: Heath Lexington, 1971, pp. 192–93.

Scott, James C. *Weapons of the Weak: Everyday Forms of Peasant Resistance.* New Haven, Conn.: Yale University Press, 1985.

———. *Domination and the Arts of Resistance.* New Haven, Conn.: Yale University Press, 1990.

Sharman, A., J. Theophano, K. Curtis, and E. Messer, ed. *Diet and Domestic Life in Society.* Philadelphia: Temple University Press, 1991.

Shin, Hei Soo. "Women's Sexual Services and Economic Development: The Political Economy of the Entertainment Industry and South Korean Dependent Development." Ph.D. dissertation, Rutgers University, 1991.

Shorrock, Tim. "Ex-Leaders Go on Trial in Seoul." *Journal of Commerce,* Five Star edition, February 27, 1996, p. A1.

———. "Debacle in Kwangju." *The Nation,* December 9, 1996, pp. 19–22.

Shukert, Elfrieda Berthiaume, and Barbara Smith Scibetta. *War Brides of World War II.* New York: Penguin Books, 1989.

Song, Young In, and Ailee Moon, ed. *Korean American Women Living in Two Cultures.* Los Angeles: Academia Koreana, Keimyung-Baylo University Press, 1997.

Spickard, Paul. *Mixed Blood: Intermarriage and Ethnic Identity in Twentieth-Century America.* Madison, Wis.: University of Wisconsin Press, 1989.

Steel, Ronald. "When Worlds Collide." *New York Times,* July 21, 1996.

Sturdevant, Saundra Pollock, and Brenda Stoltzfus, ed. *Let the Good Times Roll: Prostitution and the U.S. Military in Asia.* New York: New Press, 1992

Sunoo, Harold Hakwon, and Dong Soo Kim, ed. *Korean Women in a Struggle for Humanization.* Memphis, Tenn.: Association of Korean Christian Scholars in North America, 1978.

Tajima, Renee E. "Lotus Blossoms Don't Bleed: Images of Asian Women." In *Making Waves: An Anthology of Writings by and about Asian American Women*, ed. Asian Women United of California. Boston: Beacon Press, 1989, pp. 308–18.

Takaki, Ronald. "Reflections on Racial Patterns in America." In *From Different Shores: Perspectives on Race and Ethnicity in America*, ed. Ronald Takaki. New York: Oxford University Press, 1987, pp. 26–38.

———, ed. *From Different Shores: Perspectives on Race and Ethnicity in America*. New York: Oxford University Press, 1987.

———. *Iron Cages: Race and Culture in Nineteenth-Century America*. New York: Oxford University Press, 1979, 2d ed., 1990.

Takazato, Suzuyo, and Harumi Miyashiro. "Crimes against Okinawan Women by American Soldiers since World War II." In *Appeal to Prioritize Women's Rights*, ed. Suzuyo Takazato and Keiko Itosu. Women's Group to Disallow the U.S. Military Bases, 1996.

Theophano, J., and K. Curtis. "Sisters, Mothers and Daughters: Food Exchanged and Reciprocity in an Italian-American Community." In *Diet and Domestic Life in Society*, ed. A. Sharman, J. Theophano, K. Curtis and E. Messer. Philadelphia: Temple University Press, 1991.

Thiesmeyer, Lynn. "U.S. Comfort Women and the Silence of the American Outrage." In *Hitting Critical Mass: A Journal of Asian American Cultural Criticism*, vol. 3, no. 2 (Spring 1997), pp. 47–67.

Thornton, Michael C. "The Quiet Immigration: Foreign Spouses of U.S. Citizens, 1945–1985." In *Racially Mixed People in America*, ed. Maria P. P. Root. London, Sage Publications, 1992, pp. 64–76.

Truong, Thanh-dam. *Sex, Money, and Morality: Prostitution and Tourism in Southeast Asia*. Atlantic Highlands, N.J.: Zed Books, 1990.

Uchida, Aki. "The Orientalization of Asian Women in America." *Women's Studies International Forum*, vol. 21, no. 2 (1998), pp. 161–74.

Villapando, Venny. "The Business of Selling Mail-Order Brides." In *Making Waves: An Anthology of Writings by and about Asian American Women*, ed. Asian Women United of California. Boston: Beacon Press, 1989, pp. 318–36.

Virden, Jenel. *Good-Bye Piccadilly: British War Brides in America*. Urbana: University of Illinois Press, 1996.

Warde, Alan. *Consumption, Food and Taste*. Thousand Oaks, Calif.: Sage Publications, 1997.

Waters, Mary C. *Ethnic Options: Choosing Identities in America*. Berkeley: University of California Press, 1990.

Watson, James L., ed. *Golden Arches East: McDonald's in East Asia*. Stanford: Stanford University Press, 1997.

Wood, Roy C. *The Sociology of the Meal*. Edinburgh, UK: Edinburgh University Press, 1995.

Yim, Sun Bin. "Korean Immigrant Women in Early Twentieth-Century America." In *Making Waves: An Anthology of Writings by and about Asian American Women*, ed. Asian Women United of California. Boston: Beacon Press, 1989, pp. 50–60.

Yoo, Chul-In. "Life Histories of Two Korean Women Who Marry American GIs." Ph.D. dissertation, University of Illinois at Urbana-Champaign, 1993.

Yoon, In-Jin. *On My Own: Korean Businesses and Race Relations in America*. Chicago: University of Chicago Press, 1997.

Yoshikawa, Yoki. "The Heat Is on Miss Saigon: Organizing across Race and Sexuality." In *The State of Asian America: Activism and Resistance in the 1990s*, ed. Karin Aguilar-San Juan. Boston: South End Press, 1994, pp. 275–94.

Yu, Eui-Young. "Ethnic Identity and Community Involvement of Younger-Generation Korean Americans." In *Korean Studies: New Pacific Currents*, ed. Dae-Sook Suh. Honolulu: University of Hawauu Press, 1994, pp. 263–82.

KOREAN LANGUAGE SOURCES

Ahn Il Soon. *Bbaet-bul*. Seoul: Gonggan Media, 1996.

Alternative Culture, ed. *Jubu: Geu Makhim-gwa Teu-im (Housewife: That Closing and Opening)*. Seoul: Alternative Culture Press, 1990.

Bahk Sunyoung, and Ryu Baochoon. *I Could Not Destroy Myself (Na-neun Na-reul Jook-il-soo-ubtsudda)*. Seoul: Kipeun Sarang Press, 1995.

Chang, Edward (Jang Taehan). *Heukin: Geudeulee Nugu Inga? (Blacks: Who Are They?)*. Seoul: Korea Economic Daily, 1993.

Cho Haejoang. *Hangug-ui Yosong-gwa Namsong (Men and Women in Korea)*. Seoul: Munhak-gwa Jisongsa Press, 1988.

Cho, Hyoung, and Chang Pilwha. "Perspectives on Prostitution in the National Assembly: 1948–89." *Women's Studies Review*, vol. 7 (December 1990). Seoul: Korean Women Research Institute of Ewha Women's University.

Edwards, Chon S. (Song Jun-Gi). *Na-do Hangug-ui Ddal (I Am also a Daughter of Korea)*. Seoul: Mirae Munhwasa Press, 1988.

Han Kyung-Koo. "Some Foods Are Good to Think: Kimchi and the Epitomization of National Character." *Hankuk Munhwa Inryuhak (Korean Cultural Anthropology)*, vol. 26 (1994), pp. 51–68.

Kang Suk-kyung. "Nat-gwa ggum (Days and Dreams)." In *Bam-gwa Yoram (Night and Cradle)*. Seoul: Min—sa, 1983, 1993.

Kang Sungchul. *Juhan Migun (American Military in Korea)*. Seoul: Ilsongjung, 1988.

Kim Sil Dong. "Ko-jaengi byungsa-wa honin-han hanguk yuhja chilmanmyung-eu sijib sari (The Marriage Life of Korean Women Who Married the Big-Nosed Soldiers)." *Bburi Gipun Namu (Deep-Rooted Tree)*, October 1979, pp. 60–67.

Kim Yumee. *Migug Hakgyo-ei Hangug Aideul (Korean Children in American Schools)*. Seoul: Il Sa Jun Suh Books, 1988.

Kwon, Kyu-Sik, and Oh Myung-Kun. "Yullak Yosong-ui Silt'ae (Report on Prostitutes)." *Yosong Munje Yongu (Journal of Research on Women's Issues)*, no. 3 (1973), pp. 149–71. Taegu, Korea: Hyosung Women's College.

Lee, Changhee. *Philadelphia Haninsa, 1945–1995 (History of Koreans in Philadelphia, 1945–1995)*. Philadelphia: Korean Association of Philadelphia, 1995.

Min Pyong Gap et al. *Migug Sok-eu Hangugin (Koreans in America)*. Seoul: Yurim Munhwa Sa, 1991.

Oh Yun Ho. *Du Isang Oori-reul Seul-peu-gae-ha-ji Ma-ra (Stop Making Us Sad)*. Seoul: Baiksan Sundang, 1990.

———. *Sikminji-ui Adul-ae-gae (To the Sons of the Colony)*. Seoul: Baiksan Sundang, 3d ed., 1994.

Sohn Jung-Mok. "Iljeha-ui Maech'unop: Kongch'ang-gwa Sach'ang (Prostitution under Japanese Rule in Korea: Legal and Illegal Red Light Districts)." *Tosi Haengjong Yongu (Urban Administrative Review)*. Seoul: Seoul City University, no. 3 (1988), pp. 285–360.

Yi Soong Sun et al. "Housewife Movement." In *Jubu: Geu Makhim-gwa Teuim (Housewife: That Closing and Opening)*, ed. Ddo Hana-eu Munhwa. Seoul: Ddo Hana-eu Munhwa Press, 1990, pp. 308–20.

Yoon, Ilwoong. *Maechun: Jongguk Sachanggawa Changnyo Siltae (Prostitution: The Reality of Prostitution Districts and Prostitutes in Korea)*. Seoul: Dongkwang Press, 1987.

Yoon Chongmo. *Gobbi I*. Seoul: P'ulbit, 1988.

NEWSPAPERS AND MAGAZINES

Korea Times, New York edition.
Korea Times, Atlanta edition.
Dong-A Ilbo, Philadelphia edition.
Mal, Korea.

REPORTS/NEWSLETTERS/PAMPHLETS

Korea Church Women United, *Great Father, Great Army: The USFK and Prostitution in Korea*, 1996.

My Sister's Place, untitled report on camptowns and camptown prostitution in

South Korea, 1997. (My Sister's Place is the American name for Durae Bang, a community center for camptown women. Located in Uijongbu near Seoul, it is sponsored by Korea Church Women United.)

My Sister's Place. Newsletters, nos. 1–18, 1988–97.

National Fellowship of Inter-Cultural Family Ministries (a Methodist-sponsored organization for Korean military brides and their families, based in Killeen, Texas). Newsletters, 1995–97.

Rainbow Center (a community and advocacy center for Korean military brides in New York). Newsletters, 1995–98.

Sae-oom-tuh (a community and advocacy center for camptown women and children in Tongduchon, South Korea). Newsletters, nos. 1–17, 1996–98.

Second Infantry Division, 102nd Military Intelligence Battalion Soldiers Book. 1987 rev. ed.

INTERVIEWS WITH SERVICE PROVIDERS

Faye Moon, cofounder of My Sister's Place and staff of the Rainbow Center, December 1997, at the Rainbow Center in New York.

Kim Myungboon, staff member, My Sister's Place, and cofounder, Sae-oom-tuh, February 1997, near Uijongbu, Korea.

Rev. Geumhyun Yeo (Hanna Hahn), founder and director of the Rainbow Center, December 1997, at the Rainbow Center in New York.

Rev. Park (pseudonym), minister of the Korean military bride where author conducted research, 1996, at the church.

Rev. Son, minister of Korean immigrant churches in the American South and the American East Coast, 1995–96, in Philadelphia.

DOCUMENTARIES

Camp Arirang, produced by Diana S. Lee and Grace Yoonkyung Lee, 1995.

"Gugjae Gyulhon Yosong: Geu Myung-gwa Ahm, 1, 2 Hwe (Internationally Married Women: The Light and the Darkness, Parts I and II)," *PD Such'up (Producer's Diary),* Munhwa Broadcast Corporation (MBC). Seoul, Korea. Broadcast September 27, 1994, and October 4, 1994.

Women Outside, produced by Hye-Jung Park and J. T. Takagi, Third World Newsreel, 1996.

INDEX

ABOUT THE AUTHOR

Ji-Yeon Yuh received a doctorate in history from the University of Pennsylvania and is an Assistant Professor of History at Northwestern University, where she teaches Asian American history and international Asian migration history. Her research interests include race and ethnicity, culture and nationalism, women and gender, memory and historical narrative, and the construction of identity. She is currently working on a comparative study of ethnic Koreans in China, Japan, and the United States.

Born in Seoul, Dr. Yuh grew up in Chicago and graduated from the Latin School of Chicago. She majored in cognitive science at Stanford University and worked in journalism after graduation, including stints as a reporter for *Newsday* and an editorial writer for the *Philadelphia Inquirer*. She and her husband have two children.